A Cornishman and his Goonhilly Years

George Williams

Copyright © George Williams

All Rights Reserved

ISBN: 9798722771001

Dedication

This book is dedicated to the people that have played their part in making my two decades at Goonhilly such a wonderful memory.

Firstly, there are the 17 apprentices from all around the country that joined me as the 1968 intake of Radio Station apprentices. During the three years when we spent so long together, we grew from children to young men, and from confused tearaways to engineers, well most of us anyway. I hope you have had as good a working life as me.

Most importantly this book couldn't have been written if it wasn't for the men and women that were at Goonhilly while I was there.

There are too many to list, and although I have forgotten names, their faces stay clearly in my mind, Sadly, many are no longer with us, and before too many decades have quickly passed, the rest of us will also stop orbiting this planet.

I feel I must mention a couple of people who have perhaps left a bigger mark on my life than others.

On that first day at Goonhilly, our little group of nervous apprentices were approached by one or two friendly faces. I am almost certain that one of those people was Shaun Bew who introduced himself and wished us the best. He was also an apprentice, but in his final year.

Like so many of the people at Goonhilly, Shaun remained approachable, and always willing to give advice, or answer questions about confusing technology, or just to chat about life. Over the years he lived quite close to us in Porthleven, and his children were of a similar age to ours and went to the same school.

He remains a friend, and I regularly see posts or comments from Shaun on Facebook, as well as swapping messages with each other. Inadvertently he has helped me with this book by reminding me of moments at Goonhilly, or updating me on colleagues who have died.

Finally, I want to thank Pip Greenaway.

We worked together on shift, and shared transport for many years. We might have had different characters, but his mischievous mind and endless pranks cheered me up on many long night duties.

Thanks to everyone who made my life at Goonhilly so wonderful. You were amazing, and I will always remember you as a family, rather than simply workmates.

What an amazing time.

Introduction

Some time ago while planning this book, I was listening to the radio, and a daily religious *'Pause for Thought'* feature came on. I don't remember who the speaker was, or what faith she was from, but the words triggered a marvellous memory.

On this day in 1967 the Beatles were part of a worldwide satellite broadcast when they sang *'All you Need is* Love', live from their Abbey Road studio.

I instantly remembered that evening (25th June 1967) as I sat in front of our black and white television, and thrilled at those few minutes of musical magic being created in that crowded studio. I was watching it on one of the only two television channels we could receive, but it was simultaneously being beamed over various satellites to an estimated world-wide audience of 350 million people.

That International programme was called *'Our World'*, and the British section was being broadcast by Goonhilly Satellite Earth Station, which was just seven miles away from where I was sitting.

I sat open mouthed at the spectacle of the Beatles in the middle of an orchestra, with choirs boosting the quite simple lyrics and creating an amazing spectacle. Abbey Road studio was also packed with sound and vision engineers and equipment as well as a host of 'hangers on'. Thrilled by the experience, I longed to be able to make music, but I had no ambitions of ever being a 'pop star'.

A major part of my excitement about the song was that I lived so close to where the science fiction of satellite communications was allowing my generation to experience such special moments.

Little did I know that barely 12 months later I would be walking through the gates of Goonhilly to begin my working career.

Time to begin work

Just after 7:30 in the morning of Tuesday 27th August 1968, I got off a bus and crossed the road to the gates of the PO Radio Station on Goonhilly Downs. I wandered along the straight entrance road towards the main buildings where a few weeks previously, I had passed a job interview to begin my working life. As I strolled the hundred metres or so, I looked to my left at the huge satellite dish where it all began in 1962. To my right was a second giant aerial that was new, and would soon become operational, beginning service by receiving some of the television material from the Mexico Olympics.

It was very early as I walked in through the main building front doors and waited for someone to appear. After fifty years I've forgotten the name of the person who greeted me, but he cheerfully said hello and took me to the canteen to sit and wait until he could find someone to look after me. It wasn't long before one of the training group came and organised a cup of tea while I waited for the other new starters to arrive.

Over the following 30 minutes six other quiet boys of a similar age joined me with a drink and we began to make conversation. The seven of us would soon gel as a group as we began a three-year training programme to complete our apprenticeship.

Along with me as the 1968 Trainee Technician Apprentices intake there was:

David Slade and David Sjoholm from Porthleven.

Mark Jago, and Rodney Lister from Falmouth.

George Whitaker from Camborne, and David Webb from Penzance.

A further lad called Philip Harvey (from Falmouth) arrived a few weeks later to begin with a different department at the site.

This was the beginning of my life long career with the GPO as it morphed through various names to become today's BT. The first 20 or so years were based at Goonhilly, and they were amazing. I grew into a passable engineer, gained many wonderful experiences, and made so many friends. I woke each morning with a smile on my face, and eagerly went to work at this incredible place.

That first morning flashed by as we were officially welcomed, and then given a short tour of the site. Everywhere we went, people were smiling, and prepared to momentarily stop what they were doing to say hello to us. I certainly never registered their names that morning, but over the coming weeks and months, many of them became more than simply work colleagues, they became friends. To be honest the places the equipment we were shown meant nothing, and it really felt like I was being allowed to witness something from a science fiction story.

Totally excited and amazed at what we had already seen, we returned to the canteen for a mid-morning tea break. The canteen was busy now, and the people around us looked at this little group of newcomers, and no doubt we were the target of many jokes, but I was lapping up every minute of this adventure.

Soon we continued our tour and met yet further smiling faces. It was a very male dominated environment with some dressed in overalls while others were in shirts and occasionally with ties. As the morning rushed towards lunchtime one final visit was to the clerical support office where Gerry Hayes looked after a small group of ladies. They would assist us in so many ways as we learnt the processes of getting paid, booking our time, requesting annual leave, reporting in if we were sick, and in fact to answer the hundreds of questions that we had while developing from newbies into budding engineers. There were also many unnecessary visits to this office just to chat to the ladies who happily (usually) put up with our interruptions.

Lunchtime was a shock as we were told that as apprentices, we could order anything we wanted to eat and drink without charge. As we ate, the seven of us huddled together as a group and avoided eye contact with the strangers around us as much as possible, but one or two of them were determined to find out about us and conversations began.

After lunch we had another official welcome from the management team, including the Station Manager called Sidney Pitham. He had received a medal in the 1966 Queen's Birthday list for his services.

I was impressed!

The early part of the afternoon, was then all about paperwork. There was an immediate shock, when one of the first tasks was signing the Official Secrets Act. The Post Office was a part of the Civil Service in those days, and we had no option to refuse what felt to be something rather sinister.

More paperwork and forms followed a talk with the Secretary of the Post Office and Engineering Union, and we all duly signed up as members.

After another tea break, we settled into a more formal session with the training team, who described what we would be doing over the coming months and years. The main training manager involved was called John Apperley, and he remained a part of my life for the next 20 years. One dramatic bit of news he passed on to us was that we would be travelling to the middle of Oxfordshire at the weekend to a place called Leafield. This was where we would begin our college work on what was described as a *Block Release* series of courses.

We looked at each other with confused faces at this news.

I think it was obvious by now that we were a little overawed by all the things that had happened that day, and we were relieved to be told that it was time to go home.

I think the conversations with my mum that evening was very much one way, as I described all the amazing things I had seen, and done, plus the news that I was going away for several weeks at the weekend.

Goonhilly Downs

In the middle of a lump of Cornwall known as the Lizard Peninsular, about eight miles from Helston, and perhaps five miles from the most southerly point of mainland Britain, is Goonhilly Downs.

The name apparently means Hunting Downs in old Cornish. *'Goon'* is the old word for Downs, and *'Hilly'* comes from *'Helghya'* meaning Hunting.

To be honest, this bleak, regularly damp, and misty expanse of moorland, was probably not used for anything else except scavenging for food for hundreds of years until it became one of the many temporary airfields used during the 2nd World War. Then at the beginning of the 1960s, the engineering wing of Britain's Post Office became interested.

On the 4th October 1957, the space race was born with the Russians launching a tiny object called Sputnik 1'. It was a crude object that whistled around the earth and transmitted simple 'beeps' to anyone with a suitable radio receiver. It amused college students and radio amateurs around the world, but the Americans were terrified of the possibility that Russia were better than them, and an unstoppable series of rocket improvements by the two superpowers, allowed bigger and more sophisticated lumps of metal to be propelled into space.

During the second world war, an RAF radio operator, called Arthur C Clark, came up with a concept of using carefully positioned satellites around the globe that would allow worldwide communications. It was total science fiction at that time, but by the early 1960s the rocket technology was making the idea possible.

It was the USA that led the way now, and they worked with a number of countries in western Europe to be ready for some impending satellite experiments. This would require the building of suitable aerials to transmit to, and receive signals, from satellites.

In Britain, the responsibility fell to the GPO, and they began looking for an ideal site. Goonhilly Downs was one of the places considered. It allowed a clear line of sight to the south where the satellites would eventually be positioned, and with no nearby industries or major development, it meant the area was free of man-made noise. Also, rather important in the decision making, was that the Crown owned some of this land, making it easy to get planning permission. It was a perfect spot to take part in the experiments.

By 1962 Goonhilly was ready. The aerial was designed by a company called 'Husband and Co' and based on the huge radio telescope in Cheshire called Jodrell Bank. Goonhilly 1 stood proudly with its almost 100-foot parabolic dish looking towards the horizon, from where the first experimental satellite transmission would come. Late at night on 10th July 1962, the engineers, scientists, television crews and press were sitting in anticipation for the beginning of a new era of telecommunications to commence.

How it all began

I think I should briefly describe a little of what happened on this bleak Cornish moor nearly 60 years ago.

Around 1960, a group of scientists, engineers, and technological groups got together with a plan to build the infrastructure and hardware to begin experimental satellite communications. In America the 'National Aeronautics and Space Administration' (NASA) was formed, and along with the AT&T communications company and the Bell Telephone Laboratories, they became the main players. The American organisation linked up with the GPO in Britain, plus the equivalent French PTT. The very complicated and expensive aim was to launch a satellite into orbit above the earth, to allow communications between America and Europe.

That satellite would become known as Telstar (officially Telstar 1) and was developed and built by Bell Telephone Laboratories. Most of the technology within this quite tiny sphere was brand new, and had to be small enough to fit into the payload space available on NASA's Thor Delta Rocket. The satellite body was less than a metre end to end, and weighed about 77 kilograms. To be stable in space the sphere would have to spin, so motors had to be included to de-spin the middle section of Telstar containing the important radio elements, so that they were always pointing towards earth.

Its design used a single radio channel (called a transponder) that could receive a single signal from the earth, amplify it, and then transmit it back to earth to be received by anyone with the appropriate equipment.

The outside of the satellite was covered in panels of solar cells to charge batteries that powered the de-spin motors, and the electronics.

On 10th July 1962, NASA launched the Delta rocket from Cape Canaveral in Florida with its precious cargo. Telstar was eventually sent into what is referred to as a Medium Altitude

Elliptical Orbit. It raced around the earth in loops that were at about 45° to the equator, and it was orbiting the globe once every 2 hours and 37 minutes. The orbit reached about 3600 kilometres at its furthest point from the earth (Apogee), whilst just 950 kilometres at its closest point (Perigee).

At the American Satellite Earth Station called Andover, in the State of Maine, the engineers, scientists and press waited for the all clear to begin the experiments. Across the Atlantic Ocean in Europe, a similar group of people tapped their fingers in anticipation at Goonhilly, and a little over 100 miles to the south-east at the French Earth Station (Pleumeur Bodou), others were also waiting.

Very early in the morning of the 11th July 1962, history was about to be made.

Telstar was launched into space at a very high speed to maintain its orbit. To complicate matters, the orbit wasn't passing over the same area of earth each time. There were long periods of several hours between moments when Telstar was actually visible to both Europe and America. When those moments occurred, there was only around 20 minutes when the experiments were possible, before the satellite disappeared out of site over the horizon again. Hence it was important that everybody was ready when Telstar made one of its fleeting appearances.

Once NASA were content that Telstar was where it should be, the electronics were switched on, and the satellite was operational for the first time. Andover (America) locked its aerial onto Telstar and began transmitting television pictures towards it.

At Goonhilly, the engineers sitting at the aerial steering control desk, pointed the huge parabolic dish towards the predicted spot where the tiny object would appear over the horizon. The predictions were correct, and they locked onto Telstar's tiny signal. Goonhilly's aerial was then carefully driven to follow the satellite across the sky. The dish used its huge motors, capable of moving at 100 degrees per minute, and drove the 1000 tonnes of concrete and steel very accurately. The vast dish began by going upwards as Telstar passed overhead, then the giant dish seamlessly spun around, before dropping down to the opposite horizon as Telstar disappeared from view.

While those aerial steering engineers maintained a physical lock onto Telstar, down below them, a group of engineers sat in front of an operational control desk with its indicator lamps, switches, and small television monitors. Sitting in front of the desk that night in July 1962, the engineers concentrated on their meters and controls. They twiddled knobs while staring at the meters and television monitors, hoping that eventually the snowy noise on the screens would clear and become a real picture.

On the other side of a vast window behind that control desk, the BBC had cameras and a production team led by Raymond Baxter. This was part of a very popular programme of that era called 'Tomorrow's World' introduced by Richard Dimbleby.

By now it was 1:00 in the morning, and at my home, I was one of the hundreds of thousands of people who stayed up to watch this moment of science fiction becoming fact.

I could remember the excitement in Raymond Baxter's voice as the engineers twiddled the controls.

"Here we are…. here we are…. it's a bar!

… that's a man's face!

… there we are…."

Sadly, there was a technical issue at Goonhilly, and the picture remained snowy and never stabilised.

Although not commercially satisfactory, these noisy pictures were technically the first to ever be transmitted and received live in Europe from the USA.

Just a few seconds after Goonhilly's disappointment, the official first ever commercial television pictures via satellite were received in France at the Pleumeur Bodou Satellite Earth Station. The French had no technical hitches, and instead of Goonhilly's grainy images, they received perfectly clear pictures and sound.

By the time Telstar's orbit passed over Goonhilly again, the problem had been resolved, and at 18 minutes past midnight on 12th July, acceptable pictures and sound were finally received.

Technical bit - The problem at Goonhilly was a device called the receive polariser that had been fitted to the wrong setting. No-one will ever know if this was an error at Goonhilly, or if the Americans had given them the incorrect setting.

Although Goonhilly was never credited with those first satellite television pictures, the station would celebrate many 'firsts', and witnessed numerous historical moments in the following 40 years.

Six years later, as I was shown around Goonhilly, I was at the very spot where Raymond Baxter stood. He was describing the scene as the first live satellite television pictures between the USA and Europe were received, and I was now a part of the story.

Although remembered simply as 'Telstar', that satellite should really be referred to as Telstar 1. It remained active for several months transmitting landmark television broadcasts, plus the first ever satellite telephone calls, and data transmissions. Sadly, it seems Nuclear Explosive Tests in space by the Superpowers damaged the satellite, and it finally failed in February 1963, and was switched off.

On 7th May of that year, Telstar 2 was launched, and carried on the experiments. It survived for two years before it was also switched off with its mission completed.

These two little satellites began a revolution in communications. They are also some of the first pieces of mankind's rubbish to pollute space, and continue to fly around the globe several thousands of kilometres above us.

… but there has been a lot more space junk since then.

A Quick Look around the Main Building

I excitedly went back to work at Goonhilly for the rest of the week. The seven of us started to get used to each other and our characters were beginning to be displayed and friendships were forming.

We didn't have the chance to spend too long with each other except at breaks, as our main activities for the week were to go and spend a day in different areas of the station.

Perhaps this is a good moment to describe what I remember of Goonhilly from 50 years ago.

From the main road from Helston to St Keverne and Coverack, the entrance drive led to a car park that was to the left and in front of the typical 1960s single story building. Although the main entrance to the building was further on, there was a smaller door into the building from the car park. The corridor initially passed by the kitchen and canteen area on the left, with the toilets and first aid room on the right. Continuing for perhaps 30 or 40 metres, this corridor went down a slight slope with the conference room and an attached projection room on the right, and then there were a few steps up to the left to the administration area with the general office. Beyond that office were a couple of smaller rooms for senior engineers, then an open area and desks for the first level managers of the different disciplines around the station.

Going further down the corridor there was a couple of the highest management offices to the right, and then a secretarial office and the telephone switchboard just in front of some double doors. These opened into the main entrance lobby of the station with seating for visitors, and a sliding glass window to gain attention from someone in the secretary's office.

To the left was a set of doors to the Operational Control Area (OCA) which had only just been brought into service. In here engineers monitored and controlled the various communications equipment that made the station tick. This was the hub of the site where people would meet to discuss technical issues, or sometimes to just socialise and have chats with each other.

Passing by this vast room, the corridor continued through tall copper lined wooden doors into the original engineering part of the station. The first thing on the right was an area with sliding doors that would become our training room. It had bunk beds, and was described as a nuclear fallout shelter, and this area of the building was lined in copper.

Yes, this was still the 'Cold War' era, and the world lived under an almost constant threat of Armageddon.

In front of another pair of copper lined wooden doors, there was a corridor to the right that led to what was known as the 'Aerial Steering' room. This was a quite dark room with several cabinets of equipment that controlled the motors to move the aerials up and down, or round and round. For the technically minded, this control equipment was mainly made up of hundreds of printed-circuit boards with individual transistor devices.

There was also a spiral stair-case that took you up into the control tower. At the top of those stairs there was a viewing gallery going around the room's 360° of windows allowing a tremendous panoramic view of the site. Up a further couple of steps was a control desk with a vast array of meters, knobs and switches. Sitting at this desk, the operator could focus perhaps a quarter of a mile away to the original monstrous aerial, while watching the displays showing the time, the angle that the aerial was pointing, or others showing the direction and speed of any movement. This was where Goonhilly 1 was steered as it tracked the satellites.

It fascinated me, and remained a favourite spot for many years to come.

Back to the corridor that I was describing. Going through that second set of huge copper lined doors there was another room which was referred to as the 'I.F. and Baseband' area. One of the most important parts of this room was an old control console, where operational aspects of the station's equipment were controlled before the newly added OCA. This desk was about three metres long with more switches, meters and knobs as well as some small black and white television monitors. Behind that console was the wall to the corridor which included a huge glass window. This allowed people to see the control desk, and anything the control engineers were up to. Further into the room there were numerous cream painted racks of equipment that meant absolutely nothing to me 50 years ago.

Onwards, and at the end of the I.F. and Baseband area there were further rooms to choose from. On the left was the East Wing, which was the interface with the British Terrestrial Network. Here telephony and television signals came from, and went back to London. My first impression of this room was complete confusion, as it had row upon row of those cream painted racks again. Most seemed to be covered in hundreds and hundreds of cream-coloured cables, although there were also occasional shelves of equipment, that were slightly more interesting, but still unidentifiable.

The room to the right was the West Wing. This vast room contained the equipment taking the telephony and television signals from the East Wing, and converted them into signals to be transmitted to the satellite, and also in the reverse direction for any signals received.

My small 17-year-old brain was once again completely mesmerised by the rows of racks and equipment, but one thing did catch my eye and my imagination.

I was thrilled with a small desk in a corner of the room with a banner displaying it to be for NASA engineers. Through the years as Telstar continued and was replaced by more sophisticated satellites, NASA used Goonhilly as a monitoring station. By the time I arrived, the desk was no longer used, and soon that part of the site's history disappeared.

That just about completes the main building at Goonhilly when I arrived, although there were several other rooms that didn't leave a significant impression on my memory from that time.

One of my more memorable experiences of that first week I was at Goonhilly, was when I spent a day with John MacNelly of the Power Group. This group of four or five men looked after the array of motors, and generators, plus electrical switchgear. That day John had to replace a faulty aircraft warning light on Aerial 1. This was to be the first time I got a close up look at this wonderful aerial.

Goonhilly Aerial 1

Aerial 1 at Goonhilly is very special.

Most people who spent any serious time working at the station, will almost certainly say that this is their favourite.

Of the original four 1960s aerials that came into service between the USA and Europe, Goonhilly 1 was the first to use a parabolic reflector. The others at Pleumeur Bodou (France), Raisting (Germany), and Andover (USA) were based on a 'horn' shaped aerial.

A Horn shaped aerial is similar to an ear trumpet, but far bigger, and very effective. They were the first method used by terrestrial microwave radio systems to direct the signal energy between the stations, and perhaps the most obvious solution for those early experiments with satellites.

However, there was a slight difference for transmissions between terrestrial radio stations, and those to and from a satellite. Terrestrial systems are fundamentally operating between towers, and the signals are in a horizontal plane. The satellite is thousands of kilometres above the ground, and that huge opening in the horn was pointing upwards, and hence open to the elements. Rain, or snow, could go down and cause chaos to the communications equipment.

To overcome this serious problem, the horn-based aerials were covered by a Radome (**Ra**dar **Dome**) which did not affect the radio signals, but protected the metal structure.

These Radome aerials can still be seen, and look a bit like golf balls on tops of hills.

When the GPO were invited to get involved in the Telstar experiments, thoughts turned to the tried and tested radio telescope at Jodrell Bank in Cambridgeshire. It used a giant 76metre diameter parabolic dish to capture radio energy from space. The Jodrell Bank construction team 'Husband & Co' were asked to design and build the aerial at Goonhilly.

Their parabolic solution was a risk. The chosen reflector shape had a technical weakness compared to the horn design. The horn aerial could direct radio energy very effectively, with little wasted signal strength from a phenomenon called 'sidelobes'. The parabolic aerial could be much bigger and hence create an even bigger beam of radio energy, but some of it was wasted by sidelobes.

The risk was seen to be worth taking, and Goonhilly 1 was erected on the bleak Cornish moor.

It should be noted, that it was simply called Goonhilly at that time. There were no others.

The Physical Structure

At ground level, there is a circular base building. Inside it there is a huge cog wheel that is connected by an enormous drive chain to a motor and gear box, known as the Ward Leonard Set.

When the motor was operated, the chain pulled the giant cog around in either a clockwise or anti-clockwise movement. As the cog turned, it produced what is known as Azimuth movement. That cog is attached to the equipment room above, which has an 'A' frame on either side supporting the giant dish and its backing structure. So as the motors are operated, the equipment room and the dish rotate, and in excess of 1000 tonnes of concrete and steel turn through the complete 360 degrees, at a maximum speed of over 100 degrees per minute. The drive and positioning accuracy is amazing, to minutes of a degree.

On the reflector backing structure, there is a segment of a cog wheel, which meshes with another motor and gearbox. It allows the reflector to be moved from horizon (0 degrees), to vertical (90 degrees). This is called 'Elevation Movement' and can again achieve 100 degrees a minute of accurate movement.

The reflector is approximately 27 metres in diameter, and originally had a four-legged support system holding the signal feed equipment. In the receive direction, the parabolic shape of the dish collected the radio energy coming from the satellite, and focussed it into a small receive horn of the feed system. That radio signal then travelled inside a rectangular metal conductor box, known as waveguide, which ran down one of the feed support legs. At the other end of that waveguide was the input of the all-important 'Maser' Low Noise Amplifier (LNA) receive equipment.

When Goonhilly was transmitting towards the satellite, the signals from the High Powered Amplifier transmitter (HPA), were sent along waveguide again to the feed system, where the shape of the horn spread the energy to all of the main reflector dish, which in turn sent it away into space.

After the Telstar experiments ended, there were some physical alterations to the reflector. The important one was to re-sculpture the parabolic shape by fitting a second skin over the original. Then the original four-legged feed support was replaced by a three-legged (tripod) system. These changes made the aerial more effective, and ready to begin full time operation in the mid-1960s.

Heebie Geebie Chamber

Because the equipment room and reflector are movable, all the power and signal cables have to come via the base building, and routed upwards. Worse still, those cables have to be able to move without damage as the structure rotates potentially 360 degrees.

This is common to most satellite aerials, and uses clever techniques of wrapping cables so that they have sufficient slack to unwind or rewind as the aerial structure moves. For Aerial 1 the hundreds of signal, control, and monitoring cables are brought from the main site building in trunking, that gets to the cable wrap point under the base building through an underground tunnel. This quite low tunnel is rather dimly lit, and eerie, hence known by many as the 'Heebie Geebie' Chamber.

I was taken there on a couple of occasions, and never felt very comfortable.

Getting the Acclaim it Deserved

On the 26th March 2003, Goonhilly 1 was officially recognised for its part in the history of satellite communications. It was Grade II Listed ensuring it is preserved for future generations.

Goonhilly has always attracted visitors. The sight of the giant dishes as you drive by, can bring gasps of amazement to those seeing it for the first time. In the mid-1980s, Goonhilly opened a visitor centre next to Aerial 1. It attracted upwards of 80,000 visitors a year, and as well as a museum and hands on attractions, there was a coach tour of the complete site.

Sadly, the guides decided to make the experience special, and named all the aerials after the Knights of the Round Table. Aerial 1 was the original so was named 'Arthur'. Let's just say that very few people on the staff could stomach this name.

It will always be Goonhilly 1 to us.

My First close up View of an Aerial

So back to my adventure with John MacNelly.

That faulty aircraft warning light was unfortunately the one right at the top of the Aerial dish, and it was 100 feet above the ground. The only way to get to the lamp was using the Simon Hoist Platform, that was commonly referred to as the 'Cherry Picker'.

Initially the experience was amazing. I sat in the passenger seat of this giant vehicle as we drove along the road to the aerial. Then the lorry's stabilisation legs were dropped into place and the cage brought to ground level.

Now, I am scared of heights, and the next 15 minutes became a period of my life that absolutely terrified me.

I was forced to get into the cage, and to hold the red replacement warning light bulb. John joined me and began pulling levers that propelled us upwards. I clung on to the cage bars and shut my eyes as the cage jolted and wobbled its way into space. John attempted to ease my obvious silence and suggested I looked around at the wonderful view. I was neither interested or impressed and maintained my efforts to ignore what was happening.

Then as we reached the required height and position, the jerky movements stopped, and my torture chamber became almost stationary. John asked me to bring the red bulb across to his side of the cage. Unfortunately, this involved opening my eyes, letting go of the rails, and actually having to move. At this point John realised just how frightened I was, and laughed loudly, which simply made the situation even worse.

With the bulb replaced we bounced our way back down to the ground. I silently vowed to never repeat this experience, and successfully avoided this mental torture for almost 20 years, but that is a story for later.

Before John drove back to the main site, he offered me the chance to get a more detailed look at the aerial. Although Goonhilly 1 was less than half the size of the reflector at Jodrell Bank which it was modelled on, it was still amazingly impressive, and huge when you stood below the dish.

After the trauma of the ride to the top, I began to enjoy myself again, and we actually went inside the equipment room of the aerial for a brief look around. Whilst inside I was introduced to yet more smiling people, and the racks of equipment in the aerial building were described. It meant absolutely nothing to me at that time, and the small group of engineers seemingly poking around within the shelves, made me feel that I was in the presence of scientists, rather than young men just a few years older than myself.

During those first few days, I remember more than once hearing an announcement made by someone on the Public-Address system. It varied slightly depending on who made it, but it was along the following lines:

"Attention please, the aerial is about to move in both azimuth and elevation. After the klaxon sounds there will be no further warning"

Our moment inside the aerial building coincided with one of those announcements, and as the speaker finished, there was a loud blast of klaxon for a few seconds. Then imperceptibly there was a slight feeling of movement as the giant structure gently revolved.

It was time to move on, and as we left the aerial through the same door as we had entered, there was a very weird sensation. The aerial was now pointing towards a different position and the view had changed. It was just one more fascinating new experience to add to the many others.

The Remainder of Week 1

My head was quickly overloaded each day as I was being whisked from building to building and room to room. I saw so many different mysterious pieces of equipment, with winking red, amber and green lights flashing unknown messages. There were meters seemingly everywhere indicating just how well, or how badly, things were operating.

I was already realising just how amazing Goonhilly was, and wondered if I would ever understand what was actually happening.

While extremely confused, I had been thrilled by different guides who showed me around during that first week. They amazed me as they brought Goonhilly to life. Many of the new people in my life told stories of how it all began, and it really made me feel as if I was becoming a part of history.

Each day the seven of us were also being given little presents.

We received a large leather bag the size of a small suitcase, plus bag after bag of tools to be stored inside it. There were screwdrivers ranging from gigantic to miniscule, several pairs of pliers whose function were unknown, different size hammers, a soldering iron, and numerous oddities that were viewed with intrigue. I can honestly say that when I eventually retired, there were still a couple of tools whose function I didn't comprehend, and certainly never used. The large leather tool bag was impressive, but was rarely more than a storage point for the most obscure items. The important and most used tools were kept inside another handier sized leather bag, that we held like a badge of honour as we moved from area to area around the site.

There were also various bits of clothing to keep us dry and clean. The most important item was a knee length brown dustcoat that we wore with pride, although we did seem to be the only people using them for most of the time.

On the Friday afternoon before being allowed to go home early, we were given instructions for our rail trip to a training school in a place called Leafield in the middle of Oxfordshire. None of us knew where it was, or what to expect, except for a few warnings and untruths from a number of the people we had met. We also received the rail travel warrants that needed to be exchanged at the station for tickets, and times when the driver would be meeting us on Sunday morning to take us to the nearest railway station.

Oh, and we also received our first little brown pay packet. It was for £6. 8s. 6d.

('s' signifies shillings, and 'd' is for old pence)

This is approximately £6. 42½p in modern money.

I couldn't believe what was happening. I had been paid for doing virtually nothing for a week.

The Journey to Leafield

Sunday 1st September 1968 was a day where my life was about to have another major change. It was the first time I had ever left home for more than the odd day.

Early that morning I was out of bed, had been given a good breakfast by my mum, and was standing in the front room looking out of the window. I had a suitcase ready and was waiting for the car from Goonhilly to arrive, and take me off to Truro railway station to begin the journey to the training school in Oxfordshire.

A green estate car pulled up outside, and I grabbed my suitcase and said cheerio to my mum. The next chapter of my adventure was about to begin.

I'm sure my mum cried the moment I left the house - she did every time I said goodbye for the rest of her life, but I didn't know that at the time. I rushed out to the car where the driver had the hatch open for me to drop my case alongside those of Dave Slade and Dave Sjoholm, who were already seated in the back. I jumped into the front beside the driver, who was called Les, or maybe Charlie, or Basil, and we were quickly on our way for the drive to the station.

The journey took around 45 minutes in those days, and us three young men chattered excitedly about our short time together so far, plus thoughts for the seven weeks to come. Les joined in with our discussion and added a few thoughts for us to consider. He had taken many apprentices to and from the station for the journeys to the training school, and had a wealth of knowledge to tell us from the stories he'd heard.

At Truro we exchanged our travel warrants for the tickets and met up with Rodney and Mark, who had already arrived from Falmouth. Soon the train from Penzance roared into the station and we clambered on-board. It didn't take long before we spotted Dave Webb and George Whittaker who had joined the train earlier. The seven of us then settled down in a compartment for a journey that would last around seven hours as we slowly made our way from the West of England to the centre of the country.

This train journey is still a slow one, but faster now than it was in the late 1960s. The train left Truro and continued through Cornwall seemingly stopping at every town. We crawled at a snail's pace, momentarily stopping at St. Austell, Par, Bodmin Parkway, and Liskeard, before crossing Isambard Kingdom Brunel's bridge over the Tamar into Devon. After a brief stop at Plymouth, our train sped up a little as it said hello to Totnes and Newton Abbot, before slowing again as we followed the south coast of Devon with its wonderful views of the sea between Teignmouth and Dawlish. Finally, the diesel locomotive could clear its throat and the speed increased as we roared through Somerset to Taunton. Being a Sunday I think we may have gone the long way via Bristol Temple Meads before moving eastwards to Reading.

We ate a meal on the train, we watched the countryside pass by, and we chattered noisily - like young men do. We gave away some information about ourselves, but this was quite limited, and in fact after working together for several decades, I don't think we ever knew very much about each other.

After lunch, we all became much quieter, and succumbed to moments of sleep, but late in the afternoon we arrived at the busy station of Reading. Here we left our train and finally had a chance to stretch our legs. We initially spent a few minutes looking at overhead screens and timetable boards to find the connecting train for the last part of the rail journey to a station called Charlbury. Our tired little gang eventually settled into another carriage of a local train that slowly made its way through Berkshire into Oxfordshire. We had short stops at Didcot with views of its enormous power station cooling towers, and then the city of Oxford. On the way we also visited almost deserted stations at such places as Tilehurst, Pangbourne and Hanborough.

At last we saw the station name of Charlbury.

We were totally exhausted, starving, and relieved to get off. Charlbury is a tiny station, and on that Sunday evening it was deserted except for seven quite confused young men. There wasn't even anyone in the ticket office as we passed through it to the station approach road outside. We looked in vain for someone to meet us. Fortunately, there was a telephone box, and the number we had been given before we left Goonhilly was rung to ask for transport.

We were seriously grumpy by now and just wanted to get this journey completed. After a frustrating wait for the green minibus to appear, we cheered and quietly took our seats as the driver greeted us. It might have been Brian, or possibly Goff that picked us up that evening, and he probably heard quite a bit of whispered abuse about our perceived hard treatment.

The minibus set off along narrow roads, and in the distance one of us spotted some radio masts, and the driver said that this was where we were going. At last we swung into a narrow lane with sheep in the fields on either side, and finally stopped at the buildings of Leafield Radio Station where the training school was situated.

Suitcases in hand we went through a door to a reception desk where an elderly, rather stern man welcomed us, took our names, gave us room keys and instructions of how to find our bedrooms. He was the evening warden and called Danny Spiers, and we soon learnt that he was someone to ask for help, but also someone to be careful of, as he had a knack of sniffing out mischief.

He also told us where to find some sandwiches and a drink.

After nearly half a day of cars and trains, we had arrived, and we demolished the sandwiches and soft drinks that had been left out for us. It was not enough, but at least made us feel a little less grumpy about our journey.

We considered the idea of going for a walk to the nearby village, but after consulting with Danny Spiers, who was the only other person on site, it was decided that after unpacking, and ringing our different homes, it was time to get some sleep.

With instructions of what time we had to meet up in the morning, and where we would be getting breakfast, we one by one slammed our bedroom doors. This would be our home for the coming seven weeks.

Leafield

The small village of Leafield hides in the Cotswolds, with the nearest town being Witney about five miles away by road, and the nearest city Oxford almost 20 miles away. Nearby train stations are Charlbury and Ascott-under-Wychwood, but neither are within a comfortable walking distance. Buses are also rare, so you need a car to survive in this village.

Nowadays, Leafield has a population of around 1000 people, and over the last few decades, many of these people are living in second homes, or using the quiet village to escape the crowd while commuting to their jobs. It has a church (St Michaels), a small community run shop, a pub, and a school for infants and primary children.

The only claim to fame I could find, is that the first King James allegedly stayed nearby in the hamlet of Langley in August 1605.

Langley is a little over a mile away from the village along what is called Fairspear Road, which is also referred to as the *'Straight Mile'*. At the end of this Straight Mile there is a crossroads with Charlbury to the right, the Wychwood villages straight ahead, and Langley along a single-track lane to the left.

This hamlet was very much for the farming community, until the GPO decided to build a radio station in 1912 on land that was the property of the Crown. Initially it was an experimental radio station with Marconi playing with his new invention, but that ceased with the first world war. When that conflict ended, the radio station began many decades as a major transmitter station for long distance radio communications.

That radio station was given the name of Leafield Radio Station.

In the 1960s the GPO decided to use some of the spare capacity created for a training school, as the radio station reduced its activities. It was initially just for the GPO radio station personnel, although that expanded into other topics in the 1970s.

The training school took over one of the buildings that had been freed up as transmitters became smaller and more efficient. There was a shared canteen for station and school people, and a handful of old workers' cottages acted as the bedroom dormitories for the students. As GPO radio station apprentice numbers increased around the country, a purpose build bedroom block was built in the mid-1960s to house 50 students.

This was where I found myself that evening in September as I began the academic training of my apprenticeship. It was somewhere that would almost become a second home. I didn't know it during my first week at Goonhilly, but I would be spending almost half of my time there during the next three years.

Leafield Technical Training Centre

At that time, the GPO had a number of training centres around the UK, and they concentrated on the telephone engineers, who made up the bulk of the company's workforce. But Goonhilly was a part of the International Telecommunications sector of the business, with a number of different radio stations around the country. The bulk of these radio stations were for High Frequency (HF) radio communications, and were either for transmitting the signals, or receiving them. Goonhilly was unusual because it was able to transmit and receive at the same time without interference.

Leafield was one of the long-distance HF transmitter stations. It had once been really busy, but now was less active. The spare space created was turned into a training centre dedicated for radio station engineers.

Although the station may have been less busy, it was still operational. It was surrounded by fields with tall masts that formed the aerials sending radio broadcast to countries far away across the world. Apart from the actual radio station buildings, there were a handful of cottages still used by some of the engineers, with two or three that had been converted into dormitory blocks for the students.

... oh, and there was a lot of sheep.

The training school occupied about a third of the original radio station buildings that were no longer required for radio equipment. Most of these buildings were of granite construction, and housed about four lecture rooms, plus the same number of practical work laboratories, and offices. To amuse the students there was initially a television room, and a lounge area, plus the reception desk also had a small shop selling sweets, soft drinks, cigarettes and essential things such as tooth paste and shampoo.

Our canteen was shared by radio staff and the training people. It was run by four or five ladies who became proxy mothers for the young men (no ladies at that time) who were away from home for weeks on end. The food was generally good, and the three meals a day, plus evening supper snacks, kept us happy.

Before we arrived in 1968, the training centre used the cottages as accommodation for the students, but times were changing. The current GPO workforce was getting older, and this meant an increase in new radio engineers was required. Hence there were more apprentices coming into the business. It was also the moment when the GPO Radio group introduced a major change of policy. Rather than sending apprentices to colleges near their homes for day release academic training, they decided to pair up with a local technical training college in nearby Witney. This would provide a central location for all Radio apprentices college work. So, the number of people being trained at Leafield increased even further, meaning more accommodation was necessary. When we arrived at Leafield, we found ourselves in an almost brand-new accommodation block.

The block was a large timber frame building with cedar coloured cladding that made it look like an enormous garden shed. It initially had 50 individual bedrooms fitted with a small bed, sink, wardrobe, chest of drawers, desk and two chairs. The front of the block was a long corridor of bedrooms with windows overlooking a green area, and there were two further corridors of bedrooms at right angles to that main one. At the end of these smaller corridors were the toilets, showers and bathrooms.

The block was looked after by a small number of cleaners who made our beds and tidied up our rubbish - unless it became too unhealthy to handle. We would then be summoned before the Principle of the centre, told off, and instructed to tidy the room immediately. One of the cleaners' role was to use a small laundrette to wash towels and bedding, and if we smiled and look suitably childish, they would do some of our personal washing as well.

So yes, they also became our proxy mothers.

As the years went by, the training school grew in student numbers, and extra bedrooms were added, as well as a new block where there was a bar and games area, plus a more comfortable (if noisier) television area.

The bulk of the students came from the mainstream radio stations who were able to get to Leafield on the Mondays to begin a course, and return home on Friday afternoons. The Goonhilly apprentices had a significantly longer journey, hence the reason we had travelled on a Sunday to be rested and ready for the Tuesday start. While most of the students went home for the weekend, we couldn't get away. If we left on a Friday afternoon, we wouldn't get home until very late, and then we would have to begin the return trip early on the Sunday.

Our First visit to Witney

Monday 2nd September 1968, and the seven-wide eyed, and tired Cornish apprentices were outside the front door of the training centre waiting for a minibus.

Our first experience of training was not going to be at Leafield itself. We were to be taken to Witney to attend the West Oxfordshire Technical College, where we would begin a seven-week block release academic term. It was just us that morning, as the other new apprentices from around the country would be travelling to Leafield to begin the real class work the next day. Our visit to the college was to have an introduction to the working areas, and to meet some of the training staff.

The short journey to Witney made us realise how isolated Leafield was. We drove down lanes with high hedges for three or four miles with little more than small hamlets or isolated cottages to remind us that other people did actually live here. We had even taken a back road and avoided getting to see the village of Leafield, so our first view of local civilisation would have to wait. Things became a slightly busier as we drove through the little village of Minster Lovell, where our minibus squeezed its way along a particularly narrow bit of tarmac, before crossing over the River Windrush and finally coming to a major road. This was the A40 that was a busy route between London and Fishguard in Wales. We had just two or three miles on this main road before entering the town of Witney, where we turned right at an intersection that took us to the town centre. Very soon we were tumbling out of the minibus at the entrance to the College.

Just a few weeks earlier, I had left school where I struggled to get any enthusiasm to gain qualifications, but now my career was to begin by going back into academia once more.

The college, that we quickly renamed 'Witney Tech', wasn't open yet to the normal students, so it was virtually deserted with just us and a handful of training staff. Our day was a bit of a blur - as was becoming usual for us – and we began with a rapid show round. One of the first places we were shown was the Student Union common room. We had been given special permission to use it, and although it didn't look very exciting, we grew to enjoy it as the local students took it over and brought it to life.

We had a quick glance at the canteen which was not open yet, and it was suggested we should use our lunch break to explore the town a little. Next we walked to look at the training accommodation. It was a series of rooms in various older buildings around the site that made up the engineering block. A number of our trainers were available to say hello that morning, and these men would become very familiar to us over the next three years.

At lunchtime we did take a look around the market town of Witney and found some food to top up our stomachs. The town seemed quite busy, had a good range of shops, and we were pleasantly intrigued by the number of young ladies making the most of the late summer sunshine. Over our time at 'Witney Tech' we rarely ate in the college canteen, preferring the town's fast-food outlets, and the young female attractions. After lunch we had a little longer looking around the college and meeting people. But we were soon bored and looking enviously at the warm sunshine outside. Our guide decided it was probably a good idea to organise the transport to take us back to Leafield... we didn't object.

The Village of Leafield

Back at the training centre we discovered that lots of people had arrived, and the bedroom block was now a different place. Young men were going in and out of the rooms, and there was the sounds of shouting and doors slamming all around us.

Suddenly I felt isolated. Strangers who all seemed to know each other, were looking at me and making comments between themselves. I needn't have worried, some of them turned out to be our fellow new apprentices, and others would become friends as the months and years went by.

Several of the Goonhilly group decided to make the most of the sunshine and take a stroll to the village of Leafield. Our walk began along the narrow Ash Track which led to the road towards the village. Occasionally we had to jump for cover as yet more engineers arrived in their cars, and who had little respect for pedestrians. Turning right towards the village we had our first experience of the Straight Mile. It looked a long way but we were enjoying ourselves, shouting, swearing, and joking about our thoughts of the experiences so far, and what was to come.

About half way along the road we spotted a small group of people coming towards us. Soon they became a little clearer and we chuckled at the sight. There were four of them, and they seemed to be lined up in height order. One was huge, both in height and girth, with the next being slightly shorter, but of bean pole stature. Then there was someone who appeared similar to ourselves, and finally there was a short squat one. All of them had long hair and appeared quite intimidating, and as we got closer, we stopped talking and eventually passed by without a sound.

Once we decided they were far enough away, we began to chat again and expressed our concerns about the group who had just passed us, who we perceived to be the locals.

Later that evening we discovered that they were new apprentices like ourselves, but from the Rugby Transmitter Station. In height order they were Dave Harrison who was a gentle giant, next was bean pole Benny Lee, followed by Jonny Allen, and finally Dave Gibson.

We were soon in the village of Leafield, and to be honest, we weren't overly impressed. Our slightly rowdy group passed by houses on either side and a garage, before coming to a junction with a small shop on the corner, and a pub called 'The Fox' set back behind it. Before us was a patch of grass in front of a typical school building. Taking the road to the left we walked around the grassy area and school with our only discovery being a telephone box and a butcher's shop. There seemed to be little else to see except for the village church ahead of us, so we crossed the grass to another narrow road on the right and turned back towards the village centre. More houses and then another shop on the left with the school to our right. There were smiles again as we came to another pub called 'The George'. A few metres further and we came to a junction with sign posts suggesting that Witney, and various other places with strange names were to the left. There was also a small post office on this corner.

To the right we saw where we had come from a few minutes previously, and we decided the excitement of Leafield had already been too much for us, and it was time to go back to the training centre. There was a long return walk, and it wouldn't be very long before dinner beckoned.

The little village hadn't been very interesting, but we agreed it would be very rude not to try out the pubs as soon as possible.

Back at the training school we found that even more people seemed to be running around. It was obviously a moment when people were meeting up with old friends from around the different radio stations. They were shouting, laughing, and there were even a few playing football on the grassy area in front of the accommodation block.

Inside the block, I realised the construction made it very hot in the sunshine, and my bedroom window was flung open. Someone in a nearby room stuck their head out of their own window and chatted to me for a moment or two, and passed on a bit of advice. He said that I should be careful not to leave the window open when out of the room, as it was common for people to play practical jokes by getting through the windows and causing mayhem inside.

I thanked this good Samaritan (whoever he was) and warned the others.

It was time for dinner.

So far, we had only experienced the late night sandwiches and breakfast, but now we had a chance to sample the dinner menu. The ladies in the kitchen did their best to provide a healthy diet with various choices of starters, main course and puddings. Most of the gang of young men seemed to prefer the roast options, or whatever could be accompanied by chips. The puddings were generally filling and we rarely left the canteen without full stomachs.

The regular post dinner period involved waiting for a bathroom or shower to become available to wash away the sweaty dirt of adolescent bodies. There were quite a few bathrooms but with upwards of 50 people wanting a wash, it could sometimes be a long wait.

That evening a smaller group of us walked to the village again to try out the two pubs we had found earlier.

Being the closest, we went to The Fox initially. It turned out to be a really oldie world pub with the main bar featuring a tiled floor, which somehow looked as if it might regularly be covered in sawdust. With just a small window, the bar was rather dark, and seating was mainly wooden benches around aging tables. For entertainment there was a dart board, and in a smaller back room I believe there was a pool table.

The aging landlord eyed us with suspicion, and probably realised that we were the latest intake at the training school. He hardly spoke, and certainly never questioned our age as he served us with beer direct from a barrel. We sat, drank our beer, and quietly chatted as we watched various locals come in for a drink. Many of them began to play dominoes, but they all stared at us, and probably made derogatory comments to each other about the latest batch of strangers to invade their village.

We quickly discovered over the days to come, that the people of Leafield put up with the engineers from the Radio Station, but rarely mixed with us.

Slightly concerned that The Fox was not really to our taste, we soon left and went across the grass to The George.

This was better. It had a bigger and lighter main bar with a dart board again, but also a jukebox to make it livelier. The main room was busier than the first pub and we were even acknowledged by one or two of the locals. There was also a lounge bar area that was almost empty, but we soon discovered it was where many of the training school regulars would drink.

After a second drink we decided The George was our favoured pub, and over the years to come I would visit it regularly as I came to the training school.

It was time for the walk back to the Radio Station and our beds. It had been a day of discovery and quite tiring. Half an hour later we said goodnight, and made our way to our bedrooms.

My room was hot, and the bed unfamiliar, but I was soon asleep wondering what tomorrow would bring.

Training Begins for the 1968 Apprentices

Although a couple of the lads were missing for that first day, the year's intake of Radio Station apprentices began our three years of training that morning.

Along with those of us from Goonhilly, there were the four from Rugby we had seen the day before, plus three from Bearley (near Birmingham) and three from the London area.

We met up at Leafield for almost four or five months of each year. There were two blocks making up 13 weeks a year of academic work at the West Oxfordshire Technical College, and then two further blocks of three weeks based at Leafield itself for in-house theory and practical skills. Occasionally some of us would attend other training courses focussed on the needs of our particular radio stations, so the little village of Leafield became very much a second home.

As a reference, here is a list of the 18 young men who began their working careers that year:

Goonhilly

- George Williams
- George Whittaker
- Dave Slade
- Dave Sjoholm
- Dave Webb
- Rodney Lister
- Mark Jago
- Phil Harvey

Rugby (in size order)

- Dave Harrison
- Benny Lee
- Jonny Allen
- Dave Gibson

Bearley

- Colin Bootle
- Phil Amos
- Tony Hampton

London

- Steve Cox
- Vince Maund
- Paul Jackson

Most of us survived the apprenticeship with just two people being asked to leave. They were Dave Webb from Goonhilly and Tony Hampton from Bearley. To be honest they were both innocent of the particular final straw accusation, but were guilty of overstepping the mark on a number of occasions.

For the next three years we met up regularly at Leafield. We laughed a lot, and occasionally argued over things that young men always argue about. We took the micky out of each other at any excuse, but never in a vicious way. Virtually all of us had a similar outlook on life, enjoyed alcohol (probably too much), were often cheeky with our college lecturers and instructors (again too much), and probably concentrated far too much on having fun, rather than absorbing the training matter.

Whatever else we achieved, we all grew up to become adults during those three years.

Phillip Harvey RIP

On a sad note, for me, I attended the funeral of Phil Harvey in 2019. I believe others have also died, but this was the first of those that were closest to me.

West Oxfordshire Technical College

Our trip to Witney on the second morning was in a full sized coach, and what had been an alarming journey the previous morning was now even worse, as the coach driver appeared to have no thoughts that someone might be coming the other way on the narrow lanes. We rolled from side to side on the bends, and although we soon became accustomed to our daily roller coaster ride, we were always glad to get back onto solid ground outside the college in Welch Way, where the college was situated.

There was a slightly briefer look around the still deserted college, but soon we began the first of our lectures.

Some of the lessons were easy going with very enthusiastic lecturers, while others were stricter, but all of them were a breath of fresh air for me. We were treated like young men rather than children. The lecturers addressed us by the term 'Mr' rather than just our surnames. As the months went by we became friends with some of the lecturers, and first names became the norm.

My least favourite person was Alan Grindrod who took us all for mathematics. I hadn't realised just how good my school mathematics teacher (Mr Skinner) had been, as I just couldn't come to terms with Mr Grindrod's teaching methods. I was one of the more successful students with the subject, and already familiar with much of the material, but there was one new branch of mathematics that I had to master, and that was Calculus. I suspect that if this had been a part of my Grammar School curriculum, I would have had less difficulty, and in fact another instructor I encountered later in a different college clarified many of the topics I struggled with in Witney.

Alan Grindrod also took great pleasure in taking the micky out of us from Cornwall. He insisted to suggest the county, and its people were backward. It was a bit of fun initially that we all played along with, but three years later he was still doing it.

At the other end of the personality scale was Lenny Armitage with the responsibility for general mechanical subjects. He was dedicated to helping anyone who sat in front of him. He never teased us for our ignorance and would spend ages allowing us every chance of grasping a topic. Now, as a Grammar School child my education was primarily academic based, and I never had the same exposure to mechanical subjects compared to those who went to a Secondary Modern school, where the emphasis was more about 'hands on' skills. The majority of the other apprentices had gone down this education route, and were far more advanced than me with a number of the subjects that Mr Armitage was responsible for.

I was able to come to terms with most topics, but one was a total mystery to me, and that was Technical Drawing. Although not important for my future career, a basic knowledge of the subject was a compulsory requirement to achieve success in the certificate we were aiming at. The others romped through drawings of brickwork, windows, and doors, or how to make convincing and acceptable pictures of various mechanical tools, but my results were more akin to modernist or Picasso versions of everyday items.

This is where I appreciated just how dedicated Lenny Armitage was. Over the weeks he drip-fed me simple things to draw and showed me how to create the basic shapes, and necessary visual effects by shading, or cross hatched lines. Then as the exam approached, he went the extra mile and continually gave me the same couple of objects to draw. Eventually he seemed happy with my attempts, and the extra 1:1 coaching stopped. What I didn't know was that he was responsible for actually setting the exam.

On the day of the exam I turned to the dreaded Technical Drawing question and immediately realised what he had been doing. I successfully reproduced a picture of a pair of pliers to get my 'tick in the box' pass for the subject.

Unfortunately, his dedication and desire to please, left him open to abuse. He was so easily led astray from the subject under discussion, and would regularly answer random questions that took him down a totally obscure road. As this was a common game played by some of our class, he would eventually realise what was happening, and after a quick chastise of the guilty person, he would return to the original subject. One person was a regular offender. Dave Gibson insisted on dragging Lenny Armitage down various blind alleys during almost every lesson with him. The chastisements became louder and more aggressive as the months passed, but Lenny could never resist the temptation to answer questions, and we all loved him.

Another lecturer was Mr Mills. He took us for Electrical Principles which was one of the most important subjects for us all. He was a tall man with long arms that seem to flail wildly to assist with his description of a topic. The material he covered was new for all of us and a struggle for many, including myself. But Mr Mills persevered and slowly over the years, my confusion of Resistive Networks, and Kirchhoff's Laws, became less clouded.

Then there was Mr Yates, who was a white-haired Welshman with a passion for his subject of Physics. One or two of the class managed to understand the principles of levers and weights through a distance, but several of us sat and stared in despair of these topics, and I have to say they never found a comfortable place to rest in my brain.

The final core subject on our technical training timetable was Radio Principles, and I will always remember Mr Stratton. He was a tall and bulky man with enormous hands and fingers. They were like this because of a medical problem, and created many amusing moments when he picked up small electrical components and tried to show us their construction. The size of his fingers only allowed minute bits of these components to actually be visible. We all did our best not to laugh during these moments when his huge digits hid the item of interest.

He was an enthusiastic and really good instructor, and I lapped up his words for this subject that was to become a major part of my future.

There were other instructors that came and went during our time at the college, but the small group of trainers mentioned were the main players during our three years of academic training.

On each Wednesday we were given time off from academia, and had an afternoon dedicated to non-technical aspects of life, loosely referred to as General Studies. They tempted us with introduction sessions into economics and business, which many of us decided was left-wing indoctrination, as everything appeared to be biased towards socialist politics. Occasionally someone would come to give us an afternoon of pastural subjects. In reality, although often presented by a religious person, we were encouraged to drive the topics under discussion, and it was rarely about bibles or the church.

But on most weeks, Wednesday afternoon was dedicated to sport. These sessions involved walking to a vast patch of grass known as The Leys. Here we played football, cricket, or some other team games to stretch our unfit muscles and generally let off steam. Once or twice a term we would have a coach trip to the Westminster College in Oxford, where we had the use of the swimming pool for a couple of hours. This college was for young ladies looking to become teachers, and we always fantasised about sharing the pool with these young ladies. Of course, our fantasy worlds remained fantasies.

The General Studies staff also organised a special week away from college work each year. Usually the fourth week of the 7-week block, we would board a coach on the Monday morning and spend four nights away somewhere to extend our knowledge.

... and have a very good laugh

In the first year we went to London and looked at the docklands area plus some factories, but the most memorable aspect of this week away was to visit the Crystal Palace sports centre. As well as seeing the tracks and gyms, we looked behind the scenes at how the centre ticked. That day ended with an hour in the Olympic swimming pool. I was not a swimmer then, and time in the water meant simple floundering. At Crystal Palace I was coaxed into having a swim, and only as I tired after a few strokes did I realise that the lifeguards wouldn't let me get out at the side, and I had to complete the 50 metres to the far end.

The general studies 'away week' in the second year saw us visiting Northamptonshire. I remember a mind-blowing visit to a steel foundry. We saw the molten steel being poured from the furnace and as it made its way along a channel the heat was unbelievable, and its brightness with sparks flying from it really terrified me. The next stage was seeing the freshly created block of steel being rolled, and it continually shot past us on what looked like a conveyer belt as it became the required thickness. All the time we were there, vast lumps of steel were being lifted overhead by cranes.

I left there with a feeling of relief that I managed to avoid getting a job where this level of fear, and the horrible atmosphere existed.

Another interesting visit that week was to the Lotus shoe factory. We spent a long time following the manufacturing process, which to be honest wasn't that exciting, but the fun came when we got to the end with hundreds and hundreds of shoes ready for delivery. The guide proudly exclaimed his satisfaction with the shoes, and said they were of a very high quality. He even gave a shoe to Rodney Lister and asked him to see if it was as good as he said. It must have been a truly unusual fluke, but with little effort, Rodney tore the sole away from the upper.

… roars of laughter and a very red-faced guide.

For the third and final year of our General Studies, our holiday experience was to the Herefordshire area near the border with Wales. Our group was bigger now, as another year of apprentices came with us.

One of the first outings was to the River Wye Valley and the Forest of Dean, in an area known as Simmons Yat. We crossed the river on an old hand pulled ferry, climbed up the road on the other side, and looked at a quite spectacular view down onto the river from a picnic spot called Simmons Yat Rock. We were given a period of freedom to explore, with instructions to meet up at a particular time at that same Simmons Yat Rock.

At the allotted time we met up for the journey back to our accommodation, but one of the younger Goonhilly apprentices (Tony Sutton) was missing. We searched for quite some time but eventually it was decided that we should go, and an official search was initiated with the police.

We had our dinner with no news, and it was no longer a laugh. Then, a car turned up, and without too much fuss Tony got out safe and well. After some time while he was being checked and questioned, we got the full story.

Now, across the river from 'Simmons Yat Rock', is another tourist spot overlooking the valley that is known as simply 'Simmons Yat'.

Tony didn't realise they were different places, and at the instructed time, he sat down at Simmonds Yat and waited. He was eventually found by some scouts a couple of hours later.

… more roars of laughter and a slightly red-faced Tony.

On another day that week we went to the Bulmer's Cider Factory in the city of Hereford. Our walk around the site was slightly boring as we saw crushing equipment, vats and barrels. Then after walking through a noisy bottling area we arrived at an old train carriage, and our demeanours suddenly became very much more positive.

This was the sampling area.

We started quite carefully just sipping the samples given, but the guide made it clear that we could have as much as we wanted, as long as it was consumed before we left. It wasn't more than a few minutes before I discovered I really liked cider, and especially one that was called Pomagne.

Many of us left the Bulmer's factory rather drunk.

The brand name Pomagne was soon withdrawn due to conflict with Champagne producers, and it became simply sparkling cider.

From the home of Bulmer's cider, we went to a JCB tractor factory. The visit was again rather uninteresting, especially as hangovers were progressing well. However, our afternoon ended with another wonderful moment, when the guide allowed one of us to try out driving one of the huge tractors and its lifting equipment. It was Vince Maund who had the opportunity, and he made us roar with laughter when he offered to give two girls in a mini car a lift with the tractor he was driving.

All in all, these General Studies extended field trips were amazing, but I do wonder if the cultural aspects we witnessed really justified the money spent.

At the end of each year at the college we would take exams. They were mainly based on the City and Guilds curriculum, but most of us also began working towards other national qualifications. One or two people excelled, and I had finally come out of my educational laziness, and passed every exam. There was a carrot dangled here for those with the very best results, as they would be given the chance to go to university on a degree course. Rodney Lister was successful and went on to get a degree.

I failed to get the required marks to go to university. It was in just one subject, and that was mathematics...

Thanks Mr Grindrod!

Life at Leafield

Those seven weeks away in Leafield were the first time I had been away from home for more than a few days, and I was missing my family and my friends. The new surroundings were exciting at times, but there were also moments when I felt a little lonely.

But there were positive aspects as well.

Even though my job felt a little like a continuation of being in school, there was the ongoing thrill of getting paid. Each Thursday afternoon we all eagerly lined up in the corridor outside the general office, and then one at a time we were given a little envelope in exchange for a signature. This was our pay packet, but it also included five shillings (25p) per day for being away from home. It was officially called *'Incidental Day Subsistence'* but more commonly referred to as *'Beer and Fags'* money. It meant that most of us were saving the majority of our actual pay packet.

Now to the more negative aspects.

It has to be remembered that during the early years of the training school, the radio station was operational, and high frequency radio energy existed in the air around us. It made personal radios make strange squealing or jangling noises, and the programmes we wanted to listen to were wiped out.

The radio energy also created a strange visual phenomenon.

Fluorescent lights glowed visibly without being switched on. Walking along the corridors was like being under light chasers, with the weird pulsing effect moving along each fluorescent tube. Worse still, the bedrooms initially had the same lighting, and it was impossible to have darkness. When electricians were walking around holding the tubes, it was as if they were holding Star Wars light sabres.

It wasn't long before the bedrooms were converted to have traditional bulbs that were not affected by the radio energy.

Moving away from unwanted lighting effects, there was also the problem of getting used to the noise.

Having forty or so other young men living close by, meant far more noise than I was used to. There was constant shouting, people running up and down the corridors, doors slamming, doors being hammered, and nearly always a drone of multiple sources of music. The walls were thin, and wobbled as immediate neighbours closed their doors noisily, and very few ever closed them quietly.

And there were a lot of pranks going on.

It was quickly discovered by the older apprentices, that the walls were so thin that they could be flexed away from the door catches, and with a well position shove, the doors could be opened without keys. When a room was empty, mates of the unsuspecting occupant would get in and carry out innocent (or sometimes less than innocent) little games.

The bed was remade with a fold in the sheet to stop legs of the tired and unsuspecting victim from going more than half way into the bed...

... this was simple innocent fun.

Wardrobes and drawers were emptied...

... annoying but still fun.

Others experimented with their new found electrical knowledge to cause mayhem by putting an old sixpenny coin in the light sockets. When the person returned at night and switched on his light, there was a little bang, and the lighting fuses failed.

... this was annoying to several people on the same lighting circuit, and potentially dangerous, but the victim did gain a slightly charred sixpenny bit.

Using the fire hoses to spray under the door of bathrooms, and drenching the relaxed bather with cold water...

... the victim's response brought incredible laughter, but it was horrible trick, and broke rules on misuse of fire equipment.

Taking bedroom furniture outside onto the grass...

... lots of laughter, but really rather annoying.

Taking everything in the room out onto the grass (including sink) and setting it up as if it was the bedroom...

... hilarious for all but the victim.

Bringing a sheep in from the field and leaving it in the room...

... tears of laughter, but really cruel on the sheep.

Fortunately, we were new and innocent, so didn't get targeted (initially) and as the years moved on the pranks stopped.

We also discovered that the night warden (Danny Spires) could sense that mischief was afoot. He came around a corner on many occasions as something was about to happen, and the sharpness of his tongue was usually sufficient to stop the pranks.

At weekends, Goonhilly's young apprentices were marooned at the centre. Because of our isolation we received special treatment, including dispensation to use the Radio Station's Social Club. It wasn't that spectacular, but it did have some comfortable chairs as well as a snooker table, dart board, and a record player. We were even allowed to use the bar, but only for soft drinks until we turned 18. Sadly, the bar was rarely open at weekends, so generally we had to go out and find our own entertainment.

We became more adventurous as the weeks went by, and regularly had a Saturday in Witney, even walking there on occasions. As the delights of Witney faded, we spread our wings further, and regularly caught a bus to take us from Witney into the busy City of Oxford.

Oxford was a real eye opener to me, it was vibrant, full of large shops, crowded with young students and their bicycles... oh an there were quite a few delightful girls as well.

A Saturday in Oxford meant soaking up the atmosphere, looking around the shops, and sub-consciously absorbing some of the architecture, although we would have never admitted it at the time. This was where I tasted Chinese food for the first time, and my mouth exploded with the intense flavours. I was hooked for life.

We also bought things to entertain our stay away from home, with books and music. We came back from one of our trips when Dave Webb had bought a copy of the latest Beatles record called Hey Jude. When we got back to Leafield, we went to the Station Social Club and he played it on the record player while the rest of us played darts. It was a superb record, but after it had been continually played for almost an hour, we all revolted. Dave was threatened that his record was about to be destroyed, and he was possibly going to be murdered.

Yes, we were a close group, but we were also prone to losing tempers with each other sometimes.

Dave and his record survived, and I still love the song, so no lasting damage was done.

Generally, the 1968 gang of apprentices were gelling very well.

Yes, most of us mucked around at the college, but the majority of us also realised that we were beginning a potentially very good career, and needed to be successful with the academic studies. From my point of view, I found most subjects challenging, but very interesting, especially those that were directly a part of my future role at Goonhilly.

Away from the college we spent hours together in each other's bedrooms chatting, listening to music, or playing cards. Many of us smoked, and the little rooms became unhealthily hot and stuffy, with a permanent haze of smoke. There was a lounge where larger gatherings allowed more people to join in with the card games. Our favoured game was Three Card Brag, and while betting was never excessive, fair sums of money changed hands at time. I don't think anyone lost much money, as over the weeks we all had lucky and unlucky moments.

Playing darts was another pastime, and this was in the lounge sometimes, but often in The George pub in the village. There we also regularly discussed ridiculous subjects over a drink, but silence would instantly descend if a girl was spotted in the pub. The male dominated environment was not the best atmosphere for post adolescent boys.

My musical tastes changed after discovering that Dave Harrison (from Rugby) was a rock guitar player. Several of us spent hours in Dave's room listening to his musical collection, and to him playing his guitar. I quickly became hooked on Led Zeppelin, and was introduced to several less familiar bands who nearly always had heavy metal guitar riffs, and drum solos. I soon decided that when I got home, one of the first things to spend my money on was a music system.

In another bedroom we found that one of the older apprentices had built and ran a pirate radio station. The enthusiast had absorbed the skills from training courses and built a transmitter hooked up to his stereo system. OK so it wasn't Radio Caroline, but could be listened to all over the site, and probably further away as well.

The time actually flew by, and soon we had completed the first seven-week block of college work, and the apprentices from all over England were packing their bags and waving a temporary cheerio to each other. We would be coming back in the following Spring to continue our studies in Witney, and to learn more about Leafield.

It was time for the seven of us to return home, and spend a few months at Goonhilly.

Back Home in Cornwall

When I got back home to be pampered by my mother again, there was a week off before returning to Goonhilly. This was a moment to catch up with family and friends, but there were some other very important things to organise.

Firstly, my mum booked an appointment with the manager of the Midland Bank. I needed a bank account, and at that time, it was only possible after a face-to-face interview with these men who were very powerful.

With that sorted, I turned my attention to getting some transport.

Although old enough to drive a car, I hadn't begun having lessons, so my only option was to turn to two wheels.

In Helston there was a motorcycle shop called Pascoes, and this was where all the local youngsters bought their first motorbike. It was quite a small shop at the top of Meneage Street, and crammed with pushbikes, motorbikes and scooters, and with a workshop behind it for repairs and services.

Most of the lads in my circle of friends began with a second hand bike, and after much discussion with the shop owner, I decided on a 175cc BSA Bantam. It was shiny blue with lots of chrome, but more importantly, it was within my budget. There were a few little extras that were needed like a helmet and gauntlets, but within a couple of days I was on the road.

So, having just sorted out my first bank account, and soon to receive my first chequebook, I also went straight into debt with a loan to buy the bike.

For the rest of that week, I rode around feeling the freedom of having transport. It was so special, and along with all the other new experiences of the previous two months, I really felt my life had changed, and I was growing up.

Meanwhile my mother was happy to have me home again, and I was spoilt rotten for a few days. I met up with my friends again and bored them silly with my experiences in Leafield. That week was a release from college work, but soon I had to go back to Goonhilly, and spend some serious time there. The mysteries of satellite communications would slowly begin to make sense.

Aerial 2

When we returned to Goonhilly after our visit to Leafield, a second aerial was nearing completion, and ready to begin service. Aerial 2 was again designed by Husband and Co, but constructed this time by the Marconi Company Limited.

I have to admit that when I first saw it, I thought it looked a bit like a barn with a reflector dish bolted onto one end.

It was a blue/grey corrugated metal building that hid much of the load bearing structure, which sat on a central pivot point. Just below the front edge of the dish, there were two electric bogey motors, that drove the aerial around on a circular twin track railway.

These rails were a fascination for most people. Once operational, any Aerial movement wasn't very much, and only a small section of the track (just a few inches) was used during a typical day. Many people performed a game of leaving a coin on the track where movement was expected, and then check later to see the now very squashed coin.

The bogey motors allowed azimuth movement of the 950 tonnes of structure at a maximum speed of 10 degrees a minute. The azimuth movement was restricted to about 200 degrees covering the southern quadrant where geo-stationary satellites are positioned.

Elevation movement was achieved by a motorised screw-drive, which allowed the dish to tilt up and down. The movement was limited again, and this time it covered approximately 45 degrees movement from horizontal. To go any higher, the screw-drive could be reconfigured to allow the dish to travel from 45 to 90 degrees.

The actual reflector was 27.4 metres in diameter, but the design was radically different to Aerial 1. The feed system this time was known as 'Cassegrain', and used a conical feed horn at the centre of the dish, which transmitted the radio transmissions to a smaller sub-reflector at the centre of a tripod structure. This sub-reflector acted a bit like a mirror, and reflected the energy back to fill the complete main dish profile. Finally the main dish radiated the signal towards the satellite.

In the receive direction, the signal path was into the main reflector, which focussed all the captured radio energy back to the sub-reflector, and from there into the conical feed.

This Cassegrain system eliminated the need for the use of waveguide in the dish, and reduced receive losses quite dramatically.

Although similar in size to Aerial 1, its design enabled far better efficiency.

Internally there was far more equipment space, and more of the communication modules were installed there, rather than in the main building.

As the years rolled by, the aerial became difficult to maintain, and in 2006, work began to dismantle it. It took many months to remove this particular chapter of the 40 years of satellite history. The dismantling project was very complex, and as well as tonnes of steel, the aerial had masses of asbestos insulation that had to be carefully removed, and disposed of.

For several decades, as visitors approached Goonhilly Downs in their cars, the first thing they saw when coming over the brow of a small hill, would have been Aerial 2. It was an incredible giant structure and sure to take their breath away. Now it is gone, but it has a special place in the hearts of the hundreds of engineers who had set foot inside it and kept it operating to the world.

Technical Terminology

While writing this book, I struggled to avoid using jargon and radio terminology, but I was very aware my life was rather full of scientific and technological, *'things'*. So, over the following chapters I could not describe my life, and the history of Goonhilly, without using at least some of those technical words and principles. Hopefully I won't make it overly complicated, and I will attempt to explain a few of the terms as we go along.

The first thing to address, is why Satellite Communications needed to have the gigantic aerials. These massive 30metre diameter structures have often been called different things. They could be described as an aerial, antenna, or maybe just as a reflector.

My Auntie Jane used to refer to them as:

"Those Statellite things up on the downs"

Anyway, I will attempt to explain why they are used.

Imagine before the days of electricity, people were restricted to using candles as a source of light. They weren't very effective, and moving around at night must have been hazardous.

It wasn't long before people discovered that by putting a piece of shiny copper behind the candle, some of the light that would have gone backwards, was now reflected by the copper, and added to the light going forward. They were better, but not by very much.

Now let's move forward a few decades to the electric torch. The little bulb's light was hardly more powerful than a candle. The best design found for a torch was a tube with the bulb slightly back from the end, and this stopped any light going sideways. There was also a silver shiny reflector behind the bulb, and the combination of bulb positioning and reflector, directed, or focussed, almost all the light to go forwards.

The same technique can be applied to radio signals.

The radio energy destined to go towards the satellite is of course far more powerful than a light bulb, but the parabolic shape of the dish acts in the same way as the shiny torch reflector, and creates a narrow concentrated beam of energy to be transmitted 36,000km into space towards the satellite.

Now let's think about receiving the signals back from the satellite.

The first issue is that the satellite only has a small amount of battery power to create the signal that is transmitted towards earth. It is hardly more than the equivalent of a radio candle. It has to make the same 36,000km journey through space and back to an Earth Station, and during that journey the radio energy spreads. The signal from the satellite uses the same reflector technique to maximise the energy towards earth, but the spreading effect is still quite dramatic. In fact, that little signal spreads so much that it can be seen by virtually all of the surface of the earth below it.

Just as a little bit of mathematics to put this into perspective. A modern efficient LED torch can produce 10 watts of light energy. This is about the same power level of early satellite transmissions. By the time the radio energy from the satellite gets back to the Earth Station, the spreading effect means that the energy at any one spot will be miniscule. In fact, it could be represented by putting a decimal point, and 18 zeros in front of the original 10 Watts.

Our approximately 30 metre diameter satellite dish now gathers the energy over the whole of its parabolic surface, and focusses it all on a single point, that is connected to the receiving equipment.

Instead of just receiving the tiny amount of energy I just mentioned, the radio signal strength at the input of the receiver is increased, so that there are now only 12 zeros after the decimal point.

OK, so we increased the signal strength by a factor of six decimal places, but it is still a very tiny little signal. At least the receiving equipment now has a chance of deciphering it.

Unfortunately, there is yet another problem.

Our tiny satellite sits in space, and behind it there are thousands of stars. Just like our own sun, these stars radiate all kinds of energy, including the identical energy as our satellite transmission. So, as well as the tiny bit of signal from our satellite, the giant dish also receives the energy from space. It is unwanted, and so it is called noise.

Fortunately, the clever scientists had an answer for this.

The receive amplifier used was known as a Maser Amplifier that would ignore much of the noise. But when the amplifier was also cooled down, it ignored even more of that noise, and concentrate on the slightly larger satellite signal. The colder you could make the amplifier, the less the noise affected the required signal.

When I said cooling, I don't mean running cold water over the equipment, I don't even mean putting it into a fridge. At that time, the sort of cold temperatures involved could only be achieved by immersing the equipment inside a large vessel, called a Dewar, which was filled with liquid Nitrogen.

To achieve this at Goonhilly, there was a small group of people responsible for the Dewars, and the liquid nitrogen. They were called the 'Cryogenics Team'.

After we had come back from our first period of time at Leafield, we spent a few weeks in various teams around Goonhilly, and one of the first groups of people I spent time with were the Cryogenics team.

Getting to know things

For several months after our return from Leafield in 1968, our little gang of new apprentices settled down to learning more about Goonhilly by spending time with different departments around the site. The training team organised a schedule and we would be introduced to a team, and then spend time with them. Initially these sample sessions would be little more than a few days, or a week at most.

Our aim involved finding out as much as possible about what the group did, and how it fitted in with the other groups and teams around the site.

The experiences varied, with some being very positive, while others left me wondering what it was all about.

One of the reasons to spend time like this, was to see if a particular group or team appealed to us. But the people we met also had to give feedback to our manager about such things as our attitude, and willingness to learn and get involved.

The following few sections are brief description and thoughts about some of the areas I spent time with during the end of 1968, and Spring of 1969.

The Cryogenic Group

There were several smaller groups at Goonhilly with quite specific roles, and one of these was the Cryogenic Team.

Satellite Communications was still very new when I arrived at Goonhilly, and the technology was little more than experimental. One very important item of equipment was the very first receiver and amplifier that captured the signals from space.

This box of electronic magic was called the 'Maser Low Noise Amplifier' or usually just referred to as the LNA.

If you remember, I mentioned earlier that the radio signals from the satellite were little more than the light coming from a torch.

After travelling through space, those signals from a satellite are absolutely miniscule, and even after the huge dishes had focussed as much of the energy as possible into the receiver, it was still difficult to distinguish a signal, from the noise that exists in space.

Scientists knew that if the receiver was cold, it could operate better. Hence at Goonhilly that receiver was placed inside a container full of liquid nitrogen. The job of creating this liquid freezer, and keeping the receiver vessel cool was entrusted to the small group who made up the Cryogenic Team.

Although we all had a chance to experience time with this group, it was only for a very short period, as although their responsibility may have been important, the job was quite straight forward.

I remember only four people who were connected with this group. They were Dennis Thackaway, John Lutener, Percy Rawlings, and Ray Thompson. They generally kept to themselves, and I struggled to move beyond the minimum of interaction needed to get an appreciation of what they did.

As far as what I did while with that group, I remember very little, but here goes.

Their workshop was between the Construction Group, and the Mechanical Workshop. They had a large unit that created the liquid Nitrogen, and also had various cylinders of other gases. One of them was Helium which I quickly learnt about, with its ability to change the sound of a voice.

I never did find out what the gas was truly used for, but it was popular at Christmas to fill party balloons.

Of course the main job was filling the receiver vessel on Goonhilly 1 with the liquid Nitrogen, and this meant getting to the Low Noise Amplifier situated up in the structure behind the antenna dish. I don't recollect actually going up there, so I learnt very little about it.

Down in the lower part of the antenna building, alongside the drive equipment, the Cryogenics team had a huge orange rubber balloon which captured the Nitrogen after it had warmed up, and was then a gas. This balloon was like a huge sausage nearly two metres long, and I was fascinated by it.

Back at the workshop I noticed more of these balloons, and I discovered that some were damaged and waiting to be scrapped. I asked if I could have one, and that night I went home with it. I split it open, and it was then used to cover my motorbike to protect it against the rain.

It proved to be an amazing cover, and survived all the years while using two-wheeled transport.

That was really all I can remember about the Cryogenics Team, except for a special mention about John Lutener.

During 1968 when Goonhilly was receiving the Olympic Games television coverage from Mexico, there was a fault with the LNA which threatened to stop it being received. John resolved the problem, and the importance of the situation was recognised by more than just the people at Goonhilly.

He was awarded the British Empire Medal.

That meant there were two people working at Goonhilly with medals. I began to dream that maybe one day I would get one...

... I kept dreaming for a long time.

Construction Group
All of the apprentices seemed to enjoy the time spent with a group called 'The Construction Team'.

It was another small team of men who planned, costed, ordered kit, and completed projects that were not directly involved in the communications side of the station. They installed equipment racks and ran cables to and from them. Sometimes wooden, plastic, or metal boxes had to be bought, or made, to house a piece of kit. They mainly carried out physical jobs that were necessary for the station to operate smoothly.

I remember the team with Doug Pawlby, George Wells, Tony James, and Guy Barber. I seem to remember that Percy Rawlings also worked here alongside his time with the Cryogenics team. They worked hard, but also had time for jokes and mucking around. Tea breaks were regular and long, and I learnt a lot about some of the basic jobs that had to be done.

Doug Pawlby was a very special man, and loved by everyone. He never stressed, and never upset people if they made mistakes or were slow. As a hobby, he painted wonderful watercolour pictures of local scenes, and drew charicatures of people. One of his other skills was to produce scripts for the pantomimes that were occasionally put on. My first ever venture into amateur dramatics was playing Buttons in one of those pantomimes, and that sparked an interest that I have struggled to do much about over the years.

Time in the construction group was both fun and informative, but the most significant memory of those days, was the closeness of the men. They all had different skills, and no one shirked a task because it was complicated or boring, they got the jobs done. But they also had fun, and they were close like a family, and that was what I would witness and experience in the majority of the groups that I spent time with.

Technical Development Team (TD)
This was where Phillip Harvey (our eighth apprentice) was taken on, and stayed throughout his career.

The TD Group was involved in research and development. They were not a part of the operational activities of Goonhilly, but many of the projects they worked on, eventually led to changes in operational ways of working.

When new transmission or testing equipment had been created, they would test it and check if the performance was as good as advertised, and recommend if it should be used, or not. Over the years they built their own antennas, and experimented with various new technologies.

This group of people were very much at the front of Satellite Communications technology.

My short spell in this group was not a pleasant one. To begin with, I didn't have a clue as to what the engineers and technicians were doing, and at least one of the people supposedly looking after me was obnoxious.

He had a saying that was frequently sent my way:

"**Apprentices are to be seen, and not heard**".

Well, that put a damper on me asking any questions, and what might have turned out to be an interesting group to spend time with, became days of simply finding somewhere to sit and watch at a distance.

As the years went by, I would often work with some of the engineers from TD, but during my training period, I learnt virtually nothing.

The Test Desk

This was completely chalk and cheese compared to my time in TD. It was little more than a desk in the corner of the West Wing, with meters, testers, reference manuals, and a pile of faulty equipment.

In charge was a man called Arthur Seager. He was older than many of the people I spent time with, didn't talk very much, and always smoked a pipe. His job was to use instruction manuals for any faulty kit, to find out what was wrong, and repair it.

At that time, engineers always tried to repair items no matter how big or expensive they were. Over the decades this has changed because equipment is generally more reliable, and it is seen more cost effective to buy new, rather than spend time repairing.

Anyway, I enjoyed this experience because he always made time to describe what a piece of kit was supposed to do, and described the test equipment he was using. One very important piece of his tool kit was a large box called a 'Valve Tester'. Transistors were rare in the late 1960s, and much of the equipment used small glass tube shaped items that were called valves.

There were many variations of these valves in terms of size, and also the arrangement of connector pins at one end. The first task was to find the details of the valve from a selection of data books, and then push the connectors into the appropriate socket on the top of the test box. Next the switches and knobs were used to ensure the correct voltages were applied to it. As the valve was switched on, it glowed, and meters would show the operational conditions. By comparing the readings with the data in the books, the valve could be declared OK, or faulty.

On other occasions, Arthur would simply open the covers of the suspect item, switch it on and then poke around the components and wires with meter probes. His knowledge and experience usually allowed him to spot the problem, and then replace the faulty resistor or capacitor, or a valve.

On more than one occasion I remember him peering into a metal box, taking his pipe out of his mouth, and sniff. He would then quickly suck on his pipe again and declare:

"That's the faulty component".

Another bonus of my time there was being told to go to the stores to get a new valve, or one of the other components, and then watch as Arthur put the new one in, and giving a satisfactory smile as the equipment worked again.

Over the days I began to use the valve tester, recognise different components and also what value they were, from coloured stripes and numbers.

My time with Arthur may not have been the most dynamic experience, but it expanded my knowledge of electrical components, and fundamental skills of fault finding.

Mechanical Workshop

The workshop was where metal objects were created from sheets of copper, steel, and aluminium, or blocks of brass. There were a lot of small jobs, or quite large projects sometimes, for various areas around the site.

Vernon Wheatley was in charge, and Ray Thompson sometimes appeared. There was also Richard Jenkins (Jinks) who was a third-year apprentice. He had enjoyed his time in the workshop so much, that he was allowed to stay there, and spent the rest of his career in the role.

This was a fascinating environment with huge bending machines, lathes, vices, welding equipment, and several tools of mass destruction. Vernon was not the most outgoing person, and I think he just tolerated apprentices, who rarely had sufficient skills to be useful. Jinks, on the other hand was great. He would spend time to demonstrate things, and give me small jobs.

My time in the workshop didn't inspire me very much, but I did manage to complete a personal project, of making a small box as an ashtray on a little stem attached to a base. It involved no more than cutting and bending the aluminium, and pop riveting the bits together, but it stayed with me for many decades.

To be honest it was pretty amateurish, and confirmed my suspicions that I was never going to be a metal worker.

The Rigging Team

These sample sessions with the various groups were an excellent way to get a flavour of what happened around

Goonhilly, but it also introduced us to people we might rarely encounter. One such group of men worked in the Rigging Team.

Traditionally the Riggers were a vital part of the radio stations around the country. They were the men who erected the radio towers, and hung the cables between them to create the aerials. At Goonhilly the team weren't responsible for that, but they were the primary people for the heavy jobs, or anything that involved climbing.

Hence, if something needed to be painted on the aerials, or if a repair was needed high up on the structures, the Riggers would be there. It might have needed ladders, or perhaps the Simon Cherry Picker, but sometimes they would be simply clambering up and around the metalwork on the rear of the dishes.

They had a dirty role, and worked outside in the cold and rain all through the year. But no matter what they had to do, they always seemed to be smiling, and willing to share a joke with anyone.

I only had a couple of days with them, but although they may not have been involved in technical aspects, it allowed me to appreciate that their role was vital to keep things going.

Luckily, I was not trained, and therefore not asked to climb, but I rode around in their vans and helped carry things. Then when they were climbing, I would go and wait in their portable hut which was a wooden cabin on wheels, and a bit like an old gypsy caravan. This was their refuge from the cold and wet, and where there was always a pot of hot and strong tea to refresh them, and to warm their frozen fingers.

This was where I found Nelson. He was one of the team, but he had been around for many decades, and no longer involved in climbing, or lifting. As far as I could tell, he was just employed to make tea.

I spent hours chatting to Nelson, with the stories of his younger exploits. He was amazing, and although I rarely saw him again, his honest approach to life and work, left a mark on me.

The riggers were a major part of Goonhilly. If there was a social event, they would be there. If someone needed help, they would volunteer to assist. Most of the names have left my brain cells, but I could never forget Danny, and Jonno who brought a smile to everyone, and shared a laugh with the world.

Time in the Stores

Another popular *'Get to Know About'* session was a week in the Stores. It was away from the main building, and in a complex that was home to several groups, including some teams I had already spent time with.

The Stores was not visually very exciting. Going through the door, there was a counter, and a small office to the left. The storeman spent most of his time in the office waiting for customers. Behind the counter, there were four or five long rows of shelving crammed with *'Things'*. Once I had explained who I was, the storeman grudgingly lifted the flap in the counter, and I was allowed into his hallowed world.

On the counter were a couple of large hard-covered folders containing pages and pages of the things that could be obtained from the stores. These books were referred to as the 'Rate Book' which was common right across the GPO, and introduced me to the amazing Civil Service method of describing items.

Why use a single straightforward word for an object when a description can be expanded to fill a line?

A broom might have become - Wooden brush, course haired, long handled No.1

Whilst a brush for a dustpan - Wooden hand brush, course haired, short handled No.1

Every item seemed to have a number at the end.

Some of the tools had unusual numbers, with one being 'Pliers, wiring, No. 81'.

Over several decades, these official Rate Book item descriptions were often simplified by the users. As an example, rather than the long-winded description above, those pliers were always referred to as a pair of 81s. Of course, if you needed to replace an item, the storeman (Jobsworth) would insist that the customer used the exact Rate Book Item description.

Anyway, many of us enjoyed the experience of working in the stores, and began to become familiar with Rate Book descriptions for the more common items.

I was allowed to take an active role as a trainee storeman, but there were no desktop computers or spreadsheets to assist us in those days. So, when a customer asked for something, I would begin by checking the Rate Book item code, and then, under the supervision of Jobsworth, I would complete a paper request docket, with the code number and description. Next, I had to use a local card index system to see how many of the items were left in stock, and where they could be found in the stores.

Sometimes the card showed the incorrect stock level, and then there was chaos.

All the completed request dockets were retained until there was time to check that stock numbers on the shelves matched the index card records. If during one of these stock checks there was a discrepancy, the completed dockets would be checked, to see if a simple mathematic mistake could be found.

If that failed to resolve the issue, all the shelves and drawers near the item location would be checked to see if someone had put things in the incorrect place.

The last resort was for the storeman to look through those dockets again, to see if an apprentice was involved. If someone like me had signed the docket, then I would get the blame, and the error was written off, by amending the figures in red ink.

I described the storeman as being a 'Jobsworth' and here is one of the reasons why. While I was helping out by creating dockets, or fetching items, someone came in for a pencil. Before sending me to fetch it from the appropriate drawer, he turned to the customer and sadly informed him that there was only one pencil left, so he couldn't have it.

When the person looking for a pencil asked why he couldn't have it, the response was:

"**There is only one pencil left, and someone might want it**".

I exchanged incredulous glances with the disappointed customer, and realised yet another aspect of the Civil Service way of working.

My time in the stores wasn't for very long, unlike our storeman. While there, I tried to appear happy in my work and always attempted to interact with the engineers coming in to get things. I was beginning to be recognised, and I felt I was starting to become a part of Goonhilly.

Study Periods

While the eight of us began a gentle introduction to all the different groups around Goonhilly, the academic aspects of our apprenticeship had to continue as well. This meant one day a week spent in the training room to look at what we had covered during the block release term, and studying a range of documentation made available to us.

Much of this extra documentation was from a monthly publication called the IEEE Journal which I believe was created by the GPO. Its aim was to help engineers to further their knowledge of electrical and radio principles and practices. This monthly booklet was available to engineers all over the world, to help them with information at levels to suit beginners through to university candidates. Much of the information went way over our heads, but there were several basic sections that were invaluable to us.

The topics we concentrated on, targeted people studying for City and Guilds qualifications, and over the next three years, we would be sitting these exams, as well as those for our college in Oxfordshire. In addition to the actual information, there were exam test papers from previous years that we could have a go at. It certainly gave me confidence by knowing what to expect, and also to spot topics that appeared in the exams almost every time.

There was however a major problem for our weekly training sessions. We were a group of easily distracted young men, and it was difficult to focus our minds on endless technical documents. It didn't help that our training room was hardly bigger than a small living room, with a block of tables in the middle, surrounded by quite uncomfortable chairs.

It was almost impossible to concentrate.

Rather than quiet study, we often chatted, and that chatter got noisier and noisier as our minds wandered.

I briefly mentioned earlier that the training room was in the copper lined section of the station, and designed as an emergency bedroom with metal bunk beds stored against the walls. It had a sliding door, and the wall with the corridor was not full height, and hence the noise we were generating was very apparent to anyone walking by.

Complaints to the training officer were common, and then we would be shouted at and warned that we must be quiet. This would work for a while, but soon quiet whispers would turn into raucous laughter and shouting once more. There were several occasions when our training officer would make it clear that this was not 'playtime', and there could be serious consequences if we didn't behave.

As 1968 came to an end, the Goonhilly gang of first year apprentices set off for Leafield again. It was time for some more training.

Leafield Again

It was only when I looked back at my training record that I realised we set off for Leafield on Sunday 29th December for a three-week training course. This meant we had a very unusual New Year's Eve that year.

This time our training was going to be at the Leafield Training School itself. We were about to have our first in-house training event known as the *'ETE Radio 1'* course. It was split into two three-week events, and this would be the first half of the course.

Leafield did not have recognised professional teaching staff. The lecturers and practical instructors were GPO engineers who had moved into full time training. Being GPO people, they were acting as our managers, and would tell us off if we mis-behaved, and had the power to officially discipline us.

It was the full group of apprentices from around the country again now. In general, we behaved far better than we did at the college in Witney, although some of the group still pushed their luck a little.

The training course was covering the basics of electrical theory, and radio communications, and the lecturers who looked after us were Reg Messer, and Jack Griffith. They were very much from an earlier time in the GPO, and wore suits and ties each day. The lecture room had a small raised area in front of the roller chalk board, and this gave the two quite small gentlemen a lift so they could look down on us.

Reg Messer was the most serious of the two, and we knew he was approaching the class room by his heavy footsteps in the corridor. He became known as *'Clip Clop Messer'*, and certainly commanded respect when he was explaining the world of radio communications to us.

Jack Griffith was a Welshman, and his accent was a pleasure to listen to. Like his co-presenter, he was quite officious, but sometimes shared a little humour with us in subjects that were rather new, and consequently often quite confusing.

The topics of the morning theory sessions were quite widespread, and gave us an introduction to many of the fundamental aspects of our jobs. Fortunately, the morning brain numbing theory lessons were accompanied by more interesting afternoons of practical sessions with some of the instructors. I am pretty confident that one of these gentlemen was Fred Owen (another Welshman) but other names have sadly been forgotten. These sessions allowed us to get our hands on simple training models and test equipment, that brought some of the theory to life.

A few of us were regulars in The George by now, and Saturday evenings were usually spent there. We were quite used to walking both ways along the Straight Mile, and with no-one to hear us, our chatter and laughter was very loud, and occasionally the language was a little strong.

One night as we made our way back to the Radio Station, we were well beyond the mildly intoxicated state, and almost every sentence had a swear word in it. The road was straight, so we could see anything approaching us, and we spotted a strange pair of dim lights. The lights were slightly apart, and one above the other. We contemplated on what it could be, and eventually we realised it was coming from a pushbike.

We loudly announced to the world. *"It's a fu****g pushbike"*.

To our horror, a response came back to us – *"Yes, it is, and I'm a fu****g policeman"*

We were spoken to very seriously, our names were noted, and we were advised to be on our way.

… but quietly.

Although the Goonhilly lads were behind others, the first cars were appearing among our apprentice year. This meant that sometimes we had a ride to or from the pub during the week, and the odd trip further away for a different evening adventure. I remember Colin Bootle (Bearley Radio Station) was one of the first on four wheels, and he took a small group of us out one evening in his Fiat 500 for a late-night visit to the Fortes Service Station on the outskirts of Oxford.

This was another eye-opener for me. I had never been to a Service Station before, and certainly never considered having a cup of coffee at midnight. To show my naivety, I explained my thrill in one of my regular letters to my mum, describing my wonder at this simple adventure, and the total amazement of seeing a toilet with urinals.

Perhaps Mr Grindrod was correct about the Cornish being a bit behind the rest of the world.

One night, Colin even took us all the way to London. There was no reason for this, but the freedom of youth didn't have any barriers. I remember little of the journey except for all of us laughing uncontrollably as we repeatedly went around the busy Piccadilly Circus roundabout.

Between moments of learning about life as we grew up, our training course continued. During those three weeks our technical and practical knowledge slowly increased, and my head began to absorb principles that would be a part of my life for the next 40 years. One obvious thing was the increase in my technical vocabulary with words and phrases such as: amplifiers, gain, attenuation, oscillators, frequency spectrum, tuned circuits, modulators, filters, bandwidth, and carriers, as well as different test equipment such as spectrum analysers, and various meters.

During three years of my apprenticeship, the emphasis was on giving us as much information as possible from first principles, which then allowed us to think rationally about how equipment worked, what we were doing as we operated it, and to consider the reasons when something went wrong.

Nowadays learning from first principles is less common, and probably not so important with highly technical processor driven equipment. Engineers generally receive less in-depth knowledge and are often naïve to what is happening inside a box. Fortunately, the modern-day equipment is much more reliable and hence rarely fails, as the vast majority of their operating processes rely on computers to monitor and diagnose problems.

Sadly, when things do go wrong, the only way to repair the problem is to replace the expensive computer-controlled black boxes, as nobody knows how they work, let alone how to physically fix them.

Those rare people who do understand the theoretical fundamentals of diagnosing and repairing, are often of a previous generation, and even they will struggle with a sealed box that contains processors and chipsets that are designed by computers, and operated by other computers. *'Mankind'* has reached a point where their role is simply to switch things on, and watch displays that prove things are happening, but if it goes wrong, even more computers have to be used to put it right.

We were all back home before the end of January to continue familiarising ourselves with the different operational areas around Goonhilly. In May we completed the second part of the Radio 1 course, and there was another seven weeks at Witney Technical College, that culminated with me taking and passing various exams.

Life was wonderful with money, transport, new friends, and an amazing number of new experiences. Without a doubt, I was beginning to grow up.

Aerial Steering

Back at Goonhilly again, and we all returned to the introductions with different areas and groups around the station.

I was finally given a chance to work with a group that was a real part of the operational side of Goonhilly. It was the Aerial Steering Group, and as well as being far more interesting, it was also when I realised there were two different types of workers.

As well as a core of daytime technicians, there was a 24-hour shift rota. Although all the engineers were similarly experienced in the disciplines, there was an obvious division of work. The day staff were primarily there to repair equipment and perform routine checks. Although available during daytime hours, the rota staff were responsible to maintain operational service. They might perhaps switch to standby equipment, or change out faulty units, but those units would most likely be repaired by the day staff.

Anyway, the aerial steering group was the first area I had experienced that had both day and shift engineers. For most of the time in the group, I was looked after by the day man, but the rota men took an interest and sometimes showed me some of the operational aspects as well. It was the first time I actually set foot in the OCA and witnessed the vast console of red, orange and green lights, plus hundreds of switches. I was there to watch the shift man do something with the steering controls, but I was totally amazed by what was going on around me.

My time in the steering group was often standing around watching the day man take readings and check how well the equipment was working. There was a schedule of routine measurements to be made each day. Occasionally a fault was detected, and a circuit board would be swapped to rectify the problem, and then the faulty board would be repaired.

There was one very special routine however, that I became thrilled with.

Each week, data would be sent to Goonhilly on a telegraph machine. This was the predicted positions that the satellite would be for each hour of the day and night. The data would be passed to the aerial steering day man in the form of a reel of punched tape.

The tape was then fed into a computer which would calculate where the satellite would be on a minute-by-minute basis.

Sounds simple, but this was 1969, and computers had only just started to appear, and this was the first one I had ever seen.

It was made by a company called 'Elliot' and the model number was 803. It consisted of three cabinets full of equipment, and was at least two metres long, with huge tape readers. The prediction data tape was transferred to the tape reader reel, and then the magic began. The huge machine whirred and clicked as each prediction was compared to the previous one. There were more whirrs and clicks as the computer then calculated the positions for the time between each prediction.

This new data could then be transferred to a larger reel of paper tape, and used to steer the aerial directly using a system called 'Computer Tracking'. Alternatively, the engineer could have a paper print out of the satellite position, to enable him to steer the aerial manually.

The Computer Tracking steering system relied on the predictions, but also needed to have a very accurate clock. Within the aerial steering room there was a radio receiver that received a very accurate clock signal from Rugby Radio Station. The output of that signal was looked at on an oscilloscope, and each week compared to the Goonhilly Station clock. Occasionally the Goonhilly clock signal had to be adjusted, and the day man showed me how to check the signals, and adjust them when required.

This was a task that I was more than happy to perform.

Another role of the group was to look after a small weather station, and each day someone walked outside to a nearby box called a 'Stevenson Screen'. Inside was a measuring cylinder to check rainfall, plus a barometer, and thermometers. I was quite fascinated by this, and very willing to get involved.

Initially I just had a few days with the Steering Team, but it was one I returned to for a much longer period. During that time I took on several of the routine jobs, and also spent a lot of time watching repair work. I could finally start to use my tool kit, and actually do something to keep Goonhilly working.

I also accompanied the more friendly of the shift engineers, and this meant seeing more of the steering equipment at the actual aerials. I began to know my way around aerial 1 and aerial 2, and could see the differences in the steering, and drive systems. The shift man would regularly take me into the OCA, allowing me to get a better picture of what was involved, and for the first time I was allowed the occasional push of a button on the console.

I had mentally made a decision that the OCA was where I wanted to work

East Wing

It was time to experience another one of the major areas at Goonhilly. This was the East Wing, also known as the 'Multiplex area', or 'Repeater Station'. The manager at that time was Phillip (Phil) Booker, and he always supported his team, but expected them to work hard. He had a reputation of being a difficult man, and apprentices would regularly feel the sharpness of his tongue.

My first experience of this part of Goonhilly was not very enjoyable.

The role of this very large room was the interface between the satellite side of the station, and the GPO terrestrial communications system. I will try and describe what this means as simply as possible.

At that time, the terrestrial communication system of Britain consisted of Microwave Radio links, or large cable networks between cities. Almost everything originated, and terminated in London, where vast electronic bundles of telephone calls, and television programmes were routed to and from exchange buildings all over the country.

Some of these bundles contained telephony calls for International services that went to and from the HF Radio Stations, or Sub-Sea Cable Terminals. During the late 60s and early 70s a small number made their way to and from Goonhilly.

These bundles of telephone calls or television programmes were referred to as **'Baseband Traffic'**.

In the East Wing the bundles of telephone calls were separated into smaller bundles, destined for the different earth stations in countries around the world.

These smaller bundles would then be packaged again, and sent to the equipment in the West Wing to begin the journey to the satellites.

At the same time, bundles of calls from the various earth stations around the world would arrive from the West Wing, and be re-packaged together into bigger bundles to return to London.

These 'Bundling' and 'Unbundling' processes are more accurately referred to as Multiplexing, and Demultiplexing.

WARNING – *There is a fair chunk of technical terms coming up, so feel free to struggle if they are not understood.*

If you imagine yourself at home making an International telephone call, your words make up what is referred to as a baseband signal. That signal is in the audible frequency band, and makes it way over a pair of copper wires towards a telephone exchange. In the exchange your telephone signal is multiplexed with other telephone calls going to the same location. The signal is now at a higher frequency, enabling it to be sent over longer distances using a single coaxial cable, rather than using hundreds of pairs of copper wire.

Your telephone call, and many others heading for the rest of the world, will be sent to London, where virtually all of the International traffic was dealt with.

In the London International Exchanges, your telephone call, perhaps destined for America, is de-multiplexed from the original cable, and multiplexed with more telephone calls destined to go via satellite to America from around Britain. This new package of International Telephone calls was then sent to Goonhilly.

Here in the East Wing, the incoming bundle was de-multiplexed again.

Goonhilly was transmitting more than a single satellite channel to America, so the traffic is multiplexed again as appropriate, with tones (known as pilots) added to act as a monitoring aid. Now the resulting multiplexed baseband bundles were sent to the West Wing on coaxial cables.

By the time I arrived at Goonhilly, we were no longer simply operating with America, and numerous countries were using satellites for International Communications. Hence there were several baseband signal cables heading for places in the Americas to the west, and in Africa, India, Asia and as far east as Australia.

In essence Goonhilly transmitted to a satellite that was either to the East towards the Indian Ocean stations, or to the West going to the Americas. Hence the eventual bundle of telephony signals sent towards the West Wing might just be heading towards one large country, or could perhaps be a mixture of calls destined for several countries.

While in the East Wing I also discovered that Goonhilly was a terminal station for submarine cables. They were going from Britain to Spain and Portugal, and the racks and suites of equipment purred with a buzzing sound from the high voltage equipment they needed. These were one of the most interesting bits of this room, and especially being able to see the actual cable, coming out of the rack that headed from Goonhilly to a local beach, and onwards under the sea.

Anyway, during my initial time in the East Wing, I didn't really understand what was happening, and the people working in there, were either too busy, or uninterested in explaining very much to me. This rather depressingly dark room was different to the other places I had visited, and I got the feeling that apprentices were not that popular. The East Wing was very much a traditional GPO working environment, so what I did experience was more about mainstream GPO practices and procedures.

Rather than show me specific jobs which might have taught me something, the first task that headed my way, was painting large new metal frames, that would be holding more of the thousands of cables coming in or out of this room. I was given a small paintbrush, a large tin of cream paint, and told to do a good job.

I didn't comprehend how this was furthering my knowledge and skills, and it was excruciatingly boring.

A slightly better way of keeping me quiet, was to read a series of documents in huge folders known as 'Technical Instructions' (shortened to T.I.s). There was a small library of these documents. Their purpose was to assist engineers with information and instructions on how to install, maintain, and repair all the different types of equipment found within the GPO sites.

The documents were boring, and I didn't understand much of the GPO gobbledygook. Fortunately, although I didn't understand much of their contents, I was able to become slightly useful. Every few weeks, updates for the different T.I.s would arrive from somewhere in Gobbledygook Land, and I was tasked to take out the redundant pages, and replace them with the new ones.

Perhaps my task might have been a teeny-weeny bit useful, but it was really tedious, and boring!

I was extremely pleased when my time in the East Wing ended.

Discovering other parts of the GPO

Although I was working in a small specialised section of the GPO, referred to as the International Group, I was still a part of a huge organisation. To make us aware of what happens in other parts of the business, the group of new Goonhilly apprentices spent four or five weeks working with our colleagues in the telephone side.

So, in the summer of 1969, instead of riding my bike to Goonhilly, I set off for Truro where I was going to be working with an engineer in a group known as 'Subs App and Fitting'. This cumbersome title actually meant the engineer fitted and repaired customer's telephones.

The engineer's name has long been forgotten, but having spent 30 minutes with him having a cup of tea at the Exchange building, we set off in his van for the first job.

I quickly discovered it **wasn't** actually to the first job.

We drove through the back streets of Truro for a few minutes, and then he stopped outside of a house and told me he had to go in and see someone. I sat in the van while he spent about 30 minutes inside the house. He then returned without any explanation, and now we did go to the first job.

This early morning appointment was repeated each day of my time with him. I'll let you decide what he was possibly up to.

Anyway, the work was quite interesting. Most of the time it was fitting a new telephone if the customer (Subscriber) was beginning service with the GPO, or fitting a new phone when the old one was faulty. I had my first experience of meeting real customers, seeing how telephone cables were installed, and having endless cups of tea.

One of the jobs that week was at the local telephone exchange, where the lady operators sat at manual desks connecting people with cables and jack plugs. This was another eye-opening experience of having my every move watched by the ladies, and more especially the supervisor. I had to work quietly, and behave myself by not annoying the operators. The ladies were not working to the same rules, and I was teased incessantly. I rather enjoyed this, but not the glare of the supervisor.

A regular job in the exchange was to replace one of the long switch board connecting cables. I was deemed capable of doing this, and it involved working at floor level while the operator continued her work above me. This resulted in various comments about being careful where I was looking, plus even more teasing.

Another task I was given, involved replacing a bell on the outside wall of the exchange building. It was another first, as I had to work up a ladder, while my experienced engineer mate watched.

Remember that I have already expressed my fear of heights, and those few minutes were not pleasant. There was a more important issue here, as I hadn't had any training to use a ladder, and didn't have a safety helmet.

That first week passed quite quickly, and I changed roles on the following Monday. This time it was at the Camborne Exchange where I teamed up with a different engineer who repaired faults outside in the network. Another routine of early morning tea before setting off in the van. At least there were no unscheduled appointments with him.

However, he had a different habit. As we drove along quite narrow Cornish lanes, he rolled a cigarette while steering with his knees. He also seemed to consider the cigarette required more of his attention than the road.

I didn't last long with this engineer.

On the first afternoon he had a job that required him to climb up a pole to diagnose a fault with the wiring. While attached to the pole with his safety belt, I watched from below not able to see anything of what he was doing. Then he shouted down for me to fetch a multi-meter from the van and bring it up to him. Reluctantly this involved me climbing up the ladder to his reaching hand.

As I handed it to him, and began to descend the ladder, he accidentally dropped the meter which fell several feet onto my head.

Back on the ground it was obvious that I was bleeding, and the panicking engineer quickly packed up, and I was taken to a local doctor for treatment.

After a day recovering from the shock, I was informed that I would not be working in the field anymore, and I had to report to Camborne Telephone Exchange for the remainder of the week. I also had an appointment to go to the local manager's office and stand in front of him and a couple of other men to explain what had happened.

These men were not happy. They asked me to describe the incident, and then quizzed me on why I was up the ladder. Now, I was rather naïve at that period of my life, but realised that the conversation was heading down a path where the accident was seemingly my fault.

They asked why I wasn't wearing my safety helmet, and responding that I hadn't been issued with one, the interview ended, and I was told to report to my training officer at Goonhilly.

The outcome was that I shouldn't have climbed without a helmet, and hence the blame was kicked sideways to Goonhilly for not kitting me out appropriately. The engineer was not apportioned any blame.

The managers at Goonhilly were furious. They immediately issued shiny red helmets to all of us, and I was told that the rest of my time with the telephone group would be inside the exchanges.

Sadly, I believe if the same scenario happened now, I would have been seen as a victim, and probably looking at a legal case for compensation. As I said, I was rather naïve.

Back at the Camborne Exchange building, I spent several days looking at the noisy clickity-clacking switching equipment, with limited input from the engineers to explain what was happening. There were occasional moments where a friendly man would point out what the equipment did, but this was a rare interval while he took a break from running hundreds of wires (known as jumpers) across the huge metal framework.

He also showed me the switching equipment, called uni-selectors, that kicked up a major racket as they connected people together. He explained what was happening, but it was many years later that I understood things. More interestingly, he also showed me how to listen in to a telephone call, and how to insert a little plug to clear a call.

While he returned to his wires, the little demons in my head urged me to experiment with my new found skill.

I would like to apologise to those people whose telephone calls unexplainably dropped out during my naughty moment.

There was also the 'Ringing Machines'. They had a cam-shaft that rotated with various notches and switches. As a notch got to a switch, the machine would send tones along the telephone line, or create the ringing signal to make the telephone bells ring.

I asked why there were two identical machines, and he said that if one stopped, or revolved too slowly, it would switch to the other machine.

Now, that was an open invitation to return to my rather naughty side. While no one was looking, I put my finger on the rotating shaft until it slowed. Sure enough, it quickly switched to the other machine. Of course, I decided I should switch it back again with the same technique.

... several times!

I spent the majority of a fortnight in that boring, noisy room.

The final week of my field experience was in the Penzance Exchange. There was another huge room of ladies sitting at their desks, but that was not why I was there. I was assigned to the records office.

Here there were rows of wooden cabinets with hundreds of drawers. These drawers contained a card for every telephone customer in the town with details of names, address, and phone number. They also detailed any historical faults or repairs, plus anything an engineer needed to be warned of when they had to make a visit. This included the location of telephones and wiring, perhaps the presence of dogs, or persistently angry customers, and history of previous faults.

I didn't do very much except to answer the odd phone call from engineers requesting information. This left me a lot of time to explore the drawers for anything interesting. One day I came to a drawer with a card that stood out because it was covered in red written comments.

This particular phone number was on the Scilly Isles, and the customer was a Mr Wilson. It was the summer residence of Harold Wilson who was the Prime Minister.

Just out of curiosity, I asked someone why there was so much red writing.

That resulted in the second time I had to explain myself to a manager.

To begin with, I should not have been looking at the cards without a reason. More importantly I should not have removed that particular card and asked about it.

Fortunately, this slight security blunder was not to be discussed further, as I should not had been given the opportunity to look at the cards without supervision.

... but it was explained in no uncertain terms that I had made a big mistake.

My time in the GPO Telephone Groups was over, and I could return to work at Goonhilly where life was far less dangerous, and where I was rarely officially told off by a manager again.

Special Moments of 1969

There were several special moments that I remember from 1969, and here are a few that stand out in my mind.

Change of Employer?

Well, not actually a change of employer, but the name changed from being the GPO to simply 'Post Office' (PO). The change was to break a little of the links with the Government, and it was no longer a Department of State, but just a Statutory Corporation.

This change was seamless as far as the public were concerned, but as a moment in history, it did away with the GPO name that had been in use in Britain since 1660, when it was established by King Charles II.

It was just the first of many name changes that I witnessed during my career.

It meant a change to letter heads, and thousands of forms, processes and procedures had to reflect the name change. I imagine it cost a lot of money to dispense with the 'G'.

Concorde

On to something more interesting.

The iconic supersonic aeroplane Concorde made some its first flights in this year, and many of the proposed routes it would use involved flying over the site.

There were some concerns that any supersonic booms might upset the electronics at Goonhilly. So, armed with information about when test flights would be made, it was decided to monitor and record the performance of the equipment as Concorde flew overhead at supersonic speed.

In the OCA we had a huge chart recorder which measured a selection of the services we were receiving from the satellites. The heat sensitive paper chart was around 40cm wide, and the plan was to run it at high speed to capture any possible interference.

When the engineers switched to high-speed recording, the paper would only last for a few minutes, so the exact time that Concorde would fly over the site had to be known, to avoid the paper running out.

A cunning plan was devised.

On the day of the flight, Arthur Seager from the Test Desk, along with two of us (myself and Mark Jago) drove to St Agnes on the North coast. We took an early type of portable radio system with us, and an aerial on a pole that we erected on the cliff top.

At St Agnes there would be about 30 seconds from the moment that we heard Concorde's boom over us, before it passed over Goonhilly.

We were all set up, and test transmissions had been made. Then we waited for what seemed to be an eternity from the estimated time, and began to suspect that the flight had been cancelled. Suddenly we heard the '**Boom Boom**' as the plane flew over us. Arthur immediately called Goonhilly with the agreed message of "***Concorde five seconds***". Sadly, the engineer on the other end of the radio was unsure if the five seconds meant it was before the expected booms, or that they had just been heard. Fortunately, someone realised what was happening and the chart recorder was switched on to high speed.

We packed up the radio equipment and returned to Goonhilly.

The mission had been successful, and the traces on the recorder paper showed no interference as Concorde boomed over the site.

The Official Opening of Goonhilly
In September 1969, Goonhilly officially began to use both of its aerials, with one facing west to a satellite over the Atlantic Ocean, and the other towards the east to another satellite over the Indian Ocean. There was a very special event organised to celebrate opening service to one of the countries in the east, and that was Japan and its earth station called Yamaguchi. There was a ceremony at Goonhilly attended by many of the 'Top Dogs' from the organisation, plus a representative from Japan.

To make the day even more special, Goonhilly Earth station was officially opened by the British Post Master General. He was a politician who became very well known, and his name was John Stonehouse.

He was the last ever Postmaster General, but was better known for faking his own death.

The least said the better here, and even the plaque that was unveiled by him went missing for a while.

Anyway, at the event there were a lot of very important people gathered together with finger buffets and booze. The apprentices were not allowed anywhere near the celebrations, but we were allowed to perform a very important mission. Just after lunch, a couple of us were told to go into Helston with Vernon Wheatly, from the mechanical workshop, driving the car. Our mission was to buy some lemons, to allow the grown-ups to enjoy a slice with their gin and tonic.

So, I was still a young apprentice, and not able to be technically useful, or to attend the celebration, but I was able to perform a very valuable task.

Another Special Goonhilly Moment
This is something I wasn't involved in, although I was watching every moment of it at home in front of my television.

From the launch of the Apollo 11 space mission to the moon on 16th July 1969, through to it splashing down on 24th July, Goonhilly relayed video material from America for Europe to watch this amazing moment in history.

More importantly, Satellite Communications became famous as it showed the actual landing on the moon on 20th July, and those magical steps on its surface by Neil Armstrong and Buzz Aldrin. Although not involved, I was one of a small number of people working at Goonhilly, and I beamed with pride at that achievement.

A Bit of History

By the time I had worked at Goonhilly for 12 months, I was starting to piece together what Radio, and more especially, what Satellite Communications was all about. Looking around me, it began to make some sense, and the functions of each group was becoming clearer.

I was also growing even prouder to be a part of this emerging worldwide industry that was no longer an experiment, and very much an accepted part of modern life. The Telstar satellites might still have been flying around the world above us, but no longer active, they had become the first lumps of space rubbish.

Since 1962 a lot of progress had been made with the design of rockets and satellites, and in 1963 an organisation called 'Comsat' was active. This was an international partnership of all the countries involved in satellite communications. The industry was no longer experimental, and quickly expanded from just a few Earth Stations in America and Europe. In 1964 the Comsat organisation became responsible for launching satellites, and a second organisation called *Intelsat*, was created to look after the use of those spacecraft.

Satellite orbits were changing. With far more powerful, and controllable rockets, it became possible to launch a satellite into a much higher orbit above the earth. This was seriously higher than Telstar, and the orbits were no longer elliptical.

Syncom Satellites

In 1963 experiments began with a new design of satellite named 'Syncom'. This was designed and built by the Hughes Aircraft Company, with a new cylindrical shape. The body of Syncom was about 30 cm top to bottom and about 70 cm in diameter. It was covered in solar cells and spun to achieve stability. On the bottom of the cylinder was a booster rocket (Apogee Booster) to reach the required height, and there were smaller nitrogen gas rockets to make sideway movements.

Syncom 1 was launched by a Delta B rocket on February 14th 1963. Sadly, although it achieved the correct orbit height, the electronics failed and it was never operational.

Syncom 2 was launched on 26th July 1963 and reached its designed orbit height. It was quickly used for experiments, and in August of that year was used for a telephone call between President Kennedy on an aircraft carrier off America, and the Prime Minister of Nigeria in Lagos.

Syncom 3 achieved a very special moment, by going into what is referred to as a Geo-stationary orbit. It was launched on 19th August 1964 and positioned at a height of 36,000 km (22,300 miles) above the equator. It was travelling through space at a speed of about 11,000 km per hour (6700 miles per hour), meaning that it flew around the earth exactly once every 24 hours. This means that it appeared to be stationary above the earth. This region of space above the earth has become known as the *'Clarke Belt'*, after Arthur C Clarke who identified that it was the ideal orbit for satellite communications to be possible.

Syncom 3 was very successful, and relayed television coverage of the Tokyo Olympic Games to the USA.

The Syncom experiments were run very much by the American military, but during the same period Intelsat was focussing on the public use of satellites. With the success of geo-stationary satellites, Intelsat were gearing up to begin commercial operations.

Intelsat 1 (Early Bird)
Their first official communications satellite was launched in 1965, and it was called Early Bird. It was built by the Hughes Aircraft Company, and after being launched by NASA in April, it was finally switched into an operational mode on 28th June. It had a planned life of just 18 months, but actually continued to operate for three years.

This little satellite was the same cylindrical shape and size as Syncom, but it had an enhanced set of radio equipment. Early Bird was covered in around 6000 solar cells, and with its batteries maintained 40 watts of energy to the transmission equipment. That is the equivalent energy of a quite low powered light bulb.

Intelsat 1 was spin stabilised again with electric motors to de-spin the communications aerial platform, to keep it pointing at the earth.

It weighed less than half the weight of Telstar and yet was packed with far more equipment. It enabled 24 hours-a-day constant communications between the USA and Europe providing either up to 240 two-way telephone circuits, or a single television channel.

For the technically minded, the electronic equipment had two separate but identical channels. These are more accurately described as *'transponders'* and allowed two-way communications.

Early Bird was positioned over the Atlantic Ocean, and America would transmit to one transponder which could be received by European earth stations. At the same time a European earth station would transmit to the other transponder that could be received in America.

These transponders enabled a power output from the satellite of just Six Watts back to earth. That is less than the light achieved by a modern torch.

One of Early Bird's major achievements was the transmission of the first ever live television pictures showing the splashdown of the Gemini 6 spacecraft in December 1965. It was carrying Walter M. Schirra, and Thomas P. Stafford, and they had been in space for just over a day.

Goonhilly became one of the three European earth stations to transmit to, and receive from Intelsat 1, and it was the beginning of 24 hour a day commercial satellite communication with the USA. In Europe Goonhilly shared the role with Pleumeur Bodou (France) and Raisting (Germany). These three European stations were connected via the European Network, and worked in partnership to transmit and receive all the international traffic between Europe and the USA. Each station was operational for a week at a time, while another was available in standby, and the third being in a maintenance mode.

Intelsat needed more than one satellite, and a second identical one was built. To distinguish between them, each identical satellite was given a second descriptor, which was its 'flight' number.

Hence the one I have been talking about was officially known as Intelsat 1 Flight 1.

A second one was also built, and was known as Intelsat 1 F2, but was never launched.

By the time I arrived at Goonhilly in 1968, they had already moved on to the next generation of satellites known as Intelsat 2.

During the three years of my apprenticeship, there was little time to absorb information about specific satellites in use, or the technical aspects of them. We simply continued with our college work, between days and weeks in the different groups around Goonhilly.

As time passed, we revisited some of these groups to get more detailed knowledge, and we would feed back our thoughts to the training team. No doubt the groups also gave feedback about us. As the end of the three years approached, most of us were already showing interest in certain groups, in the knowledge that we would eventually be assigned to one of them.

So, for now I will continue with some of my recollections and thoughts about my time from 50 years ago.

The West Wing

Another vast room, but there were more windows, so slightly less depressing than the East Wing. This was the area of Goonhilly where the real radio technology began, and it was no surprise that I had a major struggle coming to terms with what was going on.

Even in those early years, the room must have been about 30 metres long and 20 metres wide, and it would expand far more as the years passed. There were rows and rows of equipment, and seemingly more racks being added weekly as Goonhilly stretched its radio tentacles towards more and more countries. At least the equipment here was quite interesting to look at, with meters, switches, and coloured lights. It was just as technically confusing as I had already seen elsewhere, but I was getting used to that.

High up on the wall to one side of the room, a huge metal trunking came through the wall from the East Wing. It carried hundreds of cream and white cables that were individual bundles of telephony, or perhaps a television signal. These were the Baseband Signals.

A Baseband Signal from the East Wing, destined for a particular country, or sometimes to multiple countries, was connected to the input of a piece of equipment called a Modulator. Here the signals were filtered to reduce noise, and had a 60kHz Pilot tone injected to allow monitoring. The main activity within the modulator was mixing the baseband with a much higher frequency to turn it into an Intermediate Frequency (IF) signal. This higher frequency (70Mhz) could be carried on a coaxial cable for quite some distance around the site without absorbing any interference.

The final stage was to convert the IF signal to the frequency that it would be transmitted by the High Power transmitter. This was achieved in an 'Up-converter' which might have been in the West Wing, or at the aerial buildings. Our package of telephony, data, or television programme was now called a ***'Carrier'***.

... as an attempt to explain the term 'Carrier', think of it as ***carrying*** the signals through space.

The up-converter increased the frequency to the precise one allocated by Intelsat, and there was a final bit of electronic shaping to match the needs of the satellite. At around 6Ghz our lump of energy was now ready to be sent into space.

In the return direction, the receive half of your telephone call with your friend or relation in America, arrived in the West Wing as a carrier from the Aerial receive equipment. It would have to be down-converted, and demodulated back to a baseband frequency signal. This then disappeared into the trunking through the wall to the East Wing. In there, your call would be multiplexed with other bundles of calls from around the world, and returned to the appropriate International Exchange in London, and eventually to the pair of copper wires going to your phone.

The journey from your mouth, to the other person's ear, and then from their mouth back to you is very long. That conversation would have travelled in excess of 36,000 km (22,700 miles) in space in both directions. This created a new phenomenon in telecommunications. There was a *'Time Delay'* between the moment you spoke, to the time that the other person heard your voice. There is always some tiny, insignificant, amount of time delay on a radio transmission, but now it was around a quarter of a second, and very noticeable.

OK, so what did I do in the West Wing?

My time began with an engineer giving me a lengthy guided tour of the room, and its equipment. Racks of equipment shelves were pointed out to me which were called modulators, and they had a series off cards plugged into them. Each card had a specific function that my friendly engineer attempted to explain to me.

But as he showed and described more cards, my head spun with confusion.

Then he showed me other racks which were a different design of modulator.

With hardly a moment to yawn, we moved to the racks of de-modulators'.

Then there were the upconverters, double-downconverters, and dynamic tracking receivers.

Finally, there was some relief, and I was allowed to look at a teapot

The equipment names, and his description of what they did were immediately forgotten as his words were meaningless.

I knew that it was important to somehow get my head around the functions of the West Wing, and I had to understand what the equipment did, but his training method wasn't working.

The only things that grabbed my attention were flashing lights, and little meters attempting to indicate something to my cotton wool filled brain.

Eventually my obviously highly skilled Wizard said he had to do some real work, and that was when I began to feel better. He picked up one of those cream cables that seemed to be everywhere at Goonhilly. Announcing that they were called coaxial cables, he sliced one open to let me see what the inside looked like.

Inside the cream plastic outer, there was a layer of copper mesh, then an opaque plastic tube which covered the inner copper conductor. It was explained that the signal travels down the copper conductor, and was insulated from the layer of copper mesh by the opaque plastic tube, which was called the dielectric.

Then my latest technological Wizard, brought out his tools, and attached a plug on each end of a length of the cable. Now it was my turn to attempt to make up these test leads to keep me occupied while my new friend went away to cast spells elsewhere.

These plugs (and corresponding sockets on the equipment cards) were known as BNC. Nobody ever really explained the term, but it actually means '*Bayonet – Neill – Concelman*' presumably after the inventor, or maybe the manufacturer, or perhaps a very renowned Wizard.

Next I was shown numerous trolleys on which pieces of test equipment resided. My Wizard, took my test lead and plugged one end on the tester, and the other to a socket on the front of a de-modulator. The meter on the tester showed a reading, and he explained what I was seeing, and what the measurement meant.

I was then tasked to go to a rack of different de-modulators with the tester and note the measurement on them.

Hey, I was actually doing something. I didn't know what it was, but finally I felt I was achieving something that could possibly turn out to be useful.

Of course, there were several types of tester, and several different sockets on the equipment, where various measurements could be taken, but little by little over the days, I was learning new words, new terms, and new skills.

Another piece of test equipment that intrigued me was the Spectrum Analyser. This large box of tricks had a small screen that could look at the signal energy at either baseband or IF frequencies. Each satellite carrier looked like small mountains poking out of a field of grass. As the carriers had more and more telephony activity, the wider the mountain spread. The higher the mountains appeared above the grass (which was noise) the stronger, and better, it was.

OK, that's enough of the technical stuff.

The engineers in this room were always busy, and they couldn't spare much time for me, but when I was left to my own devices, I would read the instruction books, or simply look at the equipment and spot the names of the Earth stations we were working with. Some were cities in countries that I recognised, but others conjured up pictures in my mind of far-off countries. Here are just a few that spring to mind 50 years on:

- Andover (USA)
- Yamaguchi in Japan
- Ceduna in Australia
- Lanlate in Nigeria
- Umm-Al-Aish in Kuwait
- Vikram in India
- Ras-Abu-Jarjur (Bahrein)

As the weeks passed by, the magic of Goonhilly just continued to grow, and my enthusiasm to learn increased. This was a job that began as a simple suggestion from my school career's officer, but it turned out to be a dream, that I adored to be in.

Time away from work

My life away from Goonhilly changed so much during the three years of my apprenticeship.

I remained living at home where my mum continued to look after me, and spoilt me rotten. If I was out with her in the town, she would still introduce me to friends as *'her baby'*, but now she would enhance my status by pointing out that "**He works at Goonhilly on the Satellites**"

My mum was very proud of me, and I had no problem humouring her by letting everyone know what I was doing.

After all, I was also rather proud of what I was doing.

In the evenings, and at the weekends, I would meet up with my friends and go out on our motorbikes. We were a 'rag tag' group with a wide range of motor cycles. There were small bikes, scooters, mopeds, and a few more powerful machines. We acted like Hells Angel Apprentices, and although leather was the favoured jacket, many of us wore anything we felt appropriate for young adults to be seen in public. Over my years riding a motorbike I did have a leather jacket, but sometimes wore a black knee length PVC jacket, and even a Parka with fluffy lined hood.

Our little gang also enjoyed drinking, especially when we were legally old enough, and there were favoured pubs around Helston. Our preference was the Seven Stars where it was quiet enough to play darts, or a card game called Euchre. Quite quickly we became members at the Godolphin Club where the beer was cheaper, and it remains a popular social club for the people around Helston.

At weekends, we rode out of the town to several places around the Lizard Peninsular, where the village halls had regular dances with live bands. Of course they were called groups in those days. The local pubs of Mullion, Lizard, St. Keverne, and Coverack never judged our ages very well, and by the time we were 18, they saw us as regulars. My favourite venue was Mullion, and a rather strange pub called the 'Riviera Club'. The owner had worked in the variety business and enjoyed the company of young people, although we all knew he preferred the young men. His pub was always packed on dance nights.

The dances were always fun with local groups that usually had three guitarists and a drummer. The best ones had a dedicated singer, and sometimes even a keyboard. The music was nearly always the same songs with lots of soul music, plus occasional versions of one or two recent chart songs. My 'best buddy' during those years was Christopher Warner, and I was his wing man. He would regularly attract a girl, and I was useful to look after her mate.

Those evenings were always alcohol fuelled, and I spent a lot of time standing in front of the bass speaker, where I really felt the music, rather than simply hearing it. Occasionally I would have the nerve to tap a girl on the shoulder to suggest a dance, and as the years went by, I was not rejected as often. The goal was to get a girl to dance for the last song of the evening which would always be a smoochy one. These wonderful moments were when I delighted at the perfumed necks that I got close to, and enchanted by an un-identifiable aura that the girls gave off. Sometimes the night would be rounded off with a snog outside of the dance hall before the gang kitted up and rode home.

Such a wonderful time with so many memories, as I grew into a young man.

It wasn't long before I changed my little underpowered BSA Bantam motorbike for a brand-new Yamaha 125cc scream machine. Pascoe's the motor cycle shop made a lot of money from our little group, as many of us bought new machines.

At the weekend, the summer afternoons were also amazing times. A few of our gang would meet up and ride to beaches to enjoy the warmth, and the attention of the visitors ... well mainly the girls.

On other occasions there would be 20 or 30 motorbikes roaring around in a pack. I am sure we probably frightened people, but apart from the odd person, our gang was actually quite soft, and not looking for, or encouraging trouble.

In the darker evenings we would park up in Meneage Street in Helston and shelter in our favoured spot known as 'Cousin's Corner'. This was a shop on the corner of Meneage Street and Wendron Street, and it had a small area undercover without any lights. We made far too much noise, many of us smoked excessively, and there was probably a lot of un-necessary comments made to girls passing by.

We were young men at a time when this sort of behaviour was perhaps sadly all too common.

Another favoured spot to park our bikes and hang out, was the Monument area at the bottom of Coinagehall Street. There was a shelter here and we often sat there watching the traffic come down the Street. Any passing motorbikes would be waved at, and this often meant a new member for the gang.

There was also one very bad personal memory of my time there.

One night a young lad accused me of telling tales about him to his brother who I worked with. It culminated in a knife being drawn and its point was put up against my stomach. I have always avoided violence, and this was a time when '**flight**' took over from any thoughts of '**fight**'. I said I was sorry and promised not to say anything again.

This was a moment that has stayed in my mind ever since. I hate knives, and feel uncomfortable when anyone nearby is using one.

Apart from that incident, I was having a wonderful time, but now 50 years later I do regret one thing. I never kept in-touch with my Grammar School chums. Those boys and girls shared six years of my life, and I instantly ignored them when I started work. Now I remain on the barest of terms with perhaps half a dozen that I see when I am in Helston on Flora Day.

My life was slowly evolving. Being away on training courses for many weeks at a time, my circle of friends was changing, and becoming more focussed on people I worked with.

That was except for Chris Warner who remained a major part of my life away from Goonhilly for several years to come.

Operational Control Area (OCA)

One Monday morning at work, I was assigned to somewhere that would mean more to me than I could ever have anticipated. It was my turn to experience the Operational Control Area.

I will refer to it from now on as the OCA, and this was the operational hub of Goonhilly.

At that time (1969) the OCA had two entrances from the main corridor. One was through a double door direct into a room, while the other was a single door from the adjoining telegraph room where messages continually came from, and went to the earth stations of the world.

I had been in the OCA on several occasions for brief moments, but it never ceased to amaze and thrill me. Now I was going to spend more time in there, with an opportunity to really absorb the atmosphere, and find out what it was like to work there.

The room was about the size of two badminton courts with an arc of equipment bays in front of me, and that made up what was called the 'Console'. Each bay was about two metres high, and perhaps 60cm wide, and four of these bays were associated with each Aerial. At the far left was the Goonhilly 1 suite of equipment, then a further four bays looked after the Aerial 2. Next came a couple of bays that had test equipment in them, and finally, knowing that Goonhilly would expand, there was another four bays with blank panels in readiness for Aerial 3.

On the operational bays were row upon row of little lights, meters, and switches. Most of the little lights glowed green, others were orange coloured, and a few were red. I had already realised green meant good, while orange meant the equipment was OK but not in service, and red indicated something was wrong.

At about waist height, there was a shelf that stood out from the console, with one telephone for each aerial. They were the iconic blue 'Trim Phones' that were the modern phone of the moment. There were also microphones poking out of the console with a switch to enable them. From these microphones, announcements could be made to all parts of Goonhilly.

At the extreme right of the console was the large free-standing chart recorder, that was used to monitor the Concorde Sonic Boom I mentioned earlier. This machine was about two metres high and a metre wide, and had meters, switches and adjusting knobs at the top. Below this was a wide roll of paper with several little pens scratching traces. Various parameters could be recorded, and most of these were the strength of the receive signals (or carriers) from the earth stations around the world.

While I initially glanced at the console, I was aware of a large and rather posh desk to my right, that was almost in the centre of the room. One person sat at the desk in a tall backed swivel chair, and others regularly came and talked to him. This was where the Station Controller sat, with responsibility for all the operational decisions that needed to be made.

Behind him was a long glass window and a viewing gallery for visitors, or anyone generally wanting to have a look at what was going on. The OCA was a busy place at that time, with Goonhilly being rather new, and rather special. It was almost a weekly occurrence for visitors, or VIPs, to look around the station, and the OCA was always a highlight.

A little further across the room was another smaller console with different equipment, including a number of television monitors. That would become somewhere I would always move towards if it was quiet. This was the television console where incoming, or outgoing programmes were switched to and from the satellite and monitored.

... oh, and they always had a monitor looking at the normal terrestrial television channels.

Behind that console were windows looking into the telegraph room with the constant chattering noise of the machines. They were always churning out page after page of information and instructions being sent to and from Goonhilly. Each machine also produced a white punched tape for each message so that it could be sent to somewhere else without being re-typed.

And finally, a few feet away from the Controller's desk, and the Television desk, was a single small telephone switchboard. It had rows of circular shapes like eyes, with holes below them where plugs on the end of red cables could be inserted. This was the Engineering Order Wire (EOW) switchboard. Each earth station had the ability to add a simple telephone and telegraph circuit, onto their carrier, to enable them to speak or send messages to the other earth stations they worked with.

During the traditional working hours, an operator sat at the switchboard, and if someone called Goonhilly, one of those circular shapes would blink and make a rattling sound. The operator then plugged in a lead into the hole below, and spoke to whoever was calling. That looked intriguing, although I would quickly learn to keep away from it when the operator wasn't there.

Answering the switchboard would become something I was expected to do when the operator was missing. Once given a short training session, if an eye blinked and rattled I had to answer it. Each of the eyes had the name of the earth station calling, and with America or Australia it was a simple conversation, but when it was someone from perhaps Nigeria, or Japan, I had to try and understand their attempts to ask a question for assistance. Once understood, I could patch the call through to the person they wanted to speak to. This might be the controller, or the television man or maybe the telegraph operator.

I was often asked to answer calls. They were usually from the distant earth stations, but sometimes it was someone in an office at Goonhilly wanting to speak to a station. That meant answering the person, and then patching his call through to whatever station he needed. This was when I met someone who would play a big part in my working life at Goonhilly.

It was John Sherbird. He was the manager of a small group of people who acted on behalf of the International Control Centre (IOC) in Washington. John's small group managed the Indian Ocean region earth stations which couldn't be directly monitored from America. His role was known as the Indian Ocean Region Technical Operations Control Centre, or IOR TOCC.

He would often ask to be patched to the IOC or an earth station, but he could be short tempered, and if I got things wrong, he would come into the OCA and make it clear that I should know better.

Little did I know that I would be working alongside him in ten years time.

Uncomfortable maybe, but using the EOW switchboard was another job that I could just about do. My ability to make out an African, or Japanese attempt at English improved. But it took a long time to feel relaxed with this little job.

There was a fundamental difference in the OCA compared to most of the other groups around the station that I had spent time with. The vast majority of the engineers working in here were on a shift rota. They changed working times on a weekly basis, going from days to evenings and then nights on a five-week pattern. Hence having got comfortable with one group of men for three days, it suddenly changed to a different group.

I didn't mind this, because virtually all of these men were fun to be with. Life in here was never serious, and a good deal of the day was sitting down and chatting until a phone rang, or an alarm bleated from the console. When that happened, the guys would leap up and do whatever was necessary to repair the fault.

My time in there was not long, but as the days went by, I quickly understood what a red light meant, and what switch may have to be pushed, to perhaps change-over a modulator or demodulator. I grew in confidence to answer phones, or make an announcement on the microphones. I also learnt about basic measurements that could be made on the test equipment. These were generally either an Out of Band Noise reading (OBN) for one of the receive carriers, or a 60kHz pilot reading which was a measurement of baseband signal levels.

These were the same measurements that I had been making in the West Wing, but they could also be made remotely in the OCA. At the console monitoring bay, the engineers could remotely plug into the equipment (in the West Wing) and take readings without leaving the room. This was a job I was happy to do when someone needed a measurement, and helped me feel like I was really doing something.

A more tedious job was to change faulty bulbs on the console. This was a never-ending task as they constantly failed. To aid this job there was a series of buttons that were to test the lights. When pressed, that section of the console glowed like a beacon of colour. It was easy to spot any offending bulbs, but to change them was not so simple. They were tiny, and after unscrewing the coloured bulb cover, a short piece of rubber sleeving could go over the bulb and hold it secure enough to unscrew it.

I quickly learnt that pressing the lamp test button was also an effective way of impressing visitors in the gallery. On occasions when the press were visiting, I would be tasked to work my lamp test magic to produce a special colourful photo moment.

My brief few days introduction to the OCA was enough to instantly sew a seed in my mind to wonder how I could work in there permanently. … but that would have to wait for a few years yet.

The Apprenticeship comes to an end

Before I knew what was happening, the 1960s had come to an end, and the world was dipping its toes in the 1970s. I didn't realise it at the time, but somehow my stubbornness, and rebelliousness, that plagued my school years had gone, and I thoroughly loved to learn and expand my knowledge. Instead of failing exams, or just scraping a pass, I worked much harder and was enjoying the experience. OK, I still joined in with the 'mucking around' and had a laugh with my peers. While some of my gang of apprentices struggled with college work, and more importantly the exams, I was doing what I had to do, and achieved Credits or good Passes in the annual round of formal testing.

At the end of the first year in Witney I passed a series of exams that allowed me to get the G2 certificate - which I assume meant a 'General Part 2' certificate. In 1970 there were formal exams for City and Guilds Part A, and I came away with good passes, and even a distinction in the Radio exam. In the same year there were also exams for an ONC Part 2 certificate, and again I came away with good results, and awarded a real Certificate.

OK so this wasn't the same as the Degrees that my school chums might have been getting, but it was certainly on a par with the 'A' Levels that I missed out on.

Alongside the college work, I also completed the Post Office based Radio A (Parts 1 and 2) courses that were a mandatory part of successfully completing my apprenticeship. I was truly getting my head around the theory and practicalities of Radio Communication, and absorbing what was going on at Goonhilly became far simpler.

In the weeks that we were at Goonhilly rather than Leafield, we spent longer periods in the important groups around the station. Several of us were formulating what we would really like to do at the end of the three years, and our aspirations were getting an airing during conversations and interviews with our training management.

In 1970 there was also an incident, that made us all open our eyes to the realisation that completing our apprenticeship wasn't a given.

I enjoyed life at Leafield, and kept my nose clean with our lecturers at the college, and those on our PO courses. Sadly, some others spent more time on having fun.

At the midway point of one of our college terms, our little gang of Goonhilly apprentices were on our way home for the weekend. We left Leafield early on the Friday morning in the mini-bus and noticed some words painted on the Ash Track. It was a very derogatory comment about the Leafield Principal who was called Mr Coles. The white painted words were perhaps 30cm high, and described Mr Coles by a word that begins with 'C', which is still seen as disgustingly unnecessary 50 years on.

We were shocked, but laughed about it.

On our return to Leafield, there was no bus to take us to the college in Witney in the morning. Instead, we were instructed to gather in the conference room. The Principal was absolutely fuming with what had been done, and asked for the guilty people to make themselves known. It seems that after we had left on the Friday, the other apprentices had to clean away the graffiti before they were allowed to go home.

Of course, no one owned up, and eventually we went to Witney and continued with our work, but there was an air of concern about what would happen next.

The next day, things started as normal, but part way through the morning, two people were taken out of the class, and returned to Leafield.

They were Tony Hampton from Brierly, and David Webb from Goonhilly.

We never saw them again.

They were accused of almost certainly being involved in the prank, and with a record of several earlier wrong doings, they were sacked.

It really opened our eyes to the fact that we had been given an opportunity of a really good career, but we couldn't abuse that chance.

The last thing I will say about the incident, is that at least one guilty person did not get identified, and continued to work in the PO at one of the radio stations.

I knuckled down to my work, and took great care not to get caught up in anything similar.

There were also some other quite stupid pranks that caused many laughs.

One morning we set off for the college in Witney and noticed that the Leafield Village signs had been unscrewed and turned upside down. Yes, it was some of my peers who did it, but they were never caught, and the signs remained upside down for several weeks.

Another incident involved some of our year that now had their own transport. They regularly drove to Oxford for a night out, or just for a ride. There was a long series of roadworks on the A40 at that time, and the guilty people stole some of the orange flashing warning beacons. They brought them back and put them into the large cooling ponds of water that used to be used to cool the massive transmitter equipment.

Under about two metres of water, the beacons continued to flash for several days until the batteries finally gave up.

Once again, the guilty people were never caught.

In 1971 I had my last year at Witney Tech where I studied for the City and Guilds Part B. In the exams I had a mixture of passes and credits, and was rather proud of myself.

At the Leafield training centre we all attended the Radio B courses and another notch was made on my path towards ending my apprenticeship. During August 1971, as I was completing another Radio course, I was asked to take a phone call from Goonhilly. John Apperley, my training manager, congratulated me on finishing my apprenticeship, and I was to become a Technician 2 A on my return. He then said that I should report for duty at 11:00 at night to begin rota duties in the OCA.

I had made it, and managed to get the dream role.

More History

By the time I completed my apprenticeship, the world of Satellite Communications had moved on, so here is a little more about its evolution.

1966 and 1967

After Intelsat 1 F 1 (Early Bird) proved to be successful, the Hughes Corporation were commissioned to build more satellites, and in 1966 the second generation of Intelsat satellites was ready for service.

Named as Intelsat 2, it was very similar in shape to the Intelsat 1 with its oil drum appearance covered in solar cells. It was however about twice the size, and had a far superior communications capability, allowing multiple earth stations to transmit to it at the same time. This is referred to as Multiple-Access, and enabled true communications between countries, with two transponders providing 240 telephony calls, or a television channel.

Carrying on with the naming regime, the first satellite of this generation was Intelsat 2 F 1. On the 26th October 1966, it was launched from Cape Canaveral on the top of a NASA Delta E rocket. Its destination was a geo-stationary orbit over the Pacific Ocean, but a positioning rocket failed to operate for the correct amount of time, and meant the satellite could never be used as planned, but it did provide some communications, but not for where it was intended.

Undeterred, Intelsat 2 F 2 was completed as soon as possible, and on 11th January 1967 it was successfully launched and put into orbit above the Pacific Ocean. This opened up satellite communications to the countries in the Pacific Ocean region. Mainland USA now had traffic routes to Hawaii, Australia, and Japan. The number of Earth Stations would soon increase.

Intelsat 2 F 3 took over from Early Bird for the Atlantic Ocean communications at the end of March 1967. Satellite traffic between Europe and the USA was growing.

Finally, Intelsat 2 F 4 joined the family above the equator at the end of September 1967 and was positioned over the Indian Ocean.

The idea that Arthur C Clark had documented two decades earlier, had finally been achieved. Virtually the entire world was now able to communicate to each other with satellites.

The Intelsat 2 satellite family remained in service until 1968

Meanwhile, Goonhilly had moved from an experimental role, to a 24 hour a day commercial operation. Aerial 1 continued to speak to the world, and the Marconi company was commissioned to build a second aerial. Marconi were at the beginning of a period of years when they would build aerials all over the world.

Goonhilly Aerial 2 was nearing completion when I arrived in 1968, and was soon in full time service.

Welcome to Rota work

Goonhilly had 24-hour operational cover, that was based on a five-week shift rota.

- Week 1 - Nights
- Week 2 - Days (half a week)
- Week 3 - Days (half a week)
- Week 4 – Evenings
- Week 5 - Days – Pool Duty covering any sickness or annual leave

On that first night in late August 1971, I was told to report to the OCA at 11:00, but I discovered I was 30 minutes late, as there was an unofficial start time of 10:30.

Perhaps not the best start.

Anyway, I was greeted by a friendly bunch of men that I had seen regularly over the preceding three years.

I forget just how many of us made up that rota but they included the following:

- Controller - 1 Assistant Executive Officer (AEE) the person in overall control
- OCA – 1 Technical Officer (TO) plus a Technician 2A (T2A) and that was me
- West Wing – 1 TO
- East Wing - 1 TO
- SHF – 2 TOs plus a T2A
- Aerial Steering – 1 TO
- There was also a Power TO who was on call in event of an electrical problem

1968 and 1969

In 1968 it was time to upgrade the satellites again. This time the contract was given to a different company to build the satellite. They were called TRW and by September of that year, the Intelsat 3 family were ready to take to space.

This was the same 'Oil Drum' style construction, but now with much more powerful launch craft available, this satellite was bigger and better.

On the top of its Delta M rocket, the Intelsat 3 weighed 293 kg. Compare that with Intelsat 1 which was 149kg and Intelsat 2 was 168kg. Of course, much of that weight was launch covers and rockets to get it into orbit.

When it was in its orbit position above the equator Intelsat 3 was just 151kg.

Intelsat 1 was 39kg

Intelsat 2 was 86kg

With 183 Watts of energy from its solar cells, the Intelsat 3 electronics were much enhanced. There were still just two transponders, but they could now handle 1500 telephony circuits, or 4 television channels.

TRW were contracted to build eight of these satellites, with an expected lifetime of five years. They were not the most successful series of satellites Intelsat ever launched.

Intelsat 3 F1 was blasted off from Cape Canaveral on 19th September 1968, heading for its spot over the Atlantic Ocean. Its first mission was to relay the Mexico Olympic television pictures.

The rocket had a fault after 20 seconds, and the satellite never made it anywhere.

Intelsat 3 F2 launched on 19th December and achieved its planned orbital position over Brazil. It came into service but only lasted about 18 months before it failed. Even with faulty electronics, the satellite continued in orbit, using a valuable spot in space. Hence it was moved further away from earth using the on-board Hydrazine Gas thrusters. It became another piece of space junk.

Intelsat 3 F3 left earth on 6th February 1969, and took its position above the Pacific Ocean. It unfortunately had recurring problems and was eventually shifted to a position above the Indian Ocean.

Intelsat 3 F4 went into service on 22nd May 1969 over the Pacific Ocean. It was successfully used for many years, and is still up there in space, but no longer operational.

Intelsat 3 F5 crashed and burned in July 1969 when the launch vehicle failed before sending it into orbit. It was planned for the Atlantic Ocean.

Intelsat 3 F6 launched in January 1970 and took up an active position above the Atlantic Ocean.

Intelsat 3 F7 (April 1970) also made it into orbit above the Atlantic Ocean, but only after a launch rocket failure resulting in it having to use its own Hydrazine Gas thrusters to get to the correct position. It stayed operational for 17 years.

Intelsat 3 F8 (July 1970) was another launch failure.

During 1969, satellite communications advanced with more earth stations becoming active around the world. The three major oceans now had at least one satellite above them providing communications.

The Intelsat 3 satellites may not have been the most reliable satellite ever used, but they provided service for an almost worldwide network.

I was working in an industry that was making sensational news around the world.

But one of the greatest achievements for satellite communications was when it relayed the moon landing in July 1969. The first steps by Neil Armstrong were broadcast live to an estimated audience of 500 million people around the world. I watched this from home, with a buzz in my head at the achievement of the moon landing, but also with the knowledge that Goonhilly was involved, and knowing I would be going to work there the next morning.

Ranks

It might be useful to just outline the grades and ranks of people at Goonhilly.

At the very top was the Station Manager, and he was a **Senior Executive Engineer** (SEE).

Below him the rest of the executive management for the station were **Executive Engineers** (EE).

Then came the normal managers known as **Assistant Executive Engineer** (AEE). There were quite a few of them in charge of each section or group.

Now came the engineering grades starting with **Technical Officers** (TO), followed by my level which was a **Technician 2A** (T2A).

In some of the groups where there was perhaps less technical equipment responsibility, the starting level was **Technician 2B** (T2B) looked after by a **Technician 1** (T1). We didn't have a lot of those at Goonhilly.

My Duties

I was there to primarily help the TO in the OCA, by answering telephones, taking routine measurements of receive carrier performance, or doing whatever I was asked to do.

I could also be used to assist the other TOs if necessary.

... and yes, I also made the tea for everyone, but we all shared that job.

It might sound quite a workload, but in reality, very little went wrong. This was especially true during the evening and night shifts, when virtually nobody was working on equipment. One of the regular causes of equipment failures was due to people performing routine maintenance. Hence there were often long periods of sitting down, in the very comfortable chairs, chatting with my new colleagues, and dozing.

When an alarm occurred, a bell sounded, and there was a large light display on the wall, illuminating where the fault was. There were also lights and buzzers on the console to show any specific equipment failures.

Alarms were not frequent, but when an alarm sounded, we all looked up. Virtually all of the equipment would automatically switch to a spare unit, but invariably someone would leap from their chair, and rush to the console with button fingers at the ready.

Initially I was allowed to watch when equipment failures occurred, and soon realised that most of the station equipment had a spare, that could be switched to on the console. The important alarms were when a High Powered Amplifier (HPA transmitter) went faulty, which meant we were not sending signals to the satellite, and a lot of traffic (telephone calls or television) was being lost.

I quickly recognised those situations and knew which buttons to press, and soon the TO was allowing me to perform the switching. In those circumstances we also rang the SHF (Super High Frequency) team, who looked after the transmitters, or made an announcement over the Public Address system for the SHF staff to go to Aerial 1 or to Aerial 2.

Another equally serious concern was if the main Low Noise Amplifier (LNA) receiver failed, as that meant all of the receive traffic on that aerial was gone. Switching was again possible to a standby unit, but that would occasionally upset the Aerial Steering system, so the Steering TO had to be available as well.

The console had Trimphones at each aerial bay which might have been visually great, but trying to dial a number was a real headache. The console had a shiny surface, and the very light phone would move around as you dialled a number. You might have noticed that as time passed, these phones were fitted with push buttons to dial the number, rather than the rotary dial.

If an individual receive carrier was lost, we again had a standby, but quite often it was the distant earth station that had failed, and all we could do was to make a note of the times, and watch for the red lights to go green again.

On the console there was one other small red light which came on if the electronic logic had seen so many alarms that it declared a satellite failure. This single red light would also be accompanied by several other items of receive equipment showing red lights.

Luckily that alarm was rarely seen.

Finally, there was the ultimate disaster situation. Quite regularly during the early years, the power to the site would fail. This was easy to identify, as the first thing to happen was the room lights going off. The console equipment lights were all battery powered and glowed, but the OCA became eerily dark, but was certainly not quiet. The main battery-operated alarm panel rang its bell, and several battery powered buzzers cried out in distress.

In these situations, we would always sit quietly for a second or two. Hopefully the power would return quickly and then we had to simply silence the alarms and make any necessary equipment switchovers. If it didn't come back on, we hoped the stand-by generators would start up, but that took several seconds to happen, and it often felt like an eternity. On very rare occasions the stand-by generators failed to switch on, and we had no option but the call the Power TO at home to come in.

This would only happen perhaps once or twice a year, and as time passed, we even had a second diesel generator installed, providing further redundancy, and avoiding too much down time.

I absolutely loved the atmosphere and the job in the OCA.

There was always an air of suspense waiting for faults to occur, and then the rush of adrenalin when multiple failures meant everyone jumping up and rushing to the console. But there were also long periods of chatting and relaxation when I could learn more about the technical aspects of Goonhilly, as well as the people in my team, and a little about the social aspects of the place.

I spent several hours in the night talking with one of the controllers called Mike Dawson. His nickname was 'Digger' and he enjoyed life to the full. He enjoyed his food and drink, played rugby at the weekends, and spent a lot of time laughing about life. He was the first person I came across who studied with the Open University. He was taking a course in Psychology, and his studies often led to some deep discussions.

After months of considering his future, he decided to emigrate to New Zealand. He became one of the first people who left Goonhilly before retirement, and we were all sad to lose a wonderful man.

Sadly, once in New Zealand, a dental appointment discovered he had mouth cancer. It was terminal.

He came back to Goonhilly to say goodbye to us all. Now a skeleton of the man I knew, he philosophically talked about the situation, but the strained smiles and laughter could not hide his predicament.

He died a few weeks later.

I will always remember him as someone who spent time to chat to me about life. He taught me to think ahead, and plan my way forward. He also showed that life was really about making the most of the time we have, and fill it with laughter as often as possible.

On a much brighter note, there was a major financial perk from my job. as I had a pay rise to match my new grade as a T2A. On top of that I was also getting a special allowance for each time I was on a shift. The weekends were special and there was always one 12-hour Saturday, and a 12 hour Sunday night per shift rotation which meant overtime. One of the rota weeks was called the 'Pool' duty, when we could be asked to cover someone who was sick or on leave. Occasionally, but not often, this was a weekend shift, and then it was major overtime.

To be honest I was feeling incredibly rich, and had money to burn for evenings and nights when not working.

Out and About

Time away from Goonhilly was becoming confusing when it came to meeting up with my friends. My shift pattern, and especially evenings and weekends, meant not seeing the gang for quite long spells. But when we did meet up, it was very much about 'hanging around' either in a pub, or the Cornerhouse Café at the lower end of Trengrouse Way in Helston.

The café was warm and dry, and provided a cheap way of passing an evening. We could make a cup of tea last for an hour, and then a shilling (5p) for a record on the jukebox, or three for two shillings (10p). There was also a pinball machine to amuse those with spare cash.

The favoured pub in Helston was the Seven Stars, but sometimes we went posh in the Red Lion with more comfortable seating, but being busier, we were not quite so welcome. We would sometimes venture out from the town, and the New Inn at Wendron, or the Halzephron in Gunwalloe were popular. I think we maintained visits to them as a silent thanks for serving us while we were too young.

At weekends the gang would make a beeline to the villages where dances were being held. Mullion and The Lizard were the best, with our mid-dance breaks taken in the Riviera Club (Mullion) or the Top House (Lizard). In the second half of the dance we would become much braver, and attempts to have a dance with a girl were sometimes accepted.

Elsewhere the dance halls at Coverack and St Keverne would always attract the gang of bikers. Each dance evening would feature the same crowd of youngsters, and often entertained by the same bands, or groups. These dances were only for 50 or so people, and never attracted any well-known musicians, but there were several four-piece groups that played around the Lizard Peninsular, and the Cousin Jacks probably had the best following.

During 1971 Chris Warner moved to four wheels with a Morris 1000 van. He loved to drive, and would regularly take three or four of us to the dances, or just out to a pub. Chris was a serious drinker - and yes, he did regularly drive when he shouldn't have - but he was slow and steady at the wheel and never attracted the police. He was doing well with the local girls by now, and I was the useful wingman to look after the *'other girl'*, and yes, sometimes they were rather nice to spend time with.

There were no serious relationships for me, but I was getting known as a bit of a nutcase, and that was improving my popularity.

We were beginning to get invited to, or gate-crashed, parties. They would be someone's house, where a friend of a friend was having an evening of fun while parents were away. Chris and I were regulars, and never turned away. It was all about free booze and music, and occasionally a little dancing as the evening wore on. I remember on one Saturday afternoon, Chris and I jumped into a little blue mini with someone we'd met at a party, and he drove us to another in Plymouth. It was full of total strangers, but there was plenty of alcohol available, and we slept on the settees overnight. When I got back on the Sunday morning my mother was not amused, and I quickly realised I should have told her before we went.

I still had numerous trips to Leafield during and after the apprentice days, and my liking for alcohol did not change. The ex-apprentices of 1968 would spend many evenings in The George, and although we didn't go out of our way to encourage it, several of the local girls were quite happy to be bought drinks, and a few were even walked home. Apparently, I had a couple of girls who liked me, but we never quite got onto the same wavelength.

I was working very strongly on my weirdness by now, and had a spell of wearing a small red silk handkerchief around my neck when in the pub. This led to my first brief romance when a girl took a serious interest, and we spent a couple of evenings together. She rarely appeared, but on the evenings she was there, I would be accompanied by her. Only being in Leafield for short periods at a time, I soon disappeared, and she was gone for ever.

... I wonder what she was called!

Although one or two of the Goonhilly lads were now driving cars, we still didn't go home at the weekends. One Saturday I wasn't with the others and simply spent the evening in The George on my own at the bar of the snug. I think I was hoping to see one of the girls who allegedly liked me, but she didn't make an appearance. Alone and missing company, I managed to clear a shelf of brown ale before wandering home to the training school. That was the last time I spent alone there for many years.

Four Wheels and a Girl Friend

It was the Spring of 1972, and I was continuing to ride to and from work, and around the area, on my Yamaha 125 motorbike, but the gang was getting smaller as four wheels appeared, and the time came to do something about it.

I was lucky during my time on motorbikes.

Our gang enjoyed being a part of a group, and there were often 10 or 20 bikes roaring around the Cornish countryside on a Sunday afternoon. We all enjoyed the freedom of our transport, and yes, we often drove too fast, but in general we were not stupid, and didn't cause any trouble.

When I said I was lucky, it was because little accidents were quite common with someone misjudging a bend and falling off the bike. Once in a while the little accidents meant badly damaged bikes, and an injury requiring a sling, or a plaster cast. There were other motorbike enthusiasts that we came into contact with, where one or two had serious accidents, with permanent life changing consequences, and yes, a couple of deaths. Fortunately, we were a long way away from being Hell's Angels, and we all survived to move on healthily in our lives.

Having said this, I did have a couple of mad moments, when my Guardian Angel looked after me.

One evening on the way back from a dance in St Keverne, I completely misjudged a tricky bend, and careered onto the wrong side of the road, and almost into the hedge before I regained control. Luckily nothing was coming the other way.

There was another occasion when riding along the road by Culdrose Airfield, where I decided I wanted to turn around and go back. My mind was obviously miles away, and I simply stopped, turned straight across the road and back the other way. Again there were no cars either behind me, or coming the other way. I realised my stupidity immediately, and sighed with relief.

Then there were mechanical issues as well. I was on a straight fast road across Goonhilly Downs towards Ruan Minor, and at 80 miles an hour my throttle jammed. I could not slow down, and I knew the road would soon reach a bend. My only option was to switch off the ignition and slowly come to a halt. It was my fault. I was attempting to go as fast as I could, and wound the throttle so far, that the throttle cable came out of its housing.

So as the weeks went by, I realised I was perhaps pushing my luck too far, and maybe getting into a car might be a better option.

My mum suggested someone who was a driving instructor, so I began having driving lessons with Les Vincent. I didn't find driving a car easy to begin with, but Les soon began to relax me as I drove, and my driving test was booked.

While waiting for my test, I went to a party in an obscure village on the Lizard Peninsular. As usual, Chris drove. By now he was quite seriously involved with a girl called Sue. The party was good, but with Chris busy, I soon became quite depressed from the alcohol, and sat down behind a settee to keep out of the way.

I have no idea why, but after a couple of minutes, a girl joined me. She quietly cuddled up to me and chatted for a while. This relaxed me from my bad mood, and I enjoyed the rest of the evening with her.

She was to become my very first real girlfriend.

I will not name her for fear that somewhere a child or grandchild might recognise who I am talking about. I will simply refer to her as 'M', and she lived in Porthleven.

I was still on the motorbike at the time, but for the next few weeks (when I was not working) she spent her pocket money each evening to catch a bus to Helston, and spend time with me. At weekends 'M' would join me, and we would go out with Chris to the dances, and it was getting serious.

She was a regular at home, sitting with me on the settee and watching the television. My mum would often spend the evening sitting in the kitchen with her knitting, giving us time together. I visited her house and met her parents, and even went to chapel with her family one Sunday morning.

The relationship was becoming serious, but in my head, I realised there was a problem.

'M' was continually being told off by her mum for not revising for her exams. I suddenly had flashbacks to my own laziness and stupidity, and how this affected those important exams. I couldn't let myself ruin her future.

The next evening as I walked her back to the bus stop before she went home, I told her I wanted to break the relationship up.

She was distraught. I couldn't tell her the real reason, as that would probably push her even further away from studying. My ridiculous excuse given was that I thought she was too religious. Poor 'M' went home in tears, and I wasn't too cheerful either.

I was depressed for several days, but one afternoon my mood improved as I set off for a driving test in Penzance. Sadly, I completely messed up the reverse around a corner manoeuvre. Without thinking, I quickly put the car back in forward gear and drove back to where I had started, and tried again. Once again, I hit the kerb, so without asking, I repeated it once more. This time I was successful, but I had already decided, that passing the test that day, was not going to happen.

Back at the test centre, I answered the theory questions with a glum face. The examiner then asked about my reversing, and I said I knew I'd messed it up. He responded by saying that my confidence was apparent, and I did get it correct eventually, and he handed me a pass certificate.

I was absolutely amazed, and began to smile for a long time.

I had already bought an old rusty Morris 1000 that was now my new transport. The pride of taking it out and meeting up with Chris was wonderful. We went to Falmouth for a drive, but that was when I realised my car was not roadworthy.

It had a major brake problem that meant the car ground to a halt after about 10 miles.

In total ignorance of what to do, I rang my brother (Ernest) from a phone-box, and explained what had happened. After describing the problem, he suggested my brake cylinder was faulty, and I needed to bleed the brake system. Fortunately, I had a set of basic tools in the car, and knew what he was talking about. The problem was resolved, but Ernest had warned me that the same thing would happen again, so I needed to avoid braking very much.

Chris and I drove home very carefully that night, and I felt like a total failure.

A few days later, my brother solved the braking problem by fitting a new cylinder. Now I could drive the car properly at last.

During those first few days of becoming a car driver, I was getting regular telephone calls from 'M'. She wanted to meet up with me to talk about our break-up. I eventually agreed to meet her. I was in my car by then, and we sat together in a painful silence for several minutes until she pleaded with me to tell her why I had really broken it up.

I never did tell her.

I drove her home and when I dropped her off, an angry, and tearful 'M' walked out of my life.

I don't regret doing what I did. I hoped she would take out her anger on schooling. I met her again a year or so later, and she was with another young man. We briefly exchanged painful pleasantries, but it looked as if she was heading for educational success.

'M' was a kind, beautiful young lady who was fun to be with. I hoped she has had a good life, and found the right man in the end.

Could work get any better?

Within weeks of beginning my time in the OCA, I was sure that the job was about as good as I could have found.

The close working relationship between a small group of men was strange initially, but I soon gelled with them as we worked away the evenings and nights. During those periods, Goonhilly was empty of people except for the shift guys. I spent most of my time with the same handful of engineers, and I helped anyone who wanted somebody to hold a meter, read an instruction from a manual, or take a reading on a piece of equipment, while they buried their heads in the technical bits.

They also explained far more about the equipment, and I learnt so much from them. Of course it was all about being able to help **them** initially, but as time passed I absorbed the things they did, and learnt how to do things myself.

I forget who was actually in my shift group, but certainly remember Paul Knight, John Davies, Peter Dean, John Still, and Wally Sturgess. They spent much of their time in the OCA during the evenings and nights. From the aerial team (SHF) there was John Price, and Brian Groom, but other names have drifted into the mist of growing old. The controllers weren't always the same, as their rota had differences from the rest of us, but they certainly left a mark on my development. Peter Stone was one of the first I encountered, but Don Cattran, Len Farr, and Jock Lawson, all helped to turn me from a tea boy into an engineer.

As the years went by, the controllers moved to other jobs, and some of the TO's were promoted to take on the controller's post. This in turn meant other people joined the shift roles, and quite often I moved from one rota to another. This meant a changing number of faces to get to know, and more knowledge to absorb.

To begin with, it was quite eerie to walk down the corridors at night, as the only sounds were the echo of my footsteps, with no voices to break the silence. There was just the gentle purr of equipment, the chatter of telegraph machines, and the occasional ring of an alarm bell.

I would often be tasked to go and check a piece of equipment in the West Wing, or even in the other rooms around the main building. Each room became my personal empire, and they all had their own specific sound. I quickly learnt where different equipment was located, and where to find a receiver that operated to a specific earth station thousands of miles away.

Sometimes there was a reason to go outside, and then the lack of other people, or cars, and even the lack of bird song, made it almost magical. Each aerial had a different sound from various compressors, air conditioning or even the motors.

The day shifts were completely different as we had to share the station with all the other engineers. We were also expected to perform more of the maintenance routines when on days, but I enjoyed those as well. Changing lamp bulbs was a hated chore for many, but as I lit up a lamp again, I would dream about the particular far away earth station that it was monitoring, and wonder if someone was mirroring my job on a lamp for Goonhilly.

One of my favourite moments at any time of the day, was when we were transmitting or receiving a television broadcast. In those early years of satellite communications, live television from around the world was special. I witnessed some amazing things as raw news footage, and scenes of earth quake damage, or explosions made me gasp. Of course, there were also numerous sporting events, that allowed people throughout the world to watch live action.

The world was changing because suddenly we had almost instant access to television coverage of tragedies and celebrations from countries around the globe. The basic news broadcasts on terrestrial television were suddenly getting longer, as they could talk about and show what was making the news in America, Australia, Africa, or Asia. We could see the destructions of earthquakes, volcanoes, or wars within hours rather than days. The world shared celebrations of royal weddings, or political elections, and fans of sport could watch live coverage of the Olympics, or World Cup football in whatever country was hosting it.

One of the most watched television programmes we ever transmitted at Goonhilly was the annual FA Cup Final football match. As well as the 625 Line PAL television standard of Britain, that went towards the Asian countries and Australasia, the material was converted in London to the 525 Line NTSC television standard to the Americas. There were multiple audio feeds of the commentary in different languages to suit the countries. It was a huge, and complex television programme, and had to be monitored very carefully.

When I was on duty for this special match, it felt ridiculous to be paid to watch football. But of course, if something went wrong, I realised that an equipment failure, or accidently pressing the wrong button, could affect millions of people.

I was quickly being trusted in my role, and there were often times when I would be alone in the OCA. My colleagues were rarely away from the room for long, or were just a phone call away, but these moments made me feel as if I was finally a part of Goonhilly.

On one night quite early on in my time in the OCA when I was on my own, there was an alarm that made me glance at the console. This was no ordinary alarm as all the receiver lights for Aerial 1 were red. As I rushed to get a closer look, the lights returned to green, and seconds later back to red. Then I spotted a single red light that gave me the answer, it was a Satellite Failure.

The rest of the shift guys quickly appeared, and for a while it was chaos as the complete Indian Ocean satellite communications were destroyed. The phones were ringing from various London exchanges asking what was happening, and we were quickly speaking to the American control centre known as the IOC (International Operations Control).

The problem was soon diagnosed. If you remember earlier in the book, I said that the satellites spun in space to maintain stability, but there was also a motor to de-spin the antenna system to ensure they always pointed towards earth. Well, it appears the motor became cold while the satellite was on the other side of the earth from the sun, and it seized up. Hence as the satellite spun (for stability) the antennas would point in the correct direction for a second or two, and then point away from the earth.

Fortunately, as the earth turned, and the sun warmed the satellite up again, everything returned to normal.

We had no option but to continue using the satellite, and failures occurred every now and again. There is no way to send a repair team 36,000 km into space to squirt some oil into the motor.

The only solution was a new satellite, and that would not be for quite a while.

Things were happening nearer to home as well.

On another night shift in October 1971, I was alone again in the OCA for a moment, and the television desk phone rang. I answered it, and a voice informed me that a bomb had exploded at the Post Office Tower in London. I was shocked, but didn't realise the true magnitude of that moment.

It wasn't long that night, before there was a television broadcast from Goonhilly to other parts of the world, showing video footage of the incident. Of course, the weirdness of the situation was that the television material was being transmitted to us, from the BT Tower itself.

This was the first time the IRA had actually bombed a mainland Britain target, and it was a moment when my generation were really introduced to terrorism. That threat changed attitudes, and did achieve what the name suggests. Initially it was because of the problems of Ireland, but as the decades have passed, we've seen the source of the threat change to Islamic fundamentalists.

It is 50 years later now, and terrorism has remained with us, and for most of the world.

Social Life at Goonhilly

As well as the work, which was pretty good fun, there was also an official Sports and Social Club that organised events.

The canteen had a small bar at one end, and it was a popular venue to play cards, or just chat over a pint. But occasionally there would be a social evening with a local group to play dance music. All the dining tables and chairs would be moved to one end of the room, and there was an area for the band to play at the other end from the bar.

These evenings were quite popular, and the workers would bring their families, and sometimes friends, to join in with the music and rather cheap drinks.

Being single, I would often go along and prop up the bar for an hour before my night shifts, or for an hour after the evening shift finished. Sometimes an unattached daughter would be pushed my way to have a dance with, but that was rare.

On 5th November the club organised a bonfire with fireworks, plus hot dogs and hamburgers, as well as the bar being opened. The fireworks were quite expensive and hence the displays were rather good. Volunteers would set up the rockets and other fireworks during the afternoon, and then let them off when It was time. I got involved with the social club over the years, and helped with the fireworks on several occasions.

At Christmas there were parties for staff families, where presents were given to the younger children by Santa, while the adults enjoyed a few glasses of wine.

To enhance the Christmas celebrations, a pantomime was sometimes created and performed for children and adults. These were great fun with a stage built in the canteen, with multiple backdrops and lighting. The script was usually created by someone on the staff, and Doug Pawlby (Construction Group) was one who excelled at such things. Volunteers were then invited, or dragged into taking part.

This was where I had my very first chance to be on stage. The pantomime was loosely based on Cinderella, and I played Buttons. I was absolutely over the moon with the opportunity to be an idiot on stage. The script was simple, but corny, and there were many mistakes due to a lack of rehearsal time, but it was fun.

I was becoming quite involved with many of the social events, and quickly found myself on the social club committee. I remained active in this area, for almost all of my time at Goonhilly. They were very happy times.

My First Brand New Car

After jilting my girlfriend 'M', I continued my busy social life in the bars and dance halls around the Lizard Peninsular. Most of the old gang of motorcyclists had moved into cars, but we stayed together at weekends. My involvement was perhaps changing due to my shift pattern, interspersed with trips away to Leafield for the continuing training.

After the brakes on my little Morris 1000 rust bug were repaired by my brother, it was a quite reliable car. I couldn't trust it however to make the journey to and from Leafield, so my thoughts were turning towards getting a new car.

One sunny summer Saturday, a few of us went on a search for my new transport. We drove to Falmouth initially to look at a Datsun Cherry which was a popular car in 1972. It was affordable, but I was being nagged about considering to 'buy Japanese rubbish'.

We moved on to Redruth, and changed my thoughts to a Mini. I came away from the garage after putting a deposit down on a Mini 850cc. It would not be available for several weeks, so I had to continue with my Morris. Back home I told the family the news, and my eldest brother (John) was not impressed. I was apparently paying far too much, and he said he would deal with it.

A few days later John had got me out of the deal with the garage in Redruth, and took me to Helston Garages where I signed on the dotted line for a Mini 1000cc that would be ready for me by the end of the week.

That was to become my transport for several years.

It was a lovely deep blue colour, with the registration number of FCV700L. I was so proud to drive it away from the garage, and show it off with the gang.

I will point out, that purchasing a new car then, was different compared to car buying now. There were no extras - as the salesmen described them - and that meant no fog lights, ABS, air conditioning, and no radio. I even had to pay for the passenger sun visor.

The lack of radio was the real problem, and within days I had purchased a radio/cassette player, and an aerial. The following Sunday morning, I set to work to fit the radio, and then turned to the aerial. This meant drilling a hole in the wing, and then poking the cable through various holes until it reached the radio. It was probably two or three hours before I turned it on and tuned into Radio 1.

So that completed my preparations to become the man about town with his own shiny wheels. There is now another difference from the 1970s compared to now. The radio worked, but as I drove around, there was an annoying noise in the background that increased in volume as the car went faster. A lot of this was about how well the ignition systems of modern engines have been cleaned up, plus the improvement in aerial design.

We didn't know any better at that time, so the annoying buzzing had to be accepted.

A week or so later, I was suddenly shocked to see that I had spots of rust on the wing and bonnet of my shiny car. It was quickly taken to the garage, and a metalwork expert was arranged to come and take a look.

On the day of the appointment with the metal magician, I dropped the car off at the garage for the morning. When I came back after lunch, I was shown my car which was now spotless and gleaming again.

I was so very embarrassed when the answer to the problem was given. When I had drilled the hole for the aerial, I hadn't wiped away the little bits of metal swarf. This was what had turned to rust.

There was no charge for my amateurism, and I decided to stick to satellite communications, rather than car repairs.

Comfortable at Work

By the late summer of 1972 I was comfortable in my job, and being paid a very fair wage.

There were moments of excitement when photographers or TV crews came to Goonhilly to cover a story for the press, or television news, and documentaries. There were many moments when a photographer or TV Crew would ask for someone to pose in front of the console, and perhaps do something impressive. I would always volunteer, and the favourite trick for the cameraman was to push the lamp test button.

Away from the various lamp test button photos, there is one wonderful picture of me kneeling in front of the television console, with cricket on the monitors. That's what I called working!

Satellite Communications was very special, although most of the public were mesmerized by the television programmes that we brought into the country, rather than the core business of carrying telephony services.

The public didn't associate the fact that Satellite Communications was making it easier for anyone with a phone to make international calls with little or no involvement with an operator.

Goonhilly was working to earth stations in North and South America, as well as a number of countries in Africa, plus India, Pakistan, and all the way to Australia. Both of our antennas were operational for 24 hours of every day of the year.

When I first saw the OCA, they had a blackboard with names of the earth stations chalked on it. The information showed the operational frequencies and carrier sizes. Very soon we had to expand to huge pin boards, with little plastic letters and numbers of different colours to indicate who we were working with. Keeping the information up to date became another job that fell to the likes of me.

Some of the smaller countries only had limited services with just 24 channels of telephony, while larger countries perhaps had 132 channels, or even 252. At that moment, this was the largest volume of calls possible on a single carrier. The satellites in use were filling rapidly and newer and bigger ones were being planned and designed.

Outside, another antenna was being built, and Aerial 3 would soon be in service. The OCA console now had another four bays of switches, meters and lights as Goonhilly became even busier. We began working to two satellites over the Atlantic Ocean as the traffic levels expanded.

In November of 1973 I was given a special job.

Princess Anne would marry Captain Mark Phillips at the Westminster Abbey, and everybody (well all the women) wanted to watch the ceremony live.

There was however a slight problem at Goonhilly, as we didn't have a television aerial for domestic programmes. A solution was thought up. Cables were run from the OCA to the Canteen to show the live feed that we were going to transmit to America. There was another snag however, as the feed was carrying the television material in the American 525 Line NTSC format. Not to be beaten, the solution was to use an old 525 Line NTSC colour monitor that was no longer in operational use.

This is where I came along. I was handed a large book about the red metal cased monitor, and told to make the picture as presentable as possible. So for at least two days, I spent my time with various little tools in an attempt to make the colours seen on the screen, look roughly like the real thing.

I never saw the actual results as I wasn't on duty, but apparently the ladies (and several of the men) enjoyed the wedding ceremony.

Other major news items of 1972, that gave Goonhilly television work, included:

- The Americans leaving Vietnam after the long drawn-out war.
- The Watergate scandal
- Concorde makes its first flight to New York
- Sunderland beat Leeds 1:0 in the FA Cup
- Jackie Stewart won the F1 Championship

By now, the unreliable Intelsat III satellites were being replaced by the next generation of satellites. They were the Intelsat IV, and they heralded a giant step forward in design and capability.

Intelsat IV

Intelsat chose the Hughes company to produce this series of satellites. They were considerably bigger, and offered much more capacity, to meet the growing world-wide demand for satellite communications.

It was the shape of an oil drum again, but this time it was in the region of six metres high and about 600kg when in orbit. This was about four times the weight of the previous family of satellites.

The Intelsat IV increased the number of transponders from two to twelve. This meant 6000 telephone calls at the same time, plus two television channels.

There was an option of switching the transponders to radiate to all of the ocean area below it (referred to as a *'Global Beam'*), or to concentrate the power to new *'Spot Beam'* transmissions that were restricted to either the west or east of the region. This avoided vast amounts of the radio energy from the satellite simply being sent to the ocean, where there were very few, or no earth stations to receive it.

The satellite height when in orbit, was described as being the same as the length of a double decker bus, but almost a third of this was the stack of antennas on the top. It was spin stabilised again, and hence required the de-spin motors to keep the antennas pointing towards earth. Fortunately, they had sorted out the motor failure, and this family of satellites proved to be very reliable.

They built eight of these satellites, with a planned life of seven years. In reality they were still working long after their pension dates. They were launched between January 1971 and May 1975, and the last one was switched off in 1987.

Life away from work in 1972

Our gang had been together since Primary School, and we had played as children, and grown up through the teenage years. We'd started with pushbikes, progressed to motorbikes, which had now changed to cars. We remained true friends and spent many weekend evenings and Sunday lunchtimes in the pub, but it was different. The little gang was now enhanced by partners, and romances were becoming more serious.

I think Perry was the first to announce that he was getting married to Linda.

… Wow!

The wedding was absolutely amazing, but it probably marked the moment when the gang started dissolving.

Most of the lads were now in long term relationships. Chris was with Sue, Keith Pankhurst with Heather, and Perry's sister, Katie, was with Monty. John Hall was settling with Fran, and wedding bells were becoming high on the agenda for all of them …

… except me.

I would regularly go to work early on a night shift, to have a drink at the bar, before beginning work. On a Friday evening late in 1972, I was on nights, but there was a social evening in progress so I could listen to the music before starting the shift.

Social evenings were good fun for me, and I enjoyed chatting to workmates and watch people enjoying themselves, but that night was different.

I always scanned the people to see if there was anybody new, or more particularly, for any young ladies that I hadn't seen before. And yes, there was one. She was sitting with one of my shift buddies, and when he came to the bar, I asked who she was.

The response was that she was called Lucille, and worked with his wife... and was single.

My interest must have been passed on to her, as five minutes later, she came over to see me. We chatted and had a dance, but it was soon time for me to start work, so it was just a brief moment together. But the important thing was that we made plans to meet up again.

That was the beginning of a quite serious romance. We spent a lot of time together, going to the local dances, spending time in pubs, or just sitting together watching television. Lucille and I became a couple, and as the weeks and months passed, plans for the future were being made.

In the Spring of 1973, we got engaged and started to look forward to a wedding and finding a home. I had to go on a training course to Leafield and to show our seriousness, I left my car with Lucille while I was away.

We even bought ourselves a dog. It was an Alsatian, with a pedigree name of *'Shepherdwyn Warlord 3rd*'. We simplified his name, and called him Thor, after the Norse God of war. He certainly looked like his name, and grew into quite a big dog. In reality he was more of a pussy cat than a God of war. This huge dog liked to sit on our laps, and when out on a walk, he would shy away from any other dog, or cat. I regularly took him for long walks after a night shift, and the favoured places were the park, or the Penrose Riverside area. To my embarrassment however, if our route took us along Coinagehall Street, there was a major problem.

Outside of one of the shops was a large dog shaped charity collection box, and Thor would cringe with his tail up under his belly as we approached it. It was one of the rare moments when this soft dog used his strength to refuse to pass this inanimate object. My only option was to cross the road, before continuing our walk.

My mum loved Thor, and when I was away from home, she had to do all the necessary housekeeping, although Lucille would drop in a couple of times a day to give mum some relief.

All in all, I was happy, and the future looked to be sorted.

But there were a few moments, when I meditated while walking Thor, or at work in the long quiet hours, when doubts were creeping in. I sometimes felt things were going too fast. Getting married, and buying a house might have been a wonderful idea, but I wasn't sure if I was ready for it.

Lucille was planning our life, and I slowly began to have a feeling that I wasn't being consulted very much. The future felt to be cut and dried, and I wasn't sure if I was ready to settle.

Lucille must have sensed there was a problem, and one night when she asked if everything was alright…

After a moment of thought, I said no.

In a flash, our close relationship unravelled quickly, and love turned very sour. She tried to make me change my mind, but the decision to break it up actually came as a relief, and I felt happy again. There was to be no turning back.

Coincidentally, Lucille was from Porthleven, and lived quite near to 'M'. I was determined never to get involved with girls from the village again.

After 50 years I have no regrets about my failed relationships, and hope the two Porthleven girls went on to have happy lives.

Another chapter of my love life was complete.

Aerial 3

When I arrived at Goonhilly just a handful of years earlier, Aerial 1 had been operational, and Aerial 2 was just about completed, but in 1972 I had the chance to watch the construction of a new aerial. Although the next giant dish aerial was again being built by Marconi, it was a completely different design.

In the early 1970s, many of the new aerials around the world were beginning to look rather similar, and I personally liked the shape.

Imagine a windmill. Now take away the sails of the windmill, and replace it with a giant 30 metre diameter reflector, that nearly stretches to the ground, and extends high above the top of the 18-metre concrete tower.

The static base of the concrete building has a short section at the top called the Kingpost, onto which the aerial reflector dish is mounted onto an Azimuth Beam. The Kingpost can be driven around by motors to allow 360° Azimuth movement of the dish. The Azimuth Beam also tilts up and down to create any required Elevation movement from horizontal to 90°.

In the middle of the dish, there is a hole leading to the equipment room within the movable section of the windmill shaped base building. That hole is apparently big enough to allow a mini car to go through it.

... as far as I am aware, this fact has never been tested.

Fitted around this hole is a conical horn shaped Cassegrain feed assembly. Signals passed to and from the satellite here. As with Aerial 2, in front of the feed is another smaller dish known as the sub-reflector. It points back towards the feed, and accurately mirrors the main reflector shape. Transmit signals radiate from the feed to the sub-reflector, whose shape reflects those signals to fill the main reflector. The signals are then directed by the 30m reflector towards the satellite in a concentrated beam of energy. In the receive direction, the vast reflector captures as much of the energy that it can, and then focusses it onto the sub-reflector, which sends it back down the feed to the aerial building.

A door at the bottom of the tower allows access inside, where a stairway leads up to an observation walkway around the outside of the tower. From here a rectangular tower construction houses a lift going to the Azimuth cabin at the top. This is where the bulk of the radio equipment is found.

Personally, I thought Aerial 3 was the best *looking* of all the aerials on the site ...

... except one of course

... Goonhilly 1 is the best aerial there has ever been.

Training Never Stops

By 1973 my career looked to be going well, but I was ambitious and beginning to look at getting to the next level with promotion to a Technical Officer (TO).

To even get to a point where I was eligible for promotion, I had to go on a number of mandatory training courses. Of course, they were mainly at Leafield, but some were nearer to home.

With Goonhilly's new aerial and equipment, there was a new monitoring and switching system in the OCA. I was becoming quite respected by then, and quickly got to grips with most of the quite familiar console indicators and switches.

But Aerial 3 had some differences.

A part of the training for Aerial 3 meant a trip to the Marconi factory in Chelmsford. Along with several others I was away for a week with training from the designers who created the Aerial 3 equipment. I had become used to the way training was delivered at Leafield from people who had worked on the kit. This factory instruction was from designers, and severely less effective. They simply showed diagrams and described what it was doing.

Almost everything went over our heads. We were not getting much useful information, and the training looked to me as if it was simply a designer showing off what he knew. This was the first time I realised that training has to be designed to meet the needs and ability of the students. What we received was a waste of our time, and a waste of our company's money.

Much of what I really learnt was from actually working on the equipment, or in my case, working on the OCA console.

Unfortunately, there were several things that made it more complicated getting used to the new system.

When satellite communications began, the equipment was very new, but at times, not very reliable. Hence for every major component, such as transmitters, receivers, modulators, and demodulators, there was a spare. This was referred to as having 100% equipment redundancy. As the technology improved, so did the equipment, and it was becoming far more reliable.

So Aerial 3 was the first I encountered where there was a reduced amount of spare equipment chains. This was most obvious with the multiple transmitters, where there were less spares, so a lower level of redundancy. Although the main Low Noise Amplifier receivers had full redundancy, the demodulators just had one spare for a block of maybe five.

This lower redundancy meant the switching was far more complex, especially automatic changes, and training was quite important. In reality, although the equipment itself was very much more reliable, the switching systems was more complicated, and introduced different faults. This was because the logic necessary to sense a fault, and make the appropriate switching, sometimes failed, but human error was also an occasional problem.

One morning while on a day shift, I was asked by one of the senior engineers (Don Higgs) to explain how the transmitter switching worked. I was quite confident with it, and did my best to explain it to him. He asked what would happen if certain things occurred, and I was able to tell him. Finally, a question was posed as to the outcome of a chain of different scenarios, and this stumped me. It hadn't been envisaged during training sessions with the Marconi engineers who designed the system.

He suggested we should get ourselves into that scenario, and see if it would be a problem. I explained that we were operational with live traffic, if the switching went wrong, we would lose service. He insisted we find out what would happen. I cleared the plan with the controller, and pushed the buttons to simulate the scenario.

The transmitters failed.

There was much laughter around the OCA.

I quickly reset things, and ensured that the manager was happy with what we had done. He was also amused by the outcome, and assured me that it was his request, and I was not to blame.

At least this incident confirmed that I was being accepted.

1974 – A Very Good Year

In January 1974, I began a series of training courses at Leafield, and they were to change my life.

The first course was probably the most complicated three weeks of training that I had ever had to do. The official course name was 'Microwave Theory and Measurements', and was to take me through the first principles of the radio aspects upon which satellite communications is made possible.

Things started so well, but within days the subject began to get very deep into the complexities of 'waveguide'.

I won't upset you with how it happens, but at the frequencies used for satellite communications, the radio signals do not go very far on normal wires or cables. Instead, they are launched into lengths of round or rectangular metal tubes. For those who know what I am talking about, I am sure many of you share my confusion about how this is possible, but for the rest of the world there is no urgent reason to know, so please accept that this is real.

Anyway, as some of the other people around me weakened under the pressure of mathematical and electro-magnetic magic, I did my best to keep up with the subject, but falling asleep seemed far more interesting. As the days went by, I had accepted that the metal boxes did indeed do as the lecturer and instructors said, and I actually enjoyed the practical elements of the course.

We learnt to use some very complicated equipment, and took measurements of signal strengths going from one end to the other of a little piece of this waveguide.

There was a lot of emphasis put on safety as well. Even the quite small powered sources we were using could have been dangerous, and might potentially make us sterile.

... that woke most of us up anyway!

Because this was a promotion qualifying course, there was an exam at the end, that we had to pass if we had any hope of becoming a TO.

… that also woke us up!

Fortunately, I was able to pass the exam, and I could go back to enjoy a few far simpler weeks in the OCA.

There was hardly time at work before I was driving back to Leafield again. I had another three-week course to attend (and pass) called 'Principles of Digital Logic'.

This was presented by the same lecturer and instructor as the Microwave course, but the material was far more interesting, and I relaxed into the course. The Lecturer was called Peter Evans, and the main instructor was Barry Strange. Because it was significantly less confusing, I began to make friends with the training staff.

I was thoroughly enjoying my time at Leafield.

There were some very good evenings in the local pubs, and I was getting to know a bit more about the local attractions. Nearby Witney was a common trip out in the evening, and I was feeling comfortable with the area.

With that course completed, it was nearing the end of April 1974, and there were just a few weeks before I would be back again for the final mandatory qualifying course.

In May of 1974 I was back on the road to Leafield. I was accompanied in the car by Mark Jago, and to this day I remember a song coming on the radio called *'Billy Don't be a Hero'* by Paper Lace. Mark was not into this type of music and turned it down, but I jokingly said it was great and turned it back up again.

… strange how little things stick in the mind

Anyway, we were about to begin a six-week course called 'Satellite Earth Station Principles and Practices'.

This was a training course that was respected around the world, and we had students from other countries alongside ourselves. It really took a detailed look at how satellite communications was possible, the different equipment used, and how to perform a wide range of tests.

To begin with, it wasn't overly confusing, as it was about the principles anyone on an earth station would get used to. But then the real nitty gritty of the course began showing us the calculations as to how to measure the power required at a transmitter, to enable a suitable power to be received at the distant earth station. This involved having to perform masses of mathematical calculations, that pushed our minds at time to the limit.

I was enjoying the course, as it was really all about my job, and I wanted to be good at it.

Of course, in the evenings we would regularly walk to the village and have numerous drinks in 'The George'. By now we had begun to get to know a few of the locals, and, we were recognised as regulars.

One evening, while we sat in the window of the snug bar, I spotted one of the older locals who was called Eva Prattley walking across the village green towards the pub. She was a real character of the village. But my eyes were actually looking further then Eva at a couple of girls walking across the green behind her. I dug someone next to me in the ribs to take a look, and soon perhaps a dozen of us were watching, and hoping they would come into the bar.

I don't remember the details, but I struck up a conversation with one of them, and discovered they were called Deb and Janet. I attempted to buy them a drink, but initially they refused the offer, and ignored me. As I watched the glasses empty, I tried again. Success, and a drink called a 'Blue Lagoon' made quite an impact on my money. They were now willing to talk, and one of my mates joined me at a table to get to know them better.

Deb (Thompson) lived in the village just five minutes from the pub. Janet was her best friend, and they both went to the college in Witney. After spending some more money on them, they said they had to go, but we arranged to meet up again.

For the remainder of the course, I met Deb several times a week, and we became very close. By the end of the six weeks Deb had agreed to my idea to come down to Cornwall and stay for a few days in the summer.

I passed the course exam, and went back to Goonhilly with all the qualifications I needed to get promotion, if a suitable post came along.

But my mind was elsewhere by then. Work continued as before, but I was missing Deb, and my head was wondering if there was anything else I could do, to see more of her, than just a few days in Cornwall.

A Big Decision

I couldn't get over the joy of my time with Deb. I had only known her for a few weeks, but I was truly missing her.

My mind was going 100 miles per hour wondering what I could do, and a plan began to unfold.

I talked to my mum, I rang Peter Evans at Leafield, and then spoke to John Apperley my training manager. My plan was feasible, but I had to think hard about a major change in my career.

My mind was made up, and by early July 1974 I was packing almost all of my clothes and possessions into the car. I was moving to Leafield to take up a post known as an Instructor Engineering. There were tears from my mother, and so many questions from my work mates, but my heart was leading me down a different path, and there was no stopping me.

I was going to be training people in the subjects that I had literally just completed, but having someone from a satellite earth station, meant I had some real knowledge of the working environment. The post of Instructor Engineering was only a temporary one, meaning that if everything went wrong, my job at Goonhilly was still there for me. I would be losing my shift allowance, but the new job was at the grade of a TO, plus enhancements. In other words, I wouldn't be losing any money, and I would be getting valuable experience to put on my record.

I hadn't fully discussed my plans with Deb, but she did know I was coming back to the village to work.

My arrival at the Training School was quite low key, and the first priorities were to get my possessions moved into a room in one of the old bungalows on the site. It wasn't big, but it was free, and I had all my meals in the college canteen, except at weekends when I had to sort out a different way of eating.

My job started the next morning, so in the evening I met up with Deb again and chatted over what was happening.

This was the beginning of a very special 12 months. I had no idea if I could be successful in training. Neither did I know if my relationship with Deb would be more than a flash in the pan.

I didn't care, I just had to follow my heart.

My First Few Days in Training

That first day in training from the establishment side of the desk wasn't very eventful. The standard training process was that the lecturer spent the morning with the delegates with theory. Usually, the instructors took over in the afternoon to give the delegates the practical aspects of the morning's theory. At the beginning of a course, there was traditionally far more theory around the basics of a subject, and hence practical work didn't start straight away.

So, my first day was all about getting to know people, and sorting out all the paperwork associated with my rather rapid change of working location. There were different ways of completing time sheets to record my time, and lots of new phone numbers, access codes, and security procedures.

Meeting everyone took several days, and a lot of paperwork appeared as I attempted to do each different task.

I had a desk in the small office that belonged to the Satellite Communications team. In the same office was my manager (Peter Evans) who was the lecturer for most of the courses I assisted with. There was also Barry Strange who was the senior instructor, and who also delivered some of the theory sessions. Peter was very experienced with the subjects, but Barry had a more mathematical brain, and was ideal for the microwave course.

Elsewhere in the training team were lecturers I had encountered during my apprenticeship years, such as Jack Griffith, and Reg Messer, but there were several others who were quite new to me. John Hicks looked after submarine cable training, and he was assisted by Mike Day and Fred Owen as instructors. John Boyd delivered several courses, and being another person with a mathematical skill, he also helped with the microwave course. There were also multi-purpose instructors called Eddie Page, and Bryan Hunt. Bryan assisted the satellite team, and I learnt a lot from him about the practical elements that I had to get used to.

As well as the training team, I was introduced to many of the ancillary people around the training school, such as the cooks, cleaners, and administration team. There were a couple of secretaries to assist with any documents I needed, and they were very helpful.

There was also the boss, and that was still Ron Coles.

He had an office of his own, with a personal secretary. His office door was not open very often, but he did have a chat with me to encourage me to work hard, and wishing me the best in my new career.

And yes, I did initially see it as a permanent change to my career, and wanted to be successful.

My head was in a buzz for several days as I first got used to what my role involved, before shadowing the instructors as I learnt how to set up the practical sessions, and then how to demonstrate them so that they looked simple, before watching the delegates making a mess of them.

I was noticing how many of the training team had different personas between time in the classrooms, and time outside. When they weren't actually in class, many of them were far more relaxed, and chatted, made jokes, and laughed. When they left the room to go to the class, they quite obviously switched on the presentation mode with a straight serious face, and a much slower pace of speaking.

I began my time in training thinking some of my colleagues had quite strange ways, but I soon realised the pressure and stress of trying to help delegates, was creating the same mental changes in my manner.

… and I was enjoying it.

What was my role?

The job didn't involve a lot of pressure. Although the courses I was responsible for were quite regular, there were gaps in the programme that allowed us the time to maintain practical equipment. I may have been brought into the training group because of my experience, but I was still learning a lot from the instructors around me.

So, between the courses, I would read through the exercise sheets to be sure I knew what had to be done. I also read the test equipment handbooks, and practiced taking measurements. After a few weeks I felt pretty much up to speed, and quite happy to be in front of the students without help from the more experienced members of the team.

There were always bits and pieces that needed repair, or to be sent away for calibration, and that was useful to understand more of the processes. When a course was about to start, I would help to get the student handbooks and practical exercise material ready. One of the secretaries would print off the sheets on an old fashioned Gestetner machine, and then I would put them into folders.

Student names had to be checked and sometimes we'd discover they had not been on one of the qualifying courses. In some cases this wasn't a problem as the students were simply coming to gain extra experience, rather than as an important part of the development.

On course days I would sit in on the theory sessions quite often. This was partly to be sure I understood the subjects, but also to watch the presentation skills. As time went by, I was asked to help out with some of the theory sessions. This was really a shock to my system, but I was keen to get involved as much as I could. I remembered the training style I had experienced at the Marconi factory, and was determined not to inflict that on my own classes.

And of course, I was continuing to learn more about the other staff members, and taking an interest in the courses they dealt with. It wasn't long before I could help on these courses to make myself more valuable.

The more I learnt, the more I was realising that I enjoyed being in training.

Fridays were a very special day. We would finish early, and delegates would be on their way home by lunchtime. All of us worked quickly to clear up the lecture and practical rooms, complete any end of course paperwork, and prepare for Monday.

Then it was lunchtime. The tradition was that one of the instructors – usually Fred Owen - would drive to Witney, buy some crispy bread rolls, and a large chunk of cheddar cheese. Back at the school's lounge area, the rolls would be buttered, and the cheese cut into manageable size pieces. Then accompanied by a pint of beer we would eat our lunch and chat about the students, the school, or just life in general.

After that I would return to my little room and sleep off the beer.

I occasionally drove home to Cornwall at the weekends to show mum I was well. She spoiled me for a couple of days, and I tried to explain what I was doing. But for most weekends, I stayed at Leafield, where I had to organise my own meals, but I kept it rather simple. In my room I had a kettle, and I had bought a basic set of cutlery, cups, plates and bowls. My food was limited to what could be prepared with hot water, so Pot Noodles, and Ready Brek was my staple weekend diet. It was not very healthy, but for the remainder of the weeks I used the canteen, with yet more unhealthy food.

I was still smoking, and this often resulted in me getting sore throats and coughs. There were occasional visits to a doctor in Charlbury who would diagnose tonsilitis and after a giving me a prescription for Penicillin, he would send me away with a plea to give up smoking. The antibiotics appeared to work, but one Saturday morning I woke feeling awful.

My face had swelled, and the sore throat was worse than it had been before the latest round of antibiotics. I managed to get an emergency appointment with the doctor in Charlbury, and was soon in his surgery looking and feeling very sad for myself. He said I appeared to have become allergic to Penicillin, and gave me a different box of pills to use. He then offered to send me to hospital because I was having quite a severe allergic reaction, that might get worse. I decided against this rather dramatic idea, and broke the news to Deb and her parents.

Amazingly, the new pills worked almost instantly. The swelling went away, and the sore throat recovered.

It was soon time for a cigarette again.

The Social side of Leafield

I was driving to the village on most evenings to see Deb. It was a lovely autumn, and we explored the area to give me a greater introduction to Oxfordshire, and the Cotswolds. We visited pubs in various villages which often had very unusual names.

Upper Slaughter, plus Lower Slaughter of course, the Wychwoods, or more accurately Ascot-under-Wychwood, or Shipton-under-Wychwood. Many of these places would become quite familiar, and Bourton on the Water would be visited many times, plus the nearby Blenheim Palace. Witney became almost a home town, and I learnt about its history, the shops, and the pubs. My knowledge of the City of Oxford also improved, but it was just a little too busy for my liking.

During the week, Deb was at college in Witney, and I would go and collect her on Friday afternoons when I had an early finish. On Saturdays she worked in the Co-op, and I would drive her to work, and collect her at the end of the afternoon. I was becoming recognised by a few of the Co-op workers as I hung about the shop. She worked in the drapery department, and there was little to interest me, so I often looked so out of place before Deb was allowed to go.

Our relationship was growing.

There were also occasions at Leafield when some of the students were from Goonhilly, or the other radio stations, and then I would go for drinks with them in the villages and show off Deb.

I also went back to College in the city of Oxford to continue my development. It was a day release course on a Wednesday where I completed my City and Guilds Telecommunications course. I did very well, and finally mastered Calculus that Mr Grindrod failed to teach me. At the end of that year, I passed my exams and completed what was referred to as a 'Full Certificate'. I never bothered getting the actual certificate, but I gather it was very near to achieving the equivalent of a degree in the subject.

Unfortunately my days in Oxford meant a lack of food, so each Wednesday evening I would go to Deb's house, where her parents would welcome me, and her mum would offer me a meal. Although she was more than happy to cook something special, I always asked for beans on toast. I got on well with Jim and Jean, and would regularly spend an evening watching the television with them.

Although not as often as I should have done, I did drive home to Cornwall and spend a few days with my mum. She quietly ticked me off for not staying in contact. My letters were not regular, and the weekends I came home during that summer and autumn could be counted on the fingers of a single hand.

Christmas 1974 was the special moment that I brought Deb to Cornwall to meet my family. Perhaps it shocked mum to see just how close we had become, and I'm sure my siblings (and their wives) thought things were getting serious... perhaps too serious.

Deb was introduced to my dog Thor, and we took him for walks together during that short break in Cornwall. I introduced Deb to a few of my gang, and we all looked as if we were growing up, and settling down.

One thing Deb often reminds me about that Christmas, was that my mum gave her so much to eat, that she put on half a stone in weight, and never managed to lose it.

The Spring of 1975

My life as an instructor was becoming easier, and the odd moment when I was asked to present a theory lesson no longer daunted me. The job was good, I fitted in with the people I worked with, and I envisaged that this could be my future.

There was no softening of my relationship with Deb, and the thoughts were beginning to turn to the next stage.

At weekends (while in Leafield) I often went for drinks with Deb's dad (Jim) and his best pal Jock. Deb would come with me at the beginning of these evenings, but often went home to spend time with her mum, and Jock's wife Evelyn. Meanwhile us three men talked more loudly about life as the beer loosened our tongues.

I would regularly have my Sunday lunch at Jim and Jean's house in Leafield, and sometimes Jock and Evelyn would also be there. This was another excuse for us three men to go to the pub before lunch, and we would often come back late, and a little worse for wear from the beer.

It was pretty obvious that I was accepted by Deb's parents, and now even by their friends.

During the late Spring Deb and I spent a week in Rouen in France with my brother Ronald and his wife Jane. This was my first trip away from England and opened my eyes to foreign travel. We went to Paris and saw the amazing city with its architecture. On a less happy note, I was one day asked to go and buy some bread, and discovered that my school French was pathetic, and eventually had to point to the desired loaf, and hold out a hand covered in local currency.

I was constantly reminded of my reluctance to settle down in school, and just how much I had missed.

There was another trip to Cornwall as well. This time it was warm and sunny, and I showed Deb some of the area. By now, my mum had finally given up on Thor. She was not able to control the big dog in a way he deserved. So Thor was given to someone to have a new life as a guard dog. I struggled to comprehend how such a soppy dog would ever scare anybody.

That visit to Cornwall was probably the moment when Deb and I began to speak openly about our future. I had spoken to Ronald, and now my mum was told that we intended to get married quite soon.

This was still a time of traditional customs, and I was expected to ask Deb's dad for permission to marry his daughter. Deb had already raised the idea with her mum, who turned around and expressed her happiness by saying she would go out immediately and buy a new hat for the wedding.

I still had one major concern that needed to be settled. My salary was not enough to buy a house in Oxfordshire, and even with a formal promotion from my temporary position, I would still be short. Deb and I talked about our options. One of these was to see if I could return to Goonhilly. Housing in Cornwall was much less expensive, and we could branch out into a new home.

So, I telephoned John Apperley at Goonhilly to see if there was a post for me to return to. A few days later the response was that I could return and a role would be found for me.

With that settled, I could go and ask Jim for his blessing for us getting married, in the knowledge that I had a plan for our future.

A date for the wedding was discussed, and after checking with the local vicar, we agreed that on 5th July 1975, Deb and I would get married at the church in Leafield. There was one slightly sticky moment when the vicar (P.G. Smith) told us off for not seemingly to be taking his little talk about marriage seriously. But we quickly sorted this out by apologising, and keeping straight faces for the rest of his chat.

Organising everything proved to be quite a challenge in the time available, but the arrangements for our wedding were coming together.

Deb's contacts at Witney Tech meant the reception could be held there, and a friend in the village volunteered to organise the buffet food, and make us a cake.

One of Deb's uncles (Vic) said that he would take the official photographs as a wedding present.

I was still going to college in Oxford at that time, and came home each week with bottles of spirit and several bottles of 'Pomagne' for our DIY reception. This was the champagne style cider drink I discovered on the visit to Bulmer's Cider in Hereford while an apprentice. We decided to use this as an alternative to proper champagne for the reception.

Now the final bit. I had to officially tell the people at Leafield Training School that I was leaving. The announcement was softened by handing out invitations to our wedding, but the fact that I would be leaving was quite a shock.

My team of new friends tried to convince me to stay, but they accepted the cost of remaining in Oxfordshire was too great. The manager (Ron Coles) also did his best to change my mind, and was quite angry when he realised that continuing to work at Leafield was not an option.

So, after just a year since meeting, Deb and I were hurtling towards marriage. I had spent just twelve months as an instructor, and enjoyed every minute of my time, but it was now time to move on. Some said it would never last, but over 45 years later we appear to have proved them wrong.

5th July 1975

I woke on Saturday the 5th July 1975, and knew that I was about to begin a new chapter in my life. Getting married is one of those moments in life that sits at the top of any list of momentous occasions.

On the previous afternoon, I had said the final farewell to people at Leafield Training School, and packed all my clothing and belongings from the little room where I had lived for 12 months. Some of my possessions had already been taken home to Cornwall, and now the final bits and pieces were stored at Jim and Jean's house in the village. I just retained the *'stuff'* I would need for the wedding day and honeymoon, and they were put away in the car.

My time at the training school was over, and I had a room booked in a hotel in nearby Charlbury, for the night before the wedding. That evening I was joined by Chris Warner and Sue, John Hall and his girlfriend Fran, plus Stuart Tregembo from Goonhilly. My 'Stag Do' wasn't over the top, but we did enjoy ourselves.

In a hotel in Witney, I had booked rooms for my mum, brothers John and Ernest with Joyce, plus Auntie Bessie, and Auntie Doreen and her husband. My other brother Ronald with Jane, were coming from much further away, and couldn't get there until the day of the wedding.

So, when I woke on the Saturday morning (with a hangover) I had a busy morning of collecting the flowers and checking that all was well with Deb's mum and dad, and the family in Witney. I also parked my car in a Witney car park, in readiness for us to leave as man and wife towards our honeymoon.

The morning flew by, and soon there was just time for a quick drink with my mates at the Charlbury hotel, before they took me to the church of St Michael and All Angels in Leafield.

Chris was my best man, and Stuart, plus Deb's brother David were the ushers. Chris and I stood outside enjoying a few cigarettes and greeting the guests as they arrived. It was a hot and sunny day, and the grass was burnt from lack of rain. Little did we know that this drought would last another 12 months.

Soon my family arrived, and were inside the church, along with Peter Evans and Barry Strange from the training school. Deb's family and friends were also sitting in the cool of the church, and after a last cigarette, Chris took me inside to stand in front of the Reverend P G Smith.

Like so many grooms, my mind was racing with anticipation and wonder, and I was so relieved when the organ began to announce the arrival of Deb on her father's arm, and Janet, from that very first night in the pub, was her bridesmaid. I could forget everything else for a few minutes now, and concentrate on the magical moment.

The 30-minute service was over, and although I fluffed my lines, with an agreement to *"Plythy my Trough"* I was a married man with a beautiful wife.

We walked arm in arm outside to where Ronald and Jane were the first people we saw. They were late, but had got there.

Then began the torture of photographs. It might have been a bit of a nightmare organising and squeezing everyone in, but as I looked back at those photographs while I was writing this chapter, they reminded me of who was there, and sadly, reflected on how many are no longer with us.

The Reception

With all the photographs completed, Deb and I got into the limousine for the drive into Witney, and the reception.

We had a lovely room that was a perfect size to sit everyone in comfort. Two of the guys from the training school, Eddy Page and Fred Owen, were looking after the bar, and it seemed most were fooled by the Pomagne and thought it was champagne.

The meal was a success, and soon it was time for the speeches. I had spent many hours working out what to say, but in just two or three minutes it was over, and greeted with applause from our friends and family. The cake was beautiful, and it was cut and distributed to the guests.

We had decided not to have any entertainment apart for background music. After the cake cutting, we chatted with everyone we could, before it was time to leave for the honeymoon.

I had booked a week at a Pontins holiday park near Weymouth called Osmington Bay. It would be a long drive, so it might have appeared we were rushing away far too quickly. Deb and I changed clothes for something more comfortable, and I slipped away from the reception to fetch the car. Then, while saying more goodbyes, a couple of people sneaked outside and made sure the car looked appropriate for newlyweds.

With waves, confetti, and laughter, we drove away to the sounds of rattling tins from the rear bumper. When suitably far enough away, we stopped and removed the noisy objects, and settled down to a drive to the South Coast.

It had been a lovely day. So many people had travelled hundreds of miles to share the moment with us. Although the church service, and the reception had been a blur of excitement, it had all worked out perfectly. Now we had a chance for the buzz to calm down, and turn our thoughts to the honeymoon. Deb had been to holiday parks as a child, but this was going to be my first experience of this type of holiday, and I desperately hoped it would be OK.

Our Honeymoon

We arrived late at the Holiday Park and missed our dinner. Luckily, the reception staff did their best for us, and we were given a sandwich to eat. We demolished the snack in our chalet while we unpacked. That's when we discovered that a little minx had liberally sprinkled confetti into our cases. Those little bits of paper continued to appear for many months, and reminded us of a wonderful day.

Still hungry, but very happy, we went to the restaurant, that doubled as the lounge, and enjoyed a drink while listening to the resident band.

They were very entertaining with dance music and some of the latest chart music. One song they played many times during that week, was *'January'* by a group called Pilot. The song pops up on the radio from time to time, and is another memory jerker of that very special moment in our lives.

I remember little of the week, except that the weather was glorious. We lazed by the swimming pool most days, occasionally went out for a drive to explore the area, and joined in with the camp entertainment whenever we could. I remember being in a knobbly knees competition, and Deb took part in the Miss Pontin contest. Like excited children, we were always ready to join in.

Our dinner table was at the front of the restaurant next to the stage, and we had two other couples with us, and later in the week we discovered one of them was also on honeymoon. News of our status quickly went around the campers, and the entertainers often pulled us out to act the fool. One night the visiting cabaret was a supposed Russian Cossack troop, and of course we ended up on the stage doing our best at the dancing.

Strangely, they had very strong Midland's accents for Cossacks.

The week flew by, and soon we were on the way back to Oxfordshire. After a night there with Jim and Jean, we set off on the road again towards Cornwall. We initially lived with my mum, and there were still a few days left before I had to start work at Goonhilly. We had already spent time planning where to live and what sort of houses we could afford, and during those first few days in Cornwall we looked at plans for a single bedroom bungalow that was within our budget.

By the time I went back to work, we had already bought the bungalow off plan, and sorted out a mortgage. Our new home on an estate called Carey Park would soon be ready.

Back to Goonhilly

Back at Goonhilly, I found myself at my original grade as a lowly T2A again. This meant a considerably lower wage than I was getting at Leafield, and I had an extra responsibility now to look after Deb, and a mortgage for our house.

After a few days simply getting used to the place, I was given a new role.

I was now working on the Modem equipment in the West Wing, and I was not very familiar with what went on in the room. I didn't know it at the time, but I would only be there for a handful of months, and most of that period was spent trying to understand how the equipment worked.

My previous experience, plus some new knowledge from my time in Leafield, meant I knew what each shelf of equipment did, but now I had to go to a new level. It was the moment to get far more involved in the function, and operation, of each card in the shelves, and more importantly, how to diagnose and repair faults.

Luckily, I was helped through a quite difficult time by some very friendly people. Peter Girling, and David Wain were very patient with me, and I slowly grasped enough information and skills to become actively useful again. The manager at that time was Barry Picken, and he was one of the stricter of the managers at Goonhilly, and I don't think I impressed him very much.

Initially a lot of my time involved reading the manufacturer handbooks describing the technical operating principles of the equipment. Thinking back to the Marconi Factory Course I attended, I was now just as unimpressed by their documentation, as I was by the training.

Some things were easy, as I had been trained to take basic measurements of equipment performance during my time in the OCA. That was fine to identify there was a fault, but now I had to be able to decide which equipment card might be causing that fault, and then change it. Of course, there was always spare equipment to avoid losing any service, but in a maintenance situation I would be using the spare equipment, so if any further operational failures occurred, then service would fail.

I felt out of my depth, and wasn't happy for the first time during the many years of working at Goonhilly.

Meanwhile I spent hours talking to people about my experience at Leafield, and introducing Deb to everyone when there was a social evening. At least people were happy that I was back, although many struggled to understand why I had taken the year away, and then why I had come back.

I had to sort out a more suitable job, and went to speak with my training officer again. He explained that there currently weren't any permanent roles available, but I would be offered something whenever they came up.

At the end of September, I was asked if I would like to have a job in a slightly different area. This was still based in the West Wing, but dealt with testing of new carriers, to ensure they met the required standards before they began operations on a satellite. This was referred to as SSOG testing.

Yes, more abbreviations.

SSOG stood for *'Satellite Systems Operational Guide'*, and there were various huge folders of documentation that detailed the rules and standards for any earth station operating on the Intelsat system.

I wasn't too sure about this, but as it offered the chance of temporary promotion to Technical Officer (TO) I accepted the opportunity. One thing I learnt very early on in my career was to never reject something without very good reasons. You were rarely offered chances a second time.

Anyway, the next three months meant working with distant earth stations as they began service with Goonhilly, or perhaps as an existing earth station increased their carrier sizes. I had already become accustomed to speaking with engineers from all over the world, but some proved easier to work with than others. The job would involve setting up test equipment and taking various measurements of the carrier performance, and only when the tests were satisfactory could the service be used. This occasionally involved changing our equipment because of faults, and my experience with the time in the Modem section was helping. As well as the enhanced pay of being a temporary TO, there was overtime as well when the only time available for the test was an evening, or even a night.

This role was still not what I wanted to do, and as the weeks passed, I was really wondering if life at Goonhilly would ever be like it was before.

Outside of work, things weren't going smoothly either. Our new house was taking longer than expected to be completed. Deb and I were living with my mum, and although very grateful, it was not what we had planned. Eventually the situation became even worse, when the building company became bankrupt. At least it wasn't a disaster, as the liquidators made the most of customers like ourselves, by ensuring the building work was completed.

Finally, we were given a completion date, and our excitement increased.

The magic day arrived, and we finally had the key to our new home. Its address was Plot 37, Phase 2, Carey Park in Helston, and was little more than half a mile from my mum's house. Our little bungalow was surrounded by a building site when we moved in, and there were only three or four of these little bungalows completed and occupied.

We had a bedroom, living room, kitchen and bathroom. We didn't have a garage, and couldn't even park outside the bungalow as the roads hadn't been completed. The garden was a tip, and there were several building jobs that still remained, but it was our home.

Now I just had to find a more suitable job.

Intelsat IVA

By the time I returned to Goonhilly in the third week of July 1975, I discovered that the world of Intelsat Satellites was moving into a new chapter. The latest piece of hardware being sent up into Space was an improved version of the previous satellite, and it was called the Intelsat IVA.

When I was involved with a Satellite Course at Leafield, I took the group to visit a factory near Bristol where one of the Intelsat IVA satellites was being built. One of the agreements with the member States in Intelsat, was that they could bid to help in the construction of new spacecraft. So, one factory might have made the electronics, while another fitted the solar cells, or somewhere else created the antenna stacks.

This satellite was huge, and people wearing white coats were working on scaffolding built around the huge shiny drum, that might one day have been a satellite that we worked with at Goonhilly.

I was even further inspired by my involvement in the amazing industry.

Sorry - Technical Moment
Satellite Communications was now ready for a major increase in capacity. Firstly, this family of new satellites had 20 transponders rather than 12. This didn't require any increase in frequency bandwidth, as some of the same frequencies were being used twice. This was described as *'Frequency Reuse'*, and made possible by routing the same frequency through different aerials on the satellite to keep them separate. This avoided interference between the signals.

The aerials were cleverly designed parabolic dishes (like at the earth stations) but seriously smaller. They were also shaped such that they only transmitted and received signals to and from a small geographical area of the earth.

The majority of the satellite aerials looked down on a complete Ocean Region, and referred to as giving Global coverage. Global coverage of the Indian Ocean Region for example, means everyone within Indian Ocean Region, could work with the signals operating through these aerials, and any satellite equipment connected to them. The resulting radio energy from the satellite was equally spread over the complete ocean region, creating what was known as a *'Global Footprint'*.

Technology meant these new parabolic dish aerials could be further shaped, to work with even smaller areas of a region. Dishes could be created that accurately restricted radio coverage to just the west or east of a region. The same power could now be focussed on a smaller geographical area, and hence the signals were stronger. These transmissions were referred to as Hemispheric Beams, with a Hemispheric Footprint.

Of course, if an earth station transmitted towards the satellite, the signals would be received by both the global, and spot beam aerials. That would create interference between the carriers.

To overcome this, a new method of transmission was required, and this involved a technique called Dual-Polarisation.

From the very early experimental stage, the radio signals weren't just radiated into space, they were actually spinning, using a technique called Polarisation. As the radio signals are about to be transmitted, they are actually made to rotate either clockwise or anti-clockwise.

So, if we took a typical transmission, the signal would travel through space towards the satellite with a clockwise rotation. This is described as being 'Right Hand Circular Polarisation' or **RHCP**. At the satellite, that transmission is now seen by the receiver as if it is anti-clockwise rotation.

Once received, the satellite removes the polarisation and performs the electronic stages of amplification and frequency conversion. It uses a lower frequency to re-transmit towards earth. As it begins the journey back to earth, the **RHCP** spin is reapplied. Back on earth that signal appears to have anticlockwise rotation.

Turning now to the Intelsat IVA satellite, it was designed to have the capability to transmit and receive two sorts of polarisation, and this was similarly introduced at the earth stations.

So, for a Global Coverage transmission, the earth stations would transmit to the satellite with clock-wise polarisation (**RHCP**), and the satellite would return those transmissions back to the Global Footprint.

However, if transmissions were destined to and from the Hemisphere Coverage locations, the polarisation would be anti-clockwise (**LHCP**) from earth, and the satellite would receive that on the Hemispheric Beam aerial. The re-transmitted amplified signal would then be routed to the appropriate Hemispheric Footprint aerial. The earth stations now receive these transmissions with the opposite polarisation, and routed through the correct equipment.

Hence Goonhilly might transmit a radio carrier with clockwise polarisation (**RHCP**) which could be received by anyone within the Global Footprint. But they could also transmit a second carrier at that **same** frequency, with anti-clockwise polarisation (**LHCP**), and this time it would only be received by stations in the appropriate Hemispheric Footprint.

This geographical footprint technology, and dual-polarisation, meant an almost doubling of the number of carriers that a satellite could handle, and this was vital to satisfy the worldwide demand for ever increasing satellite communications.

The IOR TOCC

Fortunately, my search for a new role at Goonhilly didn't take too long.

One of the managers I had come into contact with, was expanding the role of his group, and needed more staff. His name was John Sherbird, and he managed the 'Indian Ocean Region Technical Operations Control Centre' or the IOR TOCC.

With satellites in their geo-stationary orbits over the three main oceans, an earth station could see, and work with, two separate regions. In Britain we could work with the Atlantic Ocean Region, and the Indian Ocean Region. America could work with the Atlantic and Pacific Regions. The main control centre, called the International Operations Centre (IOC) was in America, and they directly monitored and controlled use of the satellites over the Atlantic and Pacific Oceans. But they couldn't see, and hence couldn't monitor, satellites over the Indian Ocean.

With the British Post Office being a major player in Satellite Communications, an agreement was made for the monitoring role covering the Indian Ocean Region to be performed at Goonhilly.

John Sherbird began this role with Mike Young as his assistant, but the job was proving to be quite complicated, and hence the expansion.

During my time in the OCA, I had answered calls for the TOCC and put them through to John. He sometimes came into the West Wing to ask for help, and as the junior person, it was often me that helped him.

It appears I made a suitable impression, and at the end of November 1975 I had a very informal interview with John, before beginning my role in the TOCC on 1st December. To start with, it was just a three-month period (as a Temporary TO) to see if I fitted in.

This would be the beginning of a fantastic five years.

The role was another 24-hour shift job, and there were five of us who covered the rota. Alongside of myself there was Mike Young, Don Evans, Tony Twyford and Cliff whose surname I have forgotten. John Sherbird came in for the days, and often spent many hours at his desk. We had secretarial support with Rose, then Jane, and later Jenny. We were a close little group, and although we were a part of Goonhilly, we were indirectly paid for by Intelsat, and had to answer to them, as well as local management.

John often referred our job as being like policemen of the Indian Ocean Region. We could see the satellite spectrum and after some practice I could pick out the individual radio carriers from the different earth stations. We could see when they were missing, or doing something wrong, and we spent hours on the telephone to the different stations asking them to correct their frequency, or change the power they were using.

To assist us with more accurate measurements of what was happening on the satellite, we worked with the Italian Earth Station, Fucino, who had an aerial specifically used to monitor the IOR satellites.

Satellite Communications was expanding around the world, and new Earth Stations were regularly being built, and brought in to service. When a new station was preparing for service via the Indian Ocean satellite, we would organise, and monitor a major test procedure to ensure they could do what they had to do, and wouldn't interfere with other users on the satellite. Fortunately, the international language was English, but it was still difficult sometimes to understand their attempts at English, and actually make the engineers understand what they had to do.

Around the region, there were stations that were very highly able, and fun to work with, such as Ceduna in Australia. There were some very professional ones such as Hong Kong,

Yamaguchi in Japan, Sentosa in Singapore, or Ras Abu Jarjur in Bahrain. But there were also some very difficult ones, including Lanlate in Nigeria, and Deh Mandro in Pakistan.

My role was no longer hands on with the equipment, but more about liaising with engineers and management with so many Indian Ocean countries.

Sometimes the role was extremely stressful, and although nights were generally quiet, there were times when I was exhausted at the end of a shift.

But I was enjoying the work, it was stretching my ability, but it was fun.

… and I was smiling again.

Time at Home

During 1976, Deb and I turned the shell of our house in Carey Park into a home. Even with working shifts, I still had time to help Deb to bring some colour to the walls, and putting up shelves. It was a pleasure to transform the universal wall to wall magnolia colour, into different rooms with yellows, and blues, and pinks.

Much of our furniture started as second hand items or sale items in the shops. Initially, the only expensive outlay was a new bed, but soon we were planning what else we needed to buy to enhance our home.

We didn't have a lot of money each month after paying the mortgage and utility bills, but we were managing to save a little, and every few weeks we would go and buy something new. Second hand tables became new ones with comfortable chairs, and a large settee made the living room a place to relax with a glass or two of home-made beer while watching the television. Our first colour television was rented, but the day eventually came when we finally bought one.

Within a few weeks of moving into the house, we saw an advert in the local paper, and set off one evening to fetch our first pet. It was a ginger Tom cat, and we named it Sandy. Our pet had a wonderful area to explore outside. The building site remained as it was when we moved in, so Sandy had overgrown patches between piles of sand and gravel. He would bring us presents of mice occasionally, but always left them on the doorstep rather than bringing them in. In the evenings he sat on our laps and purred contentedly while we snuggled together.

He would disappear for hours to nearby farms, and one day his exploration obviously took him further, and he didn't come back in the evening. Sandy stayed away for several days, and we assumed he was gone from us for ever. Then one evening there was a scratching sound on the front door, and there he was with a present of a young rabbit, to say sorry for abandoning us.

Sandy was much-loved, and he shared our lives for over 15 years.

Deb was proving to be a very good cook, and I have enjoyed her meals and cakes for 45 years. But a moment came when our budget changed, and our quite generous food allowance had to be squeezed.

Strangely, it was because I was given official promotion to Technical Officer. This was a salaried grade, and I would be paid every month, rather than every week. Up until then, there was enough money in my pay packet each week to allow so much for the mortgage, and utilities, with enough for food and occasional evenings out, as well as saving a tiny amount. Now suddenly we had to wait until the end of the month for money to arrive in my bank account, and that meant digging into those small savings, and putting off any extra purchases. Fortunately, they paid me every two weeks to begin with, and that eased the change, but soon it was monthly, and we had to make alterations to our lifestyle for several months.

Food wise, this meant we suddenly became very familiar with chicken. We would buy a large one each week as a roast for Sunday. Then the left-overs would be used for a pie, or a casserole, and sometimes the final bits made soup. Even with this level of being careful with our money, the savings, built up from years of little fixed expenses, dwindled to near zero.

It took many months, but eventually we became comfortable with a monthly income. Deb could begin to express her culinary skills again, and chicken ceased to be a regular feature of our diet.

Around us, the regular socialising with my gang of friends was also changing. Without really noticing it, we were all settling down. Chris married Sue, and they moved to a house just 50 metres away from us. Perry had married Linda, Katie married Monty, and Keith married Heather. We would occasionally meet up at the Wheel Inn in Cury for Friday or Saturday nights, and maybe at the Bochym Manor on a Sunday. The Wheel Inn was always our favourite pub, and we would play Euchre, or spoof as we chatted. At Christmas we would sing carols and Cornish songs, and Violet the landlady would reward us with pasties.

That childhood friendship continued, but the close bond we had while growing up together was evolving. It was more about being married couples, and our social lives were changing.

More Memories of the 1970s

British Sporting Moments

In terms of memorable sporting moments that involved Goonhilly, I first experienced extra work caused by the Olympics with the 1976 games in Montreal. This was the first Olympics to happen while I was working. I wasn't around for the 1968 games in Mexico, and the 1972 Munich games was covered by the German Earth Station at Raisting.

There was a very special moment in 1977 when Virginia Wade beat Betty Stove to win the Wimbledon singles. Any British success in tennis was, and still is, very rare, and this was one I can remember capturing my attention.

In 1978 Goonhilly was really busy for the Commonwealth Games in Canada. We received the television material from the Canadian Earth Station (Mill Village), and then re-transmitted it to the Indian Ocean countries. My role in the TOCC included monitoring all the television activity on our satellite, and it was a manic couple of weeks.

The Goonhilly Sports and Social Club

As well as work, I was becoming involved with the social club at Goonhilly. Many of the activities of the club revolved around the bar. It was only small, but stocked a good selection of beer. The drink prices were very low, and the income was enhanced by video games, of the Space Invaders, and Pacman era. After a lot of discussions, the bar also had a slot machine with quite a good jackpot, and that soon provided the biggest income after alcohol. The bar was voluntarily managed by Ralph Wallington, and a gang of people helped out. Every shift had at least one bar keyholder, to allow us to get chocolate or crisps to keep us going ... plus a drink sometimes as well.

There were Friday night social events with music most months, and they were well attended. It was often just records being played, but sometimes there was a local group to get people dancing. A popular evening was Firework Night, and of course there was always a Christmas Party featuring Santa Claus.

I quickly became a member of the Social Club Committee with monthly meetings, but before long I was giving quite a lot of my time organising events, and even volunteering to work behind the bar. Like many of the Goonhilly wives, Deb was drawn into the social club activities, and often joined me behind the bar to keep the glasses full.

Football
The sporting side of the club was also a real treat, and I found myself playing football again.

This was a shock for my body after several years of inactivity. The fact that I still smoked didn't help either, but the chance to be involved was wonderful. The games were on Sunday mornings, and we had successes and disasters. I played as a defender, where I could run around enough to be a nuisance to the attackers, and my main role was to boot the ball back up the field at every opportunity, and wasn't expected to offer any finesse.

There was one match I remember where we were up against a very poor team, and the score was well into double figures to us. We swapped the goalkeeper for a forward at one point to give him a chance to score. Sadly, I was the only member of the team not to score, and having missed several easy opportunities to put the ball in the net, I was shouted at by one of the team for being totally useless.

In another game, we had a wonderful man called Dave (Jock) Beattie in goal. He was actually a rugby player, but was serving a ban from the game because of being a bit over-aggressive. Well, he played quite successfully in goal and enjoyed himself with a round ball. I was getting a bit of a rough time from one of the opposition, and having found myself flat on the floor again, I heard the roaring sounds of Jock hammering across the pitch towards me shouting: *"**Leave the wee laddie alone!!**"* He was a lovely man, and a true gentle giant.

I did leave a bit of a weird legacy to the Goonhilly Football Team. As a Social Club Committee member, I was asked by the team if we might get help with a new set of shirts to play in. Our request was accepted by the committee, and one afternoon I drove to Falmouth and a reasonably large Sports shop.

The money allocated was generous, but a full set of shorts and socks for the team proved expensive. Almost ready to give up, I spotted a sign offering a full set at a bargain price. I couldn't resist it, and the following weekend, the team was greeted by the new strip.

The reason for it being cheap was quickly realised. The shirts had a large chequered pattern that was in the colours of the German Flag.

My team-mates were slightly shocked, and over the years we had a lot of comments about our whacky shirt colours. Luckily after initial moans about the colour scheme, our players saw the funny side.

I eventually gave up playing football after a particularly painful game. It was sometime in the mid-1980s, and the opposition were much better than us. I was singled out by one of them who saw me as an easy touch to get the ball - which I was – but he rubbed in his superiority a bit too much. My last contribution of the game was pretending to reach a high ball before he did, but as I have never really attempted to head a ball, it was an easy one for my tormentor. Sadly, instead of just beating me, he jumped up alongside my pathetic attempt to get near the ball, and planted a pointed elbow into my ribs.

I decided the time was right to give up this young man's game. After I got changed (painfully) I put my muddy Adidas boots in their little leather bag, and they never came out to play competitively again. It was many years later when I did unzip the boot bag, and those quite expensive boots were stiff, and still covered in mud.

There were never any thoughts of being good at football, in fact in any sport, but I just enjoyed the competitive experience, and tried my best.

I turned my attention to cricket, which didn't involve heading the ball, or physically competing with other players.

Table Tennis
I also began to play table tennis, and thoroughly enjoyed this quite new experience. As well as competition between other people at Goonhilly, we also had a league team, and visited many small clubs around West Cornwall. As with most of my attempts at sport, I wasn't very good, but I played my part for the team and won a few games.

At one point we had a rather successful team, and were promoted to a higher league. This proved to be a step too far for me, and I had the rather embarrassing record of being beaten by every person I played.

Table tennis was where we found new friends as well. Trevor Newborn was our star player. He was left-handed that fooled opponents, but he was also a superb spinner of the ball. We made a good doubles pair, as he knew that my serves would regularly give him a chance to smash winners. Anyway, on away matches we would share transport, and his wife Sue would also come along and keep Deb company while Trevor and I 'ping ponged' the evening away.

As well as evenings in chilly village halls, the four of us met up at our houses to share bottles of wine, or home-made beer. Sue was a hairdresser, and looked after our hair for a long time.

Holidays
Holidays had been forgotten while we were coming to terms with our budget. Our breaks were restricted to driving to Oxfordshire and visiting Jim and Jean. It was good to see the

area, and be spoilt rotten by Jean. There were evenings at the pub with their friends (Jock and Evelyn), and days out looking at places such as Blenheim Palace, the Cotswold Wildlife Park, or shopping trips to Swindon and Oxford.

Then in 1977, Jim and Jean invited us to join them on a cottage holiday. It was based in North Cornwall, and was a wonderful treat. The drive from Helston, was almost the same distance as for Jim and Jean, but we had a less than easy journey. It coincided with the Queen making her Jubilee visit to Cornwall, and almost every road we tried to use, was blocked for security reasons.

After many hours we all met up, and soon we were relaxing again with a bit of alcohol as we chatted. We took trips around the area as a group, but some days Deb and I set off on our own to explore an area I was very unfamiliar with. It was the first time I had ever visited the village of Clovelly and discovered something I never knew about. The car park for this quaint fishing village was at the bottom of a nearby hill. The road was quite steep, and I decided to turn off the engine and free-wheel. Then the road became rather twisty, and I realised my power steering was no longer powered. After a moment of struggling to maintain control, I also discovered the brakes depended on the engine power.

I stood on the brakes to bring ourselves to a very clumsy stop. Then after screams of distress and anger from Deb, I started the engine, and normality was resumed. This was a lesson that I have remembered, and have never repeated my mistake.

Madley

Goonhilly had hardly been operational for more than a handful of years, but in the early 1970s, plans were being discussed about increasing Britain's Satellite commitments. That would need a new site to avoid having all the eggs in one basket.

BT (or whatever they were called then) spent years looking for a suitable location for a second Earth Station. It had to be closer to London, have good and reliable transport links, and have sufficient space to allow expansion. Another major consideration was to find a spot with very little interference from any other radio sources.

After searching all over the country, it was decided that a suitable location might be near to the city of Hereford. Now it was time to find an actual site.

In late 1973 the result was the purchase of 140 acres of land, known as Street Hill Farm in the village of Madley, just six miles from Hereford. The plot, which was an RAF Airfield, is in a valley with good line of sight to the southern quadrant where equatorial satellites are visible. Its location was also a little further to the east than Goonhilly, making it more suitable to operate to the Indian Ocean satellites. Goonhilly's aerials had to be so low in elevation for these satellites that there was a greater chance of noise from the earth itself.

By the end of 1978, Madley Aerial 1 was completed. It was a Mitsubishi design of antenna built by the Marconi Company, who also supplied all the radio equipment. It would be the largest satellite antenna in Britain with a diameter of 32 metres (105 feet).

Two further identical aerials were built in 1980 and 1981. The geography of Madley allowed for the aerials to be built in a line. It means a single road can take engineers from the main building complex to each aerial in turn.

As far as I know, the aerials at Madley were never given silly 'pet' names.

Now over 40 years old, Madley boasts that it has more than 60 aerials, but just like Goonhilly the majority of them are small. It also has a major International Switch to process and route the traffic, rather than having to bring everything in and out from London.

My career has taken me on numerous visits to Madley, and in my small way, I helped to train some of the engineers working there. Several people from Goonhilly moved to Madley to further their careers, but most of them are now enjoying retirement like myself. After my eventual retirement in 2011, Deb and I actually moved to the nearby village of Kingstone. We often drove by the gates of the site, and the dishes were a constant memory of my time with Satellite Communications.

There is one historical fact about the Madley site. In 1945, a plane took off from there, carrying Rudolf Hess for his date with the Nuremburg Trials.

Goonhilly Aerial 4

The end of the 1970s saw the fourth aerial being built at Goonhilly.

It was much smaller than the first three, and was designed to operate to the latest satellites in a new frequency band. Aerial 4 would be specifically involved with transmitting and receiving Ku Band satellite frequencies.

The Ku band was at higher frequencies with transmissions to the satellite at around 14 GHz, and received from the satellite at about 11 GHz.

The new satellites operating at these frequencies didn't need such large aerial reflectors, so instead of the approximate 30 metre diameter dishes used so far, this new aerial was just 19 metres across.

Aerial 4 was built by the Marconi company, and was due for completion in 1978.

A circular base building housed all of the radio equipment. The reflector was mounted on a three-cornered steel backing structure. One corner was attached to a bearing supported on the base building roof. On the other two corners there were bogey drive systems with wheels that ran on a circular rail track around the edge of the base building roof. This produced the azimuth movement.

Any required changes in elevation angle were created by a traditional screw drive.

The reflector had a sub-reflector which was mounted on a four-legged support system. Radio energy was focussed back into the dish, but this time there was no obvious feed. Aerial 4 used a new method of feeding the energy, known as Beam waveguide. The energy to and from the radio equipment was reflected by a series of mirrors through a large aperture in the centre of the dish.

To make way for the necessary monitoring and control system, there had to be an extension created in the OCA. This meant the telegraph room was shifted, and the space used to have another three bays identical to those used for Aerials 1 to 3.

Goonhilly was becoming a major communications hub, and at that time was the largest in the world.

Aerial 4 was destined to come into service with the new Intelsat V generation of satellites, that were due to begin life in the early 1980s.

Time to Move House

Although we were quite short of money, the future looked to be more positive. Our little bungalow in Helston was really rather small, and a decision was made to move home.

I have forgotten exactly when we moved, but Deb and I believe it was in 1978. Our little bungalow sold quite quickly, and we were soon taking the keys for another newly built three bedroom semi-detached in West View Porthleven. It cost just over £10,000 and this time there was no problem with the builder going bankrupt.

Downstairs there was a kitchen/dining room, and a lounge. Heating came from night storage radiators, and an electric fire in the living room. Upstairs there was a bathroom, two good sized bedrooms, plus the usual box room above the stairs that was big enough for a single bed.

Outside, there was a miniscule front garden, plus a drive led down to a parking spot on a concreted base, with planning permission to build a garage. Going around to the back there was steps down to a good-sized sloping garden with a hawthorn hedge at the bottom.

Instead of the patch of grass and small vegetable patch in Helston, I had space to plan and create a garden to be proud of.

Our neighbours in the other half of the semi-detached plot were a mother and her daughter. The mother (Francis) was a retired district nurse, and her daughter (Hillary) was active in the same job. They were wonderful, and we often chatted to them over the fence outside of our kitchen door. On the other side, a young naval couple moved in. They were quite pleasant, but we didn't have much to do with them.

First Aid

The 1970s saw me continue the family tradition of being involved in the St John Ambulance Brigade. My father and mother gave many years to this voluntary organisation, and I think it was obvious that I would eventually give some time to it as well.

Initially it was just attending a first aid course. There was a good group of people involved, and I quickly committed myself to joining the Brigade. When my rota allowed, I would show up at the Ambulance Station in Wendron Street in Helston for the weekly meetings. I was one of the youngest but was made very welcome by men and women who had known my father, and my mother.

Soon I had my uniform, and was becoming active at events around the Lizard Peninsular giving first aid cover at all kinds of community events.

My interest in first aid was spilling over into work. After taking a First Aid at Work course I became one of the Goonhilly First Aiders, and this evolved into a more serious hobby. I was one of a team that was entered into the Post Office Regional First Aid Quiz. There were three of us, and we practiced regularly before going to the competition in Bristol.

We won!

This was the beginning of a period where Goonhilly had a very active first aid group of people, who looked after anyone who was feeling under the weather, or had had an accident.

Cars

During the late seventies there was a terrible period in our lives when we were regularly changing cars. Each change unfortunately resulted in a worse car than what we had before. It all began as my beautiful mini was rusting to an early death, and I eventually swapped to another mini that was hardly any better. Then it was a Simca 1301 that was registered in Ireland, so had strange number plates. It was a comfortable and reliable car, but when I needed a new MOT, the garage said it would have to be re-registered with British plates. I thought that was too complicated, so moved on to an Austin 1300.

Oh what a disaster!

It broke down on the way back from a First Aid competition in Bristol, and cost us a fortune (which we didn't have) to get it repaired in Weston Supa Mare.

It was the most unreliable car I have ever driven, and after spending too many weekends underneath it trying to fix various problems, I moved on again to a Hillman Imp. That continued along the same lines of bad cars, and the next car was a purple Ford Escort that was mechanically great, but so rusty that the boot had been welded shut by the previous owner.

These cars progressively became cheaper and cheaper rusty horrors, and something had to be done, because our lives were about to change dramatically.

In the summer of 1979, after regular, and very enjoyable attempts, Deb announced that she was pregnant.

The 1980s was going to be so very different.

More of my TOCC Role

Back at Goonhilly, and my job was going well. I really enjoyed being trusted to have so much responsibility. There were times when quite serious things were happening, and I was empowered to decide what to do.

The TOCC group changed people in the late 70s and early 80s. Several of the original five rota men had left for other roles. One left Goonhilly to work at our new Earth Station at Madley in Herefordshire, and another went to work in Washington at the IOC. Our rota group now consisted of myself, Anthony Soady, Tony Bernstein, Mark Jago, and another whose name I have forgotten.

One of the most difficult problems we encountered, was someone transmitting a carrier to the satellite when it shouldn't have been there. This was often because a station had accidently turned on their Television Carrier, but sometimes it was when a station had a problem with their carrier frequency generating equipment.

Finding a rogue television carrier, was usually quite simple. We just contacted each earth station in turn, and asked them to check if they were the culprit. We always started by working our way through a list of the most likely stations, who were frequent offenders. When one of our suspect stations had been contacted, we always waited a while before turning to somewhere else. We regularly had an initial response assuring us that there wasn't a problem at their station, but 30 seconds after our call, the rogue carrier would disappear.

When the carrier was within the telephony frequencies, it would severely interfere with hundreds of phone calls, and finding the problem could take hours, and even days sometimes. The first action was usually to send a telegraph message to all the earth stations asking them to check the frequencies of their carriers.

Our next step would be checking if any new earth stations, or carriers were planned to begin service, to ensure one of them had not radiated the carrier early.

The solution was sometimes obvious, because several receive stations would complain that they had lost contact with a particular earth station. We would try to talk to that station and ask them to check their equipment, but that could be very difficult as we might be trying to use that same carrier to contact them. In these situations, we would try International Phone Lines rather than their direct satellite engineering lines. If we were still in trouble, we would try calling earth stations that might have alternative communications with the rogue.

If we were still struggling, we had to get clever. After many incidents, we had learnt that a rogue carrier is often caused by a piece of equipment (called an oscillator) becoming unstable. It meant we had to turn to science and mathematics to identify possible sources of the stray transmission.

The rogue carrier was often due to the Upconverter Equipment accidently locking onto what is called a 'harmonic frequency', rather than the correct one. We knew what these harmonics might be, so we spent hours comparing the rogue carrier, to genuine carriers, to spot a possible culprit. If we found a plausible answer, we would get on the phone to the suspect earth station, and politely suggest they had a fault.

As a last resort, we would begin a chain of actions where we would ask stations to reduce the transmit energy of their different carriers, and watch to see if the rogue carrier also reduced. If that failed, we sometimes had to take quite drastic action, where we asked each station to switch off their transmitters for a few seconds while we watched the stray one.

Sometimes the interference would prove very difficult to locate, and it could be days before we could breathe a sigh of relief and satisfaction.

In addition to the active operational role, we all had little routine paperwork jobs that needed to be performed. My responsibility was to regularly look at every telephone and data channel that was in use on the satellite. A jiffy bag arrived every few weeks from the Washington office that had a pack of computer printout pages showing **every** transmit carrier going to the satellite, and then the name of every channel from its source to destination. It must also be noted that every transmit channel, had a receive one from somewhere as well.

… and there were thousands of channels!

The task was to compare the latest version with the previous version to ensure there were no anomalies. This would take several days to complete, and routine telephone calls, or reacting to problems, would make me lose my place on a regular basis.

Meanwhile John Sherbird looked after the higher-level management needs of the job. One such task was to be ready for a weekly telephone call with his manager in Washington. This was Jo Kearns, and he sat at the top table for operational aspects of the IOC. Each Thursday afternoon, John would clear his desk of anything unimportant, get himself a coffee, and wait for the call. They were always long calls with a lot of requests for information, or instructions for upcoming events. Quite regularly John would look across at me and ask for some information from my pack of channel allocations to assist in trouble shooting. Hence, I had to be careful my records were as up to date as possible.

When John was on leave, it was the rota man's duty to wait for the call, and I was often the one. Jo Kearns was a very 'laid back' person with a slow pace to his broad lilting accent. He loved to speak, and there would often be long monologues to listen to. I often struggled to keep alert during such one-sided discussions, but had to be ready to capture the key points, and answer any questions.

As the years rolled by, the Indian Ocean Region became very busy for satellite communications, and new Earth Stations were coming into service quite regularly. Sometimes they weren't on the main satellite, but working to older satellites that had been sub-let for domestic networks. Indonesia had their own network, and so did a group of Middle Eastern countries. We didn't get very involved with these networks, but some other systems needed our assistance.

They were the worst to communicate to, as many were small stations, that had no direct contact with us. Many of these required us to liaise with the French Earth Station (Pleumeur Bodou) as they were often involved with these smaller stations. They would take our requests and pass them on to the stations in Nigeria, or to one of the Indian Ocean islands, and then relay back answers or questions from those stations.

I remember one very complicated night. Nationally, France had decided to make a point to the world, and asked that everyone should speak to them in French for 24 hours when dealing with International business. They were frustrated that the International recognised language was English. Unfortunately, this coincided with me having to bring a new station into service in a remote area of Nigeria.

All operational tasks like this were performed using a teleprinter to keep a record of activities, so at about 3:00 in the morning I sat down for a very confusing few minutes.

My schoolboy French was atrocious, but I did my best. Being as there was no way of asking for technical instructions, I took a clever approach to keep the French happy.

I apologised for my French, and before each instruction, I asked them in English what I should type in French. After a moment or two, they gave me the French sentences, and I typed it back to them. This seemed to satisfy their pride, and they eventually asked me to simply continue in English.

1980 – Andrew James Williams

On 20th March 1980, I came home from the Bolitho Maternity Hospital in Penzance after the birth of our son Andrew. Deb had suffered a very uncomfortable pregnancy with atrocious heartburn for several months. Then there was a scare in the last few weeks when her blood pressure shot up, and she spent a couple of nights in hospital. To round it all off she spent well over 24 hours in labour before a little bundle of joy arrived.

This was the second of those landmark times in life. Getting married was one, and our first-born child became my second seriously emotional moment.

Deb and Andrew were soon home, and several months of broken nights and panic were to follow. Luckily, we had the mid-wives next door and they looked after Deb, and constantly checked Andrew if we had any concerns.

There was a short break from work to help out, but soon I had to leave Deb alone to cope as I returned to my duties. She was a good mother, and Andrew grew quickly and strongly. During the decades that followed, our son gave us so much joy, so much laughter, and so many moments of concern and sometimes downright panic. He still rocks our emotions after 40 years, but now he has his own life, and we have to trust he knows what he is doing.

We continued to have holidays with Jim and Jean, and they also came to see us and watch Andrew grow. My mum was always available and just 3 miles away. I collected her occasionally to come and share some of the magical moments with her grandson. As the months went by, my mum also gave us an odd evening out together to have a drink and meet friends. We always asked if everything had been OK while we were out, and she always responded yes. As far as we knew, she never had any issues, but did admit that she would have never told us even if there were.

Andrew grew from a baby into a toddler, and was soon walking, and exploring the world. After the initial tiredness, and constant confusion, Deb and I somehow turned into parents, and while our son still dictated much of our life, he gave us so many magical moments.

Our lifestyle was completely different, and back at work, things were changing there as well.

Satellite Communications Grows Bigger

The world was shouting out for greater availability of satellites. As well as the Global coverage from Intelsat, there were many Regional providers coming into the business. In Europe there was Eutelsat launching their own satellites providing telephony and television.

Then to look after the shipping industry there was Inmarsat. The shipping companies were getting rid of the historical radio operators, and replacing them with a world-wide network of satellites that could provide efficient communications. It was no longer for emergency purposes, it was to allow headquarters to speak directly to the ships, and manage routes and cargo. They initially used spare capacity on existing satellites, but would soon be investing in their own space-craft.

This demand for growth could only be possible with better satellites, offering new frequency bands, and more flexible services.

Intelsat V

As the 1980s began, Intelsat were about to introduce yet another generation of satellites, and it came with radical new features and capabilities.

As well as the traditional 'C Band' frequencies, Intelsat V would also expand the use of 'Ku Band' that was introduced with Intelsat IV satellites. This had virtually doubled the amount of bandwidth available, and further major improvements in spacecraft technology were possible with this new frequency band. The Ku band allowed smaller antennas to operate effectively. The giant 30 metre diameter dishes were slowly becoming unnecessary, and operating to this frequency band would be using the recently constructed Aerial 4.

New types of services were also being introduced to make the best use of the frequencies available. The first of these was called *'Single Channel Per Carrier'* or SCPC.

Over a day, there would always be times when some of the telephony channels between two countries would be idle. With a full time carrier carrying perhaps 240 channels, it meant that many would occasionally not be used, but they still occupied some of the limited satellite bandwidth.

With SCPC, there was a pool of small carriers that could be shared between several earth stations. When one of the countries needed to make a call, they would be automatically allocated one of the SCPC channels (in both directions) for the duration of the call. When the phone call ended, the channels were returned to the pool again.

The practical aspects of SCPC only worked properly when the pool of channels was made available to multiple earth stations, meaning more moments when the demand for telephone calls was low. This simple concept of sharing channels, involved quite complex processor-controlled equipment, but it did allow an efficient way of using the frequency bandwidth.

As the years went by, this became even more efficient by digitising voice channels. Now instead of allocating the channel when a call was made, the carrier was only radiated during the quite short periods when speech was present. If you think about a typical phone call, you only speak for a few seconds of the overall conversation. When the other person speaks, or even when you pause to draw breath, there is no need for the satellite carrier to be radiated, and it can instead be allocated to another person, on another call.

As well as new ways of using the bandwidth, the Intelsat V satellite was an incredible piece of space-craft, and of a totally new design.

It was built by a different company (Ford Aerospace) and was no longer the traditional drum shaped satellite. The main part of this generation of satellites consisted of a rectangular box, that was about 2m on its longest edge, and about 1.5m on the shortest. That box housed all the amazing equipment. It no longer had to revolve as there were three gyro-stabilisers that kept the box pointing in the correct direction towards earth. Attached to the box was the huge aerial stack with a mixture of horns and parabolic reflectors.

These satellites had small hydrazine gas propulsion rockets to keep it in a very precise orbit, that meant the steering systems of earth station antennas could be simplified. Hydrazine had been common with previous satellites, and as well as orbit management, the gas could be used to gently move the satellites to a position above different areas of the world, hence allowing domestic systems.

Instead of having solar cells on the traditional drum, Intelsat V satellites had two giant wings that unfolded once in space. These wings were covered in solar cells, and the wings could be turned to ensure they always faced the sun. This was far more efficient, and created 1800 Watts of power, compared to 600 Watts on the Intelsat IVA satellite. Although the equipment box was little more than a 2m cube, those wings were almost 16 metres from tip to tip.

Operationally there were 21 C Band transponders, plus 4 transponders for the new Ku Band. The C Band radio carriers were connected to Earth by a vast antenna stack that could operate globally, or as West and East Hemispheres, or even to smaller regional Spot Beams restricted just to the Northern or Southern halves of those Hemispheres.

Ku Band transponders antenna accurately pointed very small spot beams to specific areas of major population. This allowed higher powered energy carriers, and hence the ability to be operated by smaller antenna on Earth.

Bad News for me

The introduction of Intelsat V spacecraft, meant different geographical coverage, and hence Goonhilly would no longer be able to monitor all of the Indian Ocean satellite activities.

This meant the end of the Goonhilly TOCC group.

The monitoring would have to be shared by several earth stations, and the day-to-day operational functions would be moved to Washington.

So, in 1980, our little group at Goonhilly had a few months before the change happened, and during that time new opportunities came along to tempt me.

One of these opportunities was rather special.

All of the Goonhilly people involved in the TOCC office were offered a chance to take their wives and visit Washington (yes in the USA) to look at the IOC, and the lifestyle involved. The guys would then have an informal interview to consider a full time move to Washington.

I said I wouldn't be taking up this offer because of my fear of flying.

Then one afternoon I had a call from Joe Kearns. He offered me a job in the IOC without any interview, and they would pay for the move to the USA by ship. I was unbelievably flattered by the offer, and realised I was already seen as valuable.

I still turned down the offer.

In hindsight, I have no regrets. The lifestyle Deb and I could have had would have been wonderful, but it would mean accepting a different culture, and a different way of life.

It turned out that John Sherbird, and Tony Bernstein both moved to Washington, and they enjoyed their time. John came back a few years later after early retirement, but I never had an opportunity to meet him and discuss things. Tony remains in

America, and comes back to visit a few times. He was thoroughly happy with his decision.

The Goonhilly IOR TOCC continued as usual through 1980, while the job was run down and transferred to America.

This was the end of an amazing handful of years, that I will always treasure.

Treading the Boards

Away from the job, I continued to be very involved in the social club.

One of the most memorable moments of the year for me was taking part in the pantomime. The Goonhilly panto this year was an adaptation of Jack and the Beanstalk, and I played the Dame. There were a lot of rehearsals which proved difficult when so many of the cast were on rota duties, but as we neared Christmas, we were ready.

My character was one of the major roles, and, forgetting any thoughts of modesty for a moment, I think I played it rather well. As well as being in virtually every scene, I also had a solo moment singing with the audience. This proved a moment of fun with Dave who was one of our neighbours, as I sang a song to him, and even sat on his knee.

We had performances on Thursday and Friday evening with staff and friends as the audience, but on the Saturday it was the day of the Christmas party for the children with a special matinee show for them. The afternoon began with a tea-party while I played some music for them to dance around. I had built a simple disco rig for social functions, and I was holding the 9-month-old Andrew in my arms as I played the songs.

As Santa came with the presents, I had to scuttle off to get changed into my costume, and be transformed by a wig, and some very over the top makeup, to complete my character.

On stage I had many scenes with the customary troublesome fools of the show who were playing a couple of Cornish fishermen. They were played by Jock Beattie and Peter Morris who were both outgoing, and loved to play pranks. In one scene I had to sit between them on a bench sharing their jug of ale. In the first two performances this went funnily, and almost to the script, but for the Saturday matinee performance for the children, the scene changed without my knowledge.

The supposed jug of ale was actually just cold tea, and I would take a gentle swig each time the jug passed back and forth between the two fishermen. But, in this performance, Jock and Peter had swapped the cold tea for a strong local beer called Spingo. As I had my first sip, I whispered my surprise to the pair who were already giggling. At the end of the scene, as I was supposedly getting tiddly, I had to down the remaining ale. Of course, cold tea was not a problem, but this time I was left with virtually a full pint of very alcoholic beer. Keeping to the script, I emptied the jug down my throat as the curtains closed. I gave the pair, by now crying with laughter, a couple of harsh words, but I was also laughing at the prank.

I was fine again by the evening's final performance, and I will always remember this pantomime with a feeling of pride, and amusement of such happy times.

The TOCC role at Goonhilly ended at the end of the year. It was the end of a very special era at Goonhilly, and an unbelievably wonderful period of my working life. Various ideas of what I would be doing in the future were discussed, and I had the time to go on a number of training courses that might help me. Perhaps I was a little worried about my future as 1981 approached, but fortunately I was still being looked after by my guardian angel, and I was offered another rather special job.

1981 – Flying for the first time

Things were about to change for me, and very rapidly.

With the TOCC now gone from Goonhilly, I felt uncomfortable about having nothing to do. Then, out of the blue, I was asked to have a chat to one of the managers in the TD group about a possible job.

Satellites had become business as usual for communications across the continents, but it was also making its mark for communicating to and from ships, and even aircraft. Initially some of the commercial satellites had an additional package that was designed for limited operation by ships. After these experimental beginnings, it was soon destined to become the next leap in the history of satellite communications.

An organisation called 'Inmarsat' was formed in 1979, and it closely mirrored Intelsat with international agreements with all the interested countries. Before long plans were being implemented to have their own satellites to provide worldwide communication between ships, and a comprehensive ship to shore service. The job of the traditional ship's radio operators was about to become less complicated, and more like a telephone operator.

The satellites required different frequencies to enable ships that were bouncing around on the ocean to maintain contact. This frequency band was referred to as the 'L Band'. Ships would transmit and receive with the satellite on these frequencies, but the satellite would operate to the earth stations at traditional 'C' band. Because the satellites used the same frequencies as Intelsat, they were positioned far enough apart to avoid interference.

Goonhilly had been involved from the beginning, but as Inmarsat went live, plans were put in place to become a lead player. A new building was constructed to house what became known as the 'ACSE' group.

... and there also had to be a new aerial.

This is where I was about to become involved.

I was invited to an informal interview with Bill Cormack. He was the manager in the TD group tasked to implement the new aerial. The role that I was being considered for was in the Clerk of Works Team overseeing the new aerial being built. This would be Aerial No 5, and designed to work on the Inmarsat Satellite System.

The job sounded something very special, and I must have come across well at the interview, as I was offered a temporary role as a first level manager (AEE) while the aerial was being built.

There was just one snag.

The company building the aerial were called Toronto Iron Works based in California, and I was expected to go there on a training course at the factory.

I did my best to get out of the course, and even considered refusing the role, but there seemed to be no option but to fly to America for a week.

Now things happened very quickly. It was just a couple of months later, with seemingly no time to come to terms with what was happening, and the flight tickets were handed to me at work, and I was packing to go.

Fortunately, there was enough time to go and see my doctor (Dr Lansdowne) who listened to my dilemma about flying. He sympathised sufficiently to hand over a small box of pills to take before the flight. They were Valium, which he assured me would take away the fear.

I would be flying out on a Saturday afternoon, so a hotel was booked in London for the previous night. Going with me was Peter Hocking who had also been given a job on the contract. This was to be his first experience of air travel as well.

So, on the dreaded Friday I said my goodbye to Deb and Andrew, and set off for the railway station.

I would like to point out, that I really **did** think it was goodbye.

That evening with Peter in London was a blur, as I had no thoughts of anything except the flight.

On the Saturday morning, I woke and took the first of the Valium pills to settle my panic. I had another after lunch as we set off towards Heathrow Airport, and my date with a Pan Am Boing 747 on flight PA 125 to San Francisco.

There were four of us from the team on the flight that day. I was accompanied by Peter Hocking, Bill Cormack, and one other manager from London whose name I have forgotten. We met up at the airport, and before I could change my mind, we were all sitting in the Club Class Lounge.

By now I was well under the influence of Valium, and my head was refusing to make sense of what was about to happen.

The final '*Bing Bong*' announced that we had to board the plane, and I realised that Valium might be clouding my thoughts, but it wasn't taking away the feeling of dread.

With no way of avoiding my fate, we all entered the huge Jumbo Jet. It smelt like the inside of a new car, but even more so. My seat was a window one, and I could see the gigantic wing.

The hours to come confirmed every bad impression I had about flying.

I hadn't realised that I suffered from claustrophobia, but immediately felt trapped inside this steel tube.

After the obligatory welcome messages and safety instruction, a noise confirmed that the engines had started, and then as the sound increased in volume we began to move. We were quickly onto the runway and the noise increased further, and it was obvious that my prison was speeding up.

There was a feeling of being pushed back into my seat a little as we lifted into the air, and I almost screamed when I looked out of the window and saw the wing sagging.

That was quickly followed by another panic moment with an unexpected '*clunk*' as the undercarriage went up.

I really had no idea of what to expect, and these new feelings, and completely normal parts of flying, terrified me.

Fortunately, I soon settled down sufficiently to look around, and I began to get used to the drone of the engines. I just hoped that I would at least see America before the plane crashed.

The Valium had now kicked in, but after about an hour, they produced a horrible side effect.

My eyes decided to roll upwards into my skull, resulting in me not being able to see anything low down unless I physically tipped my head forward. This was also the moment when the Captain made an announcement to warn us of impending turbulence, and a little '*bing bong*' accompanied a warning sign illuminating a message saying '*No Smoking*' and '*Fasten your Seat Belts*'. Apart from the relief when I was sleeping, my eyes refused to focus on anything else except that sign.

The turbulence lasted for most of the flight, so that sign was on for a long time.

Peter and I had a meal, and that was extremely difficult to eat as my eyes refused to look down. There were free drinks on offer, but while my colleagues enjoyed the perks of Club Class flying, I dared not touch alcohol in case my Valium episode got any worse.

Our flight was scheduled to take about 10 hours, but the turbulence added an hour to this. Then, after what seemed an eternity, the Captain announced that we were just about to turn towards San Francisco airport, and that it was possible to see the Golden Gate Bridge below us.

At that moment he throttled back.

This initiated another bout of panic, as the sound that I had got used to for nearly half a day suddenly changed, and the plane rolled as we began our approach.

... but yes, I can honestly say the bridge did look rather special.

Minutes later, the seatbelts were fastened again, and I must have clenched every muscle in my body as we landed. After another set of roaring engine sounds, the movement settled, and I realised I had made it to America.

All that was audible was the air conditioning, and the babble of passenger voices, as the giant plane was manoeuvred to its parking spot at the terminal. Soon passengers were standing and taking their hand luggage from the storage boxes, and coats were being put on.

But then there was another announcement.

We were instructed to relax for a while, as there was a problem with the air-bridge being attached to our plane.

Well, that problem meant a major delay of over 30 minutes. Eventually the air-bridge idea was scrapped, and an old-fashioned set of steps was connected to the doors, and we were given the all clear to get off.

I would like to point out that my eyes were still targeted at anything above head level, and walking down the steps from a Jumbo Jet to the tarmac was not an easy task. However, the feel of that tarmac was very welcome under my feet.

We snaked our way into the terminal, and now it was another new experience of the luggage carousel. Think suitcases at almost ground level, and eyesight concentrating on objects on the terminal roof, and you can imagine my difficulty spotting, and more importantly grabbing my suitcase.

Next was the welcome from the arrival interrogation. I was tired, I felt ill, and was completely unprepared for the questions from a grumpy immigration officer. This was made even worse by a huge menacing security guard behind him with a rifle.

Finally, the four of us met up and walked outside. The heat of that San Francisco afternoon hit me, and my eyes began to relax. I was like a zombie by now. The Valium was wearing off, and all I wanted to do was sleep. Tucked up in the back of the hire car, I closed my eyes as we made the journey from the airport to our hotel. Once checked in, the discussion was about getting a meal, but I made my apology, preferring to be on my own in a bed.

The other three went back out into the city, but I decided the only thing I wanted to do was to make a phone call home to Deb. Even this was complicated, as I had to purchase a tube of coins before using the payphone. The call required the assistance of an operator who told me to feed the coins into the very hungry telephone. Deb was pleased to hear from me, but rather upset at being woken in the middle of the night.

Phone call over, and several dollars worse off, I crawled up to my bedroom, and was soon tucked up in my bed.

America could wait until tomorrow.

Good Morning America

Having been semi-conscious from Valium, and then tucked up asleep by early evening on Saturday, I was awake early on Sunday morning. Peter, in the other bed was fast asleep, but after I had worked out where I was, I stayed in bed and listened to the noises of San Francisco. There was an almost non-stop sound of cars interspersed with clanging fire engines.

I was hungry!

Apart from a strange meal in the plane, I had not eaten anything since leaving Britain. It was still very early, so I stayed as still as I could until eventually Pete stirred.

We were soon up and out of the Bay View Hotel. We headed down the quite steep hill towards the centre of the city, looking out for somewhere to eat. Eventually we saw a 'diner' on a street corner and were probably his earliest customers of the day.

After explaining who we were, we asked for suggestions about what to eat. We ended up with ham, eggs and grits. The meal was delayed quite a while as we tried to make our minds up about how to have our eggs. I never knew there were so many variations of a fried egg.

Anyway, the breakfast was delicious, and by the time we had left, our head was full of ideas as to where to go and explore.

Although the memories are a little vague, I think the plan for the day was to meet up with the others late in the morning at Pier 39 on the waterfront of this amazing city. Until then we continued our walk down to the busy city centre.

Pete and I saw quite a bit in those couple of hours, and my head was crammed with the delights of skyscrapers, the clanging bells of street cars, and entertainers who juggled, sang, and danced while conversing with everyone who passed them. This was a magical place to look around, and soon we found China

Town that was colourfully decorated as part of the Chinese New Year celebrations. There was also Lombard Street that wound its way down a hill. I instantly associated it with the Steve McQueen car chase in the film Bullitt.

My only sadness was that Deb wasn't there to share my excitement, and enjoy the atmosphere.

The only disappointment was that the infamous San Francisco fog was hiding the Golden Gate Bridge for all the time we were there.

At the allotted hour we found Pier 39, and met up with the rest of our gang. That had now swollen to a total of five with Dave Bridgewater, also from Goonhilly, joining us. He had been in the area for some time to monitor activity at the factory, and he could explain a lot of what we would be seeing and doing.

Early in the afternoon, we picked up a large hire car, grabbed our cases from the hotel, and set off for the hotel we would be staying at for the rest of the week. It was a sixty or more-mile drive south from San Francisco to the area known as Silicon Valley, and close to the city of San Jose. The drive was long, and even with air conditioning, it was hot and sticky.

Our destination was a motel from a popular company called Motel 7 (or was it 6). We each had a small lodge, with a bath and a comfortable large bed. There was no food available, so the meal we had in San Francisco had to keep us going until the following morning. Luckily there were machines for crisps, fizzy drinks and sweets.

I had a minor problem that resulted in me calling the receptionist for help. I couldn't turn the taps on in the sink. Explaining my issue took a while until I realised that they are called 'fawcets'.

The man quickly came to my rescue and with an angry look on his face, demonstrated the obvious method of using the taps.

Not to me it wasn't.

There was nothing to do for the rest of the evening. So, I snacked on my vending machine picnic, had a bath, and returned to getting over my Jet Lag with an early night.

I was hoping that we could sort out a more satisfying method of eating before much longer.

The next morning, we met up (still hungry) and jumped into the hire car again. Our first stop was a popular, and more importantly nearby, diner. Our manager Bill Cormack was paying the bills so he ordered the various bits from an enthusiastic waitress.

It was delicious, but we were running late and soon we were on the road again towards the factory of Toronto Ironworks (TIW).

TIW Factory Training

The rest of the week was a bit of a blur of sitting in a classroom looking at endless diagrams, interspersed with looking at bits of metal in the factory itself. The training was very similar to the course I sat on at the Marconi Factory in Chelmsford. It ticked a box on the contractual list, but provided very little assistance in helping me with the job to come.

The best bit was meeting the guys who would be coming to Goonhilly for the construction. There were three of them with varying roles. One of them was the notional manager from the company for the contract at Goonhilly, and he was a very laid-back American. It turned out he was a Vietnam veteran where he flew helicopters. It wasn't a surprise that nothing seemed to excite or anger him after that experience. The others were big strong Californians who said little but just got on with their tasks.

We were well treated by the company, and although I don't suppose it was some form of bribery, it certainly ensured good feedback. They did eventually get another contract for an aerial at the new Madley Earth Station. Anyway, they fed us well, including one lunchtime when we were all taken to a wonderful Golf Club overlooking the San Francisco Bay, where we had a very special meal, with plenty of wine.

The week was an experience that I enjoyed, but was it really so vital for me to go?

I forget details of the evenings in the Motel, but a couple of things stuck in my mind.

One evening, Pete and I took a walk down the side of the busy highway to a Shopping Mall. It was just for exercise and to look for some snacks, but we did stop at a bar for a drink. We got into conversation with the locals who did their best to tempt us into drinking the local beer. This began by asking if we would like a glass of their favourite British beers. The choice was Double Diamond or Red Barrel. We politely said it was not to our taste, and eventually tried the American Budweiser lager, which was most enjoyable.

When we got back to the Motel there was chaos. A woman was screaming about a man with a gun, and for everybody to take cover. Somehow, we couldn't really understand the panic, but we were quickly in our lodges. The Police came but we never found out the details. We were however told off by our workmates, and the guys at the factory, about walking. It appears that no-one walked in that area.

Sad people.

On another evening, the person from London whose name I have forgotten, asked if I would go with him to a local gym, where he was going to play squash. He drove the hire car and soon disappeared to his game. I watched for a while, but quickly became bored, and headed for the bar to top up my Budweiser tank. It was a long game of squash, and by the time he returned I was distinctly tipsy.

As we walked to the car, he tossed me the keys, and said his legs were too tired to drive. I was horrified. This was the first time I had ever driven a car of this size, on the wrong side of the road, and had drunk far too much.

The journey back to our motel was slow. One of the biggest problems was at major junctions where the traffic lights were high up above the road. We got back safely, and fast forwarding to the present, I have never driven after drinking too much again.

On the second morning, we went to the same diner for breakfast, but there was a problem.

They were not coming over to take our order. The waitresses were obviously ignoring us. Someone asked Bill Cormack if he had tipped the waitress on the previous morning, and his response of *"No"*, solved the mystery. After a quick word with a waitress and an apology, our order was taken, and that mistake was never made again.

By the end of the week I had seen numerous pictures of what our new aerial would look like, and seen various items of equipment that were destined for Goonhilly. I had a pretty good idea of how it would all go together, and was very ready to go home.

As the week progressed, a further factory visit was organised to oversee the project, and I managed to convince everyone that Peter was a much better idea than myself.

It was time to go back home again, and the prospect of another 10 hours in an aeroplane was the biggest thing on my mind. There was no way to get out of it, short of asking for asylum.

At the airport Peter and I had time for a drink, and we decided to get rid of all the small US coins to buy a final glass of Budweiser. This turned out to be a very sour way of leaving America. The barman was a red-haired Californian from Irish immigrants. It was the moment that a man called Bobby Sands was dying from self-starvation in a Belfast Prison, and we were British, and hence deemed responsible.

He snarled while grudgingly serving us, and slammed the glasses down on the bar, and threw our coins into a bin.

He was the only person we had encountered in America who had shown any animosity, but it was our last experience before heading towards the departure lounge.

All too soon I was walking along the Jumbo jet's passenger aisle to take my seat, but this time I had ignored the Valium.

I hated the ten-hour experience again, but at least had the opportunity to have a drink or two as we flew home towards London.

My experience of America was very special, but I had no intention of ever flying again, and so I assumed I would never return to America.

As a postscript to this chapter, I did return to San Francisco, but this time it was with Deb. It was on a very special three-month World Cruise to celebrate our retirement. It was a wonderful way of allowing Deb to share my thrill of this amazing city.

(This is described in a later book titled 'Around the World without Wings')

Back at Goonhilly

By the time I was back at work after my trip to America, the site of the new Aerial 5 was being prepared. The plot was on a new access road that was about midway between the main Goonhilly building, and Aerial 2. The rough moorland had been dug, flattened, and covered in hardcore. There would eventually be two office style Portacabins with one being for the BT people, and the other for the TIW contractor team.

I had little to do initially, but there were short managerial training courses to attend, to allow me to get my head around being a manager, and numerous meetings with my new team at Goonhilly, plus lots of men in suits from London. The majority of my time was spent looking at piles of books with details of the project, plans of the site, descriptions of equipment, plus test parameters and result recording forms.

Let's just say it wasn't a very dynamic couple of months.

The site of the aerial was a building area, and I had a desk to work at in the main building, but I did accompany Bill Cormack (and others) occasionally to peek at progress. From a distance I could begin to see shapes of where the equipment building would be, and the circle for the aerial itself. When construction became serious, the first physical signs of real activity was the equipment building foundations, and then walls.

Knowing my life would get very busy quite soon, I took the opportunity to take some time off, and enjoy family time.

We went to visit Jim and Jean in Leafield and it was a chance for them to spoil their grandson, and us. We visited Burford Wildlife Park to let Andrew have a first experience of different animals, and on another day, we left Andrew with his grandparents while Deb and I went to Bourton on the Water. A few hours alone at this quaint little town was a treat. We could stroll without the buggy, have coffee and ice-cream in peace, have leisurely looks in shops, and for a brief moment, we were a couple again. Sadly, the thoughts of grandparents tearing their hair out with a screaming grandson, was never far from our minds, and it was a relief to get back to Leafield.

The sleepy Cotswold town of Bourton has remained one of our favourite destinations when we visit this area of the country.

Back at Goonhilly, the project was in full swing by May, but I managed to get away from the site for a day to perform the traditional father's role on Flora Day. I did what we all do, and perched Andrew on my shoulders to watch the fun of this wonderful annual custom. There was no chance of dancing myself that year, but the time would come again.

Later in the year I managed to get time off again, and we were very brave, and went for a short holiday at a Pontin's holiday centre in Devon called St Mary's Bay. It was a bit of an experiment to see if we could enjoy a holiday with a youngster, and it turned out to be rather special. We have photos of Andrew in a paddling pool, being introduced to a donkey, and having a gentle moment or two on a swing.

There were grown up things to do as well, and Deb won first place in the Lovely Legs competition. In the evening we made use of the baby watching system to allow us to have a few minutes in the show bar. We proved that it was possible to have some time to ourselves, and enjoy a drink, and a bit of entertainment.

Sadly, such moments away from work were quite rare. My role as Clerk of Works for the new aerial became my focus from early summer throughout the remainder of 1981, and beyond into 1982.

The Project really begins

The time finally came when the site was ready for us to take up residence in our portacabin.

Both of the Portacabins were about 10 metres long, and although the TIW office was empty to begin with, our BT cabin was now officially active. I had a little office area at one end with a desk, a couple of chairs, with the walls decorated with bookshelves in readiness for the library of books and folders that I had already accumulated. In the main section of the cabin, there were several desks and chairs, for the other BT people on the team.

Peter Hocking was back from America where he watched the equipment being constructed, and factory tested. He had far more in-depth knowledge of the aerial and equipment than I did, so I had to play catchup. Over the months to come, Peter shared much of the equipment commissioning duties with Martin Webster, who had been temporarily promoted to TO. Peter and Martin would be monitoring the installation of equipment, then monitoring tests, and recording results.

Also in our cabin was Percy Rawlings from the Goonhilly Construction group. He would be watching over much of the electrical, and physical equipment installations. There was also Renfrew Bray whose primary role was as a labourer to keep the place clean, and assist the rest of us wherever possible.

But he had another skill.

Renfrew kept us all informed of rumours and gossip from around Goonhilly, and generally initiated chatting in the cabin at the slightest opportunity. He loved to talk about anything and everything, and became a useful member of the team by regularly giving our brains a break, from the sometimes quite tedious work over the weeks to come.

The spot where the actual aerial would be built was little more than a hole when I arrived. There were gangs of men digging and creating shapes with wood, with their actions being monitored by suited onlookers with their theodolites. The small equipment building was completed by now, and had basic lighting and power in the main section where the radio equipment would soon be fitted.

At this stage I had a rough idea of what the aerial would look like, and how some of the equipment racks in the building would appear when they eventually purred into magic.

Still at a relatively early stage of the project, we were treated to regular visits from managers at Goonhilly, and others from London. It was still only late Spring by now, and our visitors came in their winter coats to trudge around the site with wellington boots and armed with clipboards. One of the tasks that Renfrew excelled in, was spotting the impending arrival of visitors, and he'd give us a warning to put the newspapers away.

One of our regular suited visitors was Nigel Leeson, who was a University Graduate, and his role was to lead on the Civils aspects of the project. He knew all that was needed to know about digging holes, and filling those holes with concrete.

And then there was me. I had nothing much to do at the early stages, except attending meetings to report what little had happened. I still had the piles of contractual paperwork to read and understand, and my pile gradually increased by regular deliveries of construction and technical handbooks, that I tried to comprehend. As time progressed, there were also reams of test instructions and forms to fill in to ensure everything was completed to the required standard.

Things slowly began to happen with the arrival of the Americans, and the first major milestone was approaching when the aerial base would be created. On that day, lorry after lorry of ready-mix concrete arrived, and their contents poured into the hole that was to become the base for the aerial.

This was when I discovered something new about the use of ready-mix concrete, and that was the '*Slump Test*'.

The steel aerial would eventually be attached to bolts on a concrete plinth. That concrete plinth had to be very strong, meaning an awful lot of concrete. Around the outside of that plinth was a further area of concrete that was perhaps less strong, but still had to enable heavy lorries and cranes to stand on it.

To achieve the strength, the concrete had to be of a consistent mix, and with tens of mixer lorries arriving during the concrete pouring days, a check had to be made of the gloopy grey sludge. This was the '*Slump Test*'.

On the concrete pour days, Nigel oversaw the operation as each lorry arrived. Percy (and Renfrew) would fill a cone shaped bucket with a sample from the mixer lorry. The cone would then be upturned to allow the concrete witches hat shaped sand castle to stand. After a set time period, the height of the cone was checked to see how much it had sunk – or '*slumped*'. The wetness and mix of cement and aggregate affected the amount of slumping, and hence could be used to somehow calculate the mixture strength. If it was satisfactory, the lorry was allowed to spew its contents into the waiting hole. Each lorry had to be checked, and the drivers knew that if the slump test suggested a problem, the load would be rejected and sent back to their depot.

To ensure the mixes didn't fail the test, the drivers would stop at a layby about half a mile from Goonhilly, and perform their own slump test. On the way home I spotted a multitude of little concrete witches' hats in that layby.

As it happened, I didn't see any failures, and soon we had a circular patch of concrete, that would be the main weight bearing base for the aerial. The concrete had several days of setting and curing before it could be used. Soon another fleet of lorries arrived to complete the outer circular patch of concrete, and then everything awaited the arrival of the metalwork.

More Family Time

At home Deb and I were becoming more comfortable as parents. Little Andrew had grown into a lovely child, and we took turns to play, or read books to him. We also let him watch children's television, when we could both have a rest, while he enjoyed the simple delights of Bagpuss, Danger Mouse, Postman Pat, Ivor the Engine, Mr Benn, or Trumpton …

… *"Pugh, Pugh, Barney McGrew, Cuthbert, Dibble and Grubb"*.

It was an era of innocent cartoons with easy-to-understand stories with no violence or PC interference. Within a handful of years, the arrival of Japanese cartoons brought us Transformers, Thundercats, and an endless stream of other superhero characters, that provided children with 15 or 20 minutes of continuous loud battles between good and bad, with guns, explosions, and death.

Is it any wonder our children now accept violence is the *'norm'*?

It wasn't all about television, we regularly took walks with Andrew in his buggy. It was often a chance to get some exercise and look around the village. There were hardly any times when we didn't meet friends for a chat, or for a stranger to *"coo"* over our delightful son. Sometimes after a less than relaxed spell of child tantrums, one of us would take Andrew for a walk, to give the other ten minutes of peace, allowing vital moments to recharge parental batteries.

As the warmth of early summer came, I spent many hours digging at the back of our new house to terrace the quite steep slope, and make patches for lawn, fruit, and vegetables. There are numerous photos of Andrew playing on the lawn with me digging in the background, and others where his curiosity was stimulated by watching me closely. It was a glorious summer, and our back garden was a sun trap. We had visits from my brother Ronald, and his wife Jane, and the garden became chaotic with Andrew playing with his cousins (Nicola and Jenny) while the adults caught up on life.

There were adult treat moments as well. My mother occasionally offered to babysit for an evening while we had a drink down in the village at the Harbour Inn, or to go to Goonhilly for a social event. I was quite seriously involved with the Sports and Social Club, and regularly worked behind the bar, or played dance music to amuse people. Deb also helped behind the bar, and was almost accepted as an honouree member of the Goonhilly family.

That period in our lives was a major change to our lifestyle, with me no longer working on a shift rota, and not having to curtail family activities to disappear for a weekend, or an evening or night shift.

We were a young family really enjoying life.

Aerial 5 Takes Shape

In the Autumn of 1981, my employer changed its name again. We lost the Post Office name, and became British Telecommunications, or simply BT. I worked hard for my newly named organisation during 1981 and 1982 as the latest aerial at Goonhilly moved from drawings to the real thing.

Lorries began to arrive with huge steel structures, and massive boxes of equipment, and all the bits and pieces to construct, wire, power, and implement the electronics. Other Americans would appear and disappear as their specialist part of the construction was happening. TIW also employed local labourers for the manual aspects of creating order from the chaos of boxes.

One of the first stages was to fit the windmill style base of the actual aerial. A large crane swung the panels that made up the circular base, and one by one they were lowered onto the bolts protruding from the concrete. Everything fitted and then our building site truly began to take shape. More steel bits were lifted up and onto the top of the base, and soon girders were being bolted together to create the structure that would eventually hold the 14-metre dish.

One morning while we were having a cup of tea, Renfrew announced that two cars appeared to be heading towards us, and going very fast. This was the first warning that we were going to have an extremely strange experience.

As per Renfrew's suspicion, two cars did turn into our car park, and skidded to a halt with gravel flying in all directions. Half a dozen men in suits then got out of the cars and looked around the site. I went out to ask if I could help, and one (who appeared to be in charge) waved a police warrant card at me, and asked where the TIW office was. I pointed out the Americans' cabin, and was then told to go back inside and keep out of the way.

I told the rest of the team what was happening, and quickly rang my manager to let him know what was going on.

After several minutes, the officer returned to tell me that they had been searching for drugs. It seems that a small package of marihuana had been discovered in a packing case destined for the TIW team, and an explanation was needed.

Later when the site returned to normality, I spoke to the Americans and it seems that one of the guys was having a birthday, and his mates in California thought it would be a wonderful idea to send a card with a small sample of something to cheer him up. Of course, I believed his explanation that it was just a silly joke. The fact that he was a long haired 'aging hippy' with a drooping moustache and goatee beard didn't convince me that there was nothing else to concern myself about.

There were no more interruptions from the police, and the American team did their job without any problems.

As a postscript to this little story, I saw that detective again several years later, and innocently asked if he was still with the drug squad. He was shocked, and asked how I knew this. I told him the story, and he grunted, and although not making any comment, I was left in no doubt that I shouldn't concern myself any more.

Meanwhile, the equipment building was filling with racks and shelves of equipment, and miles of cables were being run from rack to rack and also to and from the aerial structure. The base section of the aerial was now being topped with a massive amount of steel beams and struts that would soon be supporting the parabolic dish.

While our Civils team looked after the steel work, my little gang monitored the equipment installation, and endlessly put their ticks and signatures on the check sheets denoting completion for each minute part of the process. Of course, everyone of their check sheets came to me to be countersigned. These check sheets for the installation stages, soon turned into sheets of test results as each little item of equipment was switched on and their performance checked.

Time passed very quickly, and before we drew breath, a couple of cranes appeared to lift the newly constructed dish onto its steel support structure. This was one of the days when every manager involved with the project arrived with crisp suits, and brand-new shiny safety helmets. Cameras captured every stage of the lift, and Renfrew kept the tea brewing and chatted with the managers. Soon it was all over, and the 'suits' left us in peace.

Actually, this was one of the few moments when I was invited to join them for lunch in the main building restaurant. I knew most of them by now and got the impression that I was doing my job to their satisfaction.

With the steel windmill now looking like a proper satellite aerial, it was the moment for the final physical element to be attached.

The cranes arrived again to lift and position the feed onto the main dish. This feed was enormous on the ground, but appeared quite small by the time it was attached to the dish. That feed had to be carefully positioned, and the American method of achieving this, probably broke a vast list of Health and Safety rules.

One of the TIW team actually sat astride the feed as it was lifted, and swung across by the crane, before being coaxed onto the bolts at the centre of the main dish.

To complete the obvious visual aspects of the aerial, a crane appeared a few days later to lift and fit the quadrapod legs, and sub-reflector.

It was 1982 by now, and over several weeks, the BT team worked alongside the TIW engineers to check if the aerial and radio equipment performed to the specification.

Some of this work was quite mundane and perhaps even boring. Every alarm and signal wire had to be checked to be sure it came from where it was supposed to come from, and go to where it should at the other end. Indicators also had to do what they should, so that meant pressing buttons and check that the correct indicator lit up, or an alarm appeared, as a simulated fault was applied. This meant page after page of individual wires, switches and lights to be checked and ticked off as being correct. It was time consuming, but vital.

To ensure the aerial was ready as scheduled, some of the team had to work long hours, with weekend overtime, and they were very happy of the extra money. It was not necessary for me to get involved in this, except for signing off the timesheets, but as the project got close to the end, one or two of the team were no longer required, and returned to other jobs around Goonhilly. That meant more for me to do, and one cold and frosty night, I had to come in for a very special test of the aerial's performance.

It involved measuring the signal power right at the input to the receive equipment. That meant being in the small cabin behind the centre of the dish. Unfortunately, TIW did not have the special item of test equipment to perform this task, so I had to borrow a Spectrum Analyser from the West Wing equipment. Even more unfortunate was that I had to carry it up the metal steps on the outside of the aerial.

There were three sets of these steps which were exposed to the below freezing temperatures. The Analyser was quite heavy, and carrying it meant I couldn't hang onto the stairway safety rails. Health and Safety was forgotten, and I struggled up the steps with my awkward load, and by the time I reached the cabin, I was exhausted. The test itself only took a few minutes, and soon I was struggling back down again with the tester.

With that test successful, the final equipment checks were soon completed, and the aerial was about to be handed over to BT, before going operational.

One afternoon, those of us who remained were in our cabin for a refreshing cup of tea. Although almost drowned out by our noisy chatter, I noticed a buzzing sound that I didn't recognise. Looking out of the window we noticed the TIW team were staring up at the aerial, so we joined them to try and identify where the buzzing was coming from.

Although it seemed impossible, the noise was coming from the quadrapod within the dish. It was actually moving, all by itself. I realised that the legs of the quadrapod were vibrating because of the wind, and the movement was getting worse, and the sound even stronger.

The dish was trying to self-destruct!

While the TIW team looked at the scene in amazement, I realised something had to be done in a hurry. My thoughts immediately turned to one of the procedures that we had at Goonhilly in case of any very strong winds. The aerial had to be driven to a position called Zenith. This is when the dish is turned to point upwards, so that the wind would blow straight through the legs, which would, hopefully, stop the destructive oscillation.

After getting the permission from TIW to hit the emergency Zenith button on the control rack, I rushed into the equipment building, and flipped up the security flap and pressed the Zenith button.

By selecting that command, the aerial drove the motors at maximum speed from the normal angle looking at the horizon to the safe position.

The buzzing stopped.

I had possibly saved the aerial from any further damage.

While TIW went to their office to speak with their design engineers in America, I called my boss and explained the situation.

An hour later I was forced to climb into the lifting cage of a Simon Platform Cherry Picker. This was the second time I had to take a ride in this torturous machine, but it was my duty to take a look at the structure to see if there was any obvious damage visible.

There were some cracks where the legs joined with the dish, and with the sub-reflector, but they didn't appear significant.

Back on Terra-Firma again, I talked to the very amused Cherry Picker operator, and vowed once more that I would never go back up in this machine. He laughed his head off at my fear, but I did succeed in never having to experience the rocking, swaying, cage of terror again.

The next day, another member of the team had the time of his life going up with a camera to get evidence of the damage. I was very happy to just watch.

The outcome of the incident was that TIW had to wrap and weld a steel coil around the legs. This acted as a damper that stopped the wind performing its attempts to create a large and very expensive musical instrument.

As Spring arrived in Cornwall, the project was coming to an end, and my time in the portacabin was finished. There was a very special moment when TIW invited all of us to a celebration party at the Carn Brea Castle. I had never been there before, and have never returned, but this is an amazing place where we had a delightful meal, and lots of free booze. The evening was even sweeter with Deb coming along as well to enjoy the Americans' hospitality. The American I described as a 'hippy' with long hair, moustache and beard, took great delight in lounging on a sofa like a Roman Emperor. He laughed and joked throughout the evening, and occasionally there was a faint hint of some herbal tobacco product as he smoked. That raid by the drug squad may have proved fruitless, but maybe it was well founded.

At the end of the evening, after much hand shaking, and shared thanks with those Californians, I knew that a very special moment in my working career was almost over.

What Next?

I was looking for a role at Goonhilly again.

With nothing currently available, my days at Goonhilly were spent in the West Wing, and although gaining quite a bit of new knowledge and experience with the equipment, it really didn't float my boat. I felt out of my technical depth, and was not enjoying the life in this area.

Training courses were once again a major part of my life, and I was looking in the direction of becoming more active with television. There were also courses for the latest aerial (number 6), plus various new equipment that continually appeared in the West Wing.

There was one offer of something different. My manager while working on Aerial 5 (Bill Cormack) had offered me a chance to take part in a promotion interview – known as a 'Board'. It was referred to as a 'Limited Board' because even if successful, I was only qualified to apply for certain roles.

I was naïve when it came to interviews, and probably didn't ask enough questions before it, to know what to expect.

As I sat before three managers on the other side of a large table, all seemed initially to be going well. The questions were very much on my favoured topics, but eventually I came to one that tripped me up.

I was asked for an experience that I had found difficult while working as the Clerk of Works. I wasn't prepared for this, but came up with an honest experience. There was a moment when I had to discipline one of my team for being lazy. The questioner came back and probed into why it was difficult. My response was that I knew one day I would be working alongside this person and hence trying to avoid friction in the future.

I was torn to shreds for not being firm with the person.

Any chance of permanent promotion was over.

In truth, I doubt I would have ever accepted promotion even if I had been successful, as any roles offered would almost certainly have been based in London.

Instead, I went about enhancing my First Aid experience and knowledge. In addition to the in-house training with BT, I took courses with the Helston St John Ambulance Brigade. I was becoming quite close to the St John Brigade and spent many evenings alongside my mother who was still an active member.

There was some very special news as well. In the summer of 1982, Deb announced she was pregnant again, and our family was due to grow in the following March.

Our little house was still perfectly large enough for us, but thoughts were turning to perhaps looking for something different. By now the back garden was producing vast amounts of vegetables, and sweetened by fruit. We spent some money improving our home by asking our neighbour (Dave) to build us a garage. He was the person I embarrassed two years earlier at our pantomime, by sitting on his lap and singing a song. I had always dreamt of a house with a garage, and I thoroughly loved having a man cave, and somewhere to work on our car in the dry.

In May I danced with Katie on Flora Day in the midday dance, and during the break at Lismore Gardens, a photograph shows Andrew wearing my sweaty top hat.

We went on a couple of holidays at Pontin's camps around Torbay. We spent a week at one called Wall Park, then another week at the South Devon camp. Deb continued to win the 'Lovely Legs' competition, and Andrew proved to be the 'Beautiful Baby' winner one week. Me, I couldn't even win the knobbly knees contest, but I did enjoy such wonderful experiences on our family holidays.

Closer to home we spent several hours at the 'Flambards' holiday park attraction, and took Deb's parents (Jim and Jean) to enjoy the exhibitions of Victorian times. Our bridesmaid (Janet) also came to visit, and she accompanied us there as well. The memories of those days may have disappeared into the grey of lost decades, but our photograph collection has captured the smiles and laughter of wonderful times.

Late in the summer, I took on a challenge to create a carnival float for Goonhilly, but although I had exciting ideas, it turned out to be rather amateurish. There were several people who helped with the float's construction, but although the thoughts and ambition were very impressive, our skills and ability to create them were seriously lacking. Fortunately, I had contacted the BT marketing group who lavished me with badges, yoyos, and squishy balls to give away to the public, and more especially, the loan of a full-size costume of the yellow advertising bird called Busby.

We didn't win any prizes, but we did amuse the Helston Harvest Fair crowds. Of course, I wore the Busby costume and walked alongside the float. I was attacked on many occasions by little children who punched and squeezed me as I handed out the small gifts.

One of the saddest moments of the year concerned our transport. I have already mentioned that our transport was lurching from old and rusty cars, to different old, but still rusty ones. Without really noticing what was happening, I was becoming mentally, and physically stressed. I was suffering from a quite scaly rash, and was eventually sent to hospital (in Falmouth) to break the psychological stress sequence. I was bathed in special chemicals, and then lathered in cream each day for a week.

It was hard on Deb having to travel with Andrew to see me, and I was shocked and embarrassed by what was happening to me.

That week woke me up to my issues, and it was enough to get my head in gear, and to stop myself panicking over cars.

After a couple more adventures with dodgy cars, we finally spent proper money and bought a car from the local garage, rather than back-street slimy salesmen. It was a little yellow Metro that was already several years old, but lasted us for many reliable years.

I gave up doing any maintenance on the car, except for the basic tasks, and inwardly made myself a vow to avoid getting stressed up about cars, or in fact anything. I never suffered from the scaly rash anymore, and generally remained a model calm and controlled person for the next 20 years.

1983 – Lynsey Louise Williams

On 9th March 1983, I collected my mother to come and stay overnight at our house. She would be baby-sitting Andrew, as Deb was showing signs of going into labour with our second child. Not long after going to bed, Deb announced it was time to go to the Maternity Hospital in Penzance.

In the early hours of 10th March, Deb gave the final push, and we became the proud parents of a daughter. We had no idea if it was going to be a boy or a girl before the birth, as this was a time when scans were only available to high-risk mothers to be, or if there were problems.

We had names ready, and when asked what she would be called, I announced our daughter was Lynsey Louise. I had no reason to doubt myself at the time, but I spelt Lynsey in a slightly unusual way, and this caused many problems with teachers, and people in authority, who often refused to initially accept the spelling, until prompted by an often-irate young lady, about her name.

Anyway, while the other new mums around the Bolitho hospital tried to sleep, Lynsey was very busy, and insistent, on announcing her arrival into the world. I helped the nurse with our daughter's first bath, and Lynsey screamed continuously until eventually being returned to her mum.

She has made her presence known quite positively ever since.

After I had been allowed to go home and get some sleep, I returned to the hospital later in the day to bring Deb and Lynsey home, to a welcome from Granny Williams, and our neighbours.

We were very fortunate to have a retired District Nurse (Frances) next door to us, who lived with her daughter Hillary, who was an active District Nurse. If either of us were ever concerned, we could pop next door to seek advice, and reassurance. Andrew had never quite mastered our neighbours' names, and they became known as 'Hirrary and Frankis', but they had already been spoiling our son for three years, and now Lynsey was equally adored.

Deb and I were thrust back into new parent mode with disturbed nights, but I took my turn at holding and cuddling Lynsey during many nights to give Deb as much rest as possible for when I left her alone during the daytime. Fortunately, our little bundle of energy soon quietened down, and routine returned.

Just like Andrew during any daytime tantrums, Lynsey could always be relaxed by putting her in her buggy and going for a walk. And soon, (again like Andrew) she had been "*cooed*" at by neighbours, friends, and strangers around Porthleven. Deb was heavily involved with the Porthleven Playgroup by now, and Andrew was growing into a lovely young man, who was always willing to show off his sister to other parents.

That year the Playgroup created a float for the village Carnival where Andrew and the other children (plus parents) dressed up as characters in a toybox. I was left to push Lynsey around in her buggy and taking the "*aahs*", and "*coos*" from the watching crowds.

Soon there were visits by Jim and Jean from Oxfordshire, as well as uncles, aunts and cousins as Spring became Summer. Lynsey quickly became predictable enough to be looked after by my mum to give us the thrill of an hour out alone. We also had a family trip to Oxfordshire to spend some more time with Jim and Jean, where we also introduced Lynsey to her Great Grandmother Thompson who also lived in the village of Leafield.

That visit allowed another trip out to the local Wildlife Park to see the animals that always brought a smile to the faces of our children.

Meanwhile I remained on basic day hours at Goonhilly working in the West Wing, and hoping desperately that a more interesting post would soon come my way.

First Aid

In May 1983, my interest in First Aid became a bit deeper. I was given the opportunity to go to London and attend a training course that would enable me to be an Instructor within BT.

That course was at a BT building called Manor Gardens, and the week was one of the most intense training moments I had experienced. Our little group of budding instructors were already some of the most experienced first aiders in BT, but this was about to take us to a new level. We were all warned at the start of the week, that the course was difficult, and it was likely that some of us would fail.

Instead of just performing resuscitation, we were now told how to demonstrate it, and encourage other people to do it. Bandages, slings, and various methods of treatment now had to be shown by standing at angles to allow the audience to see. But the newest skill learnt was to actually present the theory of first aid to a group of people, who were potentially completely new to the subject.

The qualification we were aiming at, was described as 'First Aid at Work Instructor'. This meant the first aid we would be providing, was in line with Health and Safety at work requirements.

Our days were full of stress from morning to evening, and as well as sitting through various theoretical sessions, we had to prepare lesson plans and practical demonstrations to be presented to very strict instructors, who would eventually be a part of the examining team. Even when we got back to our hotel, there was reading and preparation to be completed before the next day...

... but we all tried to fit in a social drink or two as well.

Anyway, at the end of the week, we were randomly assigned theory and practical sessions, that made up our exam. The Head

Doctor for BT attended with our instructors, and we did our best to reach the standards they expected.

We all passed, and I was absolutely thrilled.

Now I had a different qualification that was acceptable to the Health and Safety at Work standards, and I could begin to train other people in First Aid.

1984 - Busy Times

The mid 80s was a busy time in our lives, and 1984 was no exception.

I was working standard 8:00 till 5:00 at Goonhilly, so while Deb had the majority of the daytime parenting role to occupy herself, I did my best to give her a break when I was home.

Even the best-behaved child can drain mental and physical limits, so when I was home, I spent many hours playing on the floor, reading books (a lot of Postman Pat) putting together small jigsaw puzzles. Andrew had always enjoyed jigsaw puzzles, and it wasn't long before he was just as happy making the puzzles when the pieces were turned over, with no picture showing. This was rather useful as Lynsey also enjoyed jigsaw puzzles, but mainly to peel off the pictures.

Andrew was becoming easier as he could amuse himself for a while, but Lynsey demanded all her waking hours to be filled with parent participation. Just as with Andrew a few years before, I spent hours taking her for a walk in her buggy. It was an instant fix, and within seconds of being secured in her buggy, Lynsey would quieten down, and after five minutes she would usually be quietly surveying the world around her. It often resulted in Lynsey falling asleep as I bumped our way along pavements, purposely finding rough bits of tarmac to make the buggy rattle. If Lynsey was awake, she would giggle, but it often made her fall asleep, and then I found a smoother route.

Deb and I were getting brave, and soon looked at holiday brochures again, and we decided to experiment with a week at a Pontins camp in Devon. It was little more than three hours away, and designed very much for families. There were organised children's clubs to give parents a break, as well as more adult entertainment for us to enjoy as well. Most days we explored the area as a family, but sometimes we stayed at the camp. Andrew had been going to the Porthleven Playgroup for many months by now, and he was quite happy to join in with the Children's clubs under the supervision of the eager and friendly Bluecoats.

Meanwhile Deb and I enjoyed the sunshine, and took Lynsey to the swings and slides on the site, or allowed her the freedom to run riot around the ballroom with other youngsters, while we sat and watched the fun from the sides.

On one of those days, Deb took part in the Lovely Legs competition again, and kept up her record of winning. By winning these weekly competitions, she won a free weekend away to compete at the regional competition. This was later in the year at another Pontins site called Sand Bay, and with no way of taking the children, Deb went by herself. This was where the realisation dawned that the competition had quite a large prize, and lots of professional models were also taking part. Prize-less yes, but at least it was a chance for Deb to have a real break.

In the evening our exhausted children were usually happy to go to sleep earlier than at home. This allowed Deb and I to take advantage of the Baby Monitoring system, and we had a chance to go back to the ballroom for a drink for an hour, while we watched the evening entertainment.

There was another trip away in 1984 that tested our children with an even longer car drive. Deb's brother (David) was getting married to Diane in Bristol, and there was quite a major meet up of Deb's family for the Register Office ceremony and the reception to follow. Fortunately, the children seemed quite happy with car rides, and invariably slept for much of the journey.

As the ceremony began, Andrew sat with Deb and watched quietly, but little Lynsey finally ran out of patience and interest. She began to cry and complain about having to stay still, so I took her outside the building to allow everyone else a chance to hear what was going on. It was a rare moment for a tantrum like this, and soon she returned to her charming self, and with the marriage completed, the guests gathered in the sunshine making a fuss of her again.

Back at Goonhilly, I was doing my best to learn about the equipment and practices in the Modem area of the West Wing. Sadly, I was struggling with the technology, and regularly asked my training manager to consider me for any other roles that might come up.

On a more positive note, I continued to be quite keen on First Aid, and during the year I was given the opportunity to become the lead person on the site. I had the responsibility to keep the records up to date for training courses, and to look after the First Aid room, and numerous kits around the site. With my background of growing up with parents in the St John Ambulance Brigade, I think I was always going to get seriously involved, although I had no idea at that time just how involved I would become.

1985 A Move to East Wing

At Goonhilly I continued my career in the West Wing, where I was attempting to understand what was going on within the modulators and demodulators, plus how to operate test equipment to diagnose and repair faults.

It was not going well, and although I mastered a lot of the basics, I really struggled to reach a standard of competency. I was also back to working standard daytime hours, so my salary was not as exciting as I hoped for.

At home our little family unit was developing nicely. We had a holiday at a Pontins camp near Chichester, and it was so special as our children were developing and showing their characters. That holiday was another sunny week with time in the swimming pool. Deb and I got involved with the adult games, and Andrew managed to excel in a children's competition as well.

There was another of our regular trips to Leafield to see Jim and Jean. We had another visit to the nearby Cotswold Wildlife Park and the children got close to animals, and enjoyed the land train ride around the site with their grandparents.

I have forgotten how it came about, but Deb won a chance for a facial makeover, and a photo shoot. This was in London, so we had a family break to the capital. While Deb was being pampered, I took the children around some of the sites of London.

My major treat for the year was to dance on Flora Day again. I believe that was the last time, and I really wish that my arthritic body could still manage to get involved, but sadly it's not to be.

Back at work, and I kept watching as people changed jobs, and reminded the managers that I was looking for a different role. During the autumn, there was a suggestion of changes with some of the shift rotas in the near future, and I made it clear that I was interested. I had my eyes firmly focussed on the television officer role, and as it was based in the OCA, it was my dream job. This job had always been a long-term goal, and over the years I had been on all the relevant training courses, but sadly, this particular shift post was also popular with other people.

At the same time, a different shift post was becoming available in the East Wing. I was definitely not interested in this, but someone must have thought it was a good option for me, and I was asked to talk to the manager for this area for a chat.

In this situation, a "*chat*" is code for "**job interview**".

I have to be quite honest at this point, and say that I really did not have the technical knowledge, or skills necessary for the job. The shift role would make me responsible for a vital link in the transmission of telephony, television, and digital data coming from, and going to London. The equipment was perhaps less technologically challenging, but its maintenance and repair was totally different from anything I had been involved in so far.

There were also several very experienced and suitable day people in the East Wing who wanted a shift role, and they should have been offered the job, but I was more senior, and the historical Civil Service principles of BT always favoured seniority over suitability.

Quite rightly, the manager of the East Wing fought tooth and nail to stop me getting the job, and I was still hoping to get the television role, but as the end of 1985 approached, the television job was filled by someone else, and I realised my future was going to be in the East Wing.

So, in November 1985, I was back on shift again, and my salary improved dramatically. Over the coming months I would spend weeks and weeks going on different training courses, to cram my head with Microwave Transmission principles, and such things as Channels, Groups, Supergroups, Hypergroups, Coaxial

Systems, and really rather frighteningly, Submarine Cable Systems.

Although Goonhilly was primarily all about Satellite Communications, it was also the site where three submarine cables were powered and maintained...

... and they were a part of the East Wing's responsibility.

At that time, there were three submarine cables that terminated at Goonhilly. They went from the equipment racks in the East Wing to local beaches, and then under the sea. Two of the cables went to Spain, and the other to Portugal.

When I said they were frightening, it was because they had power applied to them from the equipment at Goonhilly, and from the Spanish or Portuguese ends. On rare moments when the cable was broken, usually by fishing trawlers, we had to connect test equipment to the cable, and more importantly, trust that the power had been removed by the engineers in Spain or Portugal.

This didn't happen very often, but I had my share of cable failures while I was on shift, and had to open the equipment doors and get to the cable head. One of the other East Wing shift engineers described the first moment of touching the central conductor of the cable, as creating bodily sensations of sweaty hands, and '**Anal Clenching**'.

... and yes, this was a very good description of how it felt.

Aerial 6

Built in 1985, Aerial 6 became the biggest antenna at Goonhilly.

The aerial was designed by Mitsubishi, but the construction project, and radio equipment was left to the Marconi Company again. The design was already tried and tested with three similar aerials already in service at the Madley Earth Station in Herefordshire.

At ground level the construction had a base building housing all the radio equipment. There was a similarity to Aerial 4 with a circular rail track on its base building roof, supporting the movable platform on which the reflector is built. This platform is square shaped with Bogie wheels at each corner. Two of these Bogies use 5.5 kW motors to enable a full 360° rotation.

Elevation movement uses an 11metre segment of cog attached to the rear of the dish and driven by another 5.5 kW motor. It can drive the antenna for 90° from the horizontal.

The steel backing structure and reflector dish are about 300 tonnes. The dish itself is 32metres in diameter and made of aluminium panels. There is a 2.9 diameter sub-reflector that is supported on a tripod within the main reflector. The radio path uses the same Beam waveguide technology as Aerial 4, although its mirrors and reflectors are very much scaled up.

The children's television programme Blue Peter was invited to be present when the aerial was brought into service. The tour guides adopted it as the Blue Peter Aerial, as well as its Arthurian name of 'Merlin'.

One of the earliest highlight moments of Aerial 6 was its use for the Live Aid Concert transmissions in 1985.

Aerial 6 is magnificent, and stands proudly looking at the Goonhilly site. By the time it was completed, I was working in the East Wing, and as far as I can recall, I never stepped inside it. Later in my career however, I did spend time looking around its sister dishes at Madley.

1986 – A New Beginning

Deb Gets a Job

As 1985 was drawing to a close, there was a significant change at home.

Deb had found herself a job at the newly opened Helston Leisure Centre. Her role was as one of the part-time reception team, but much to her surprise, this required her to become proficient as a life guard for any emergencies in the swimming pool as well.

It seemed only natural that me and the children would go swimming, and that led to us all eventually becoming trained in life saving.

At that time, we had no idea that her job was the beginning of a hobby that all of our family would get involved in. All four of us would learn or improve our swimming, and then get involved in competitive swimming for almost 25 years.

Back on Shift

Although I doubted myself, I was deemed proficient enough to be on shift as the East Wing Technical Officer. This was different to my previous experiences, as when I was on a daytime shift, I was obliged to spend the majority of my time in the East Wing to work alongside the day duty people.

Of course, when things were quiet, I would regularly disappear to the OCA where I felt so much more comfortable.

Being the shift man meant I was ultimately responsible for day-to-day operational issues, and more especially for all aspects of the sub-sea cable systems. Although some of the day people were capable of working on the sub-sea cables, I was the only person with the authority to perform any maintenance. I had been on quite intensive training courses to be capable of ensuring safety, as well as how to react if a cable failed. One of the simpler parts of the role was taking routine measurements at the beginning of a shift to record the status of the power systems, as well as the traffic quality.

But there were a lot of other things to get involved with in this room. This was the interface between the satellite systems, and the terrestrial network carrying the traffic to and from the London exchange buildings.

There was a microwave radio system from Goonhilly to London, which was predominantly used to handle any television channels coming from, or going to the BT Tower (London) where the TV services were handled. Additionally, there were also several cable systems with tens of thousands of telephony channels that passed back and forth with the West Wing. These channels were carried on thousands of cream-coloured Coaxial cables. These cables were routed through patch panels, in case of a need to change to spare circuits. Everywhere I looked in the room, there were rows and rows of racks that were either crammed with these cables, or which housed the equipment to combine or distribute the traffic.

The vast majority of the telephony was traditional analogue when I first began to work here, but digital services were appearing, and would expand over the years. These digital services had less cables to worry about, but significantly greater circuit capacity. While an analogue cable might have a maximum of a few hundred telephony calls on it, the digital services would soon be carrying thousands of circuits. If I made a mistake with an analogue cable (and I often did) I potentially interrupted a few hundred telephone calls, but with the digital circuits, my mistakes were seriously worse.

Being the primary person for operational issues, I would often take a telephone call reporting a problem from an exchange in London, or from a distant exchange in another country. Sadly, my lack of experience would often mean I had to beg for advice or assistance from the day people. One or two of them were quite annoyed at having to do my job, and I could sympathise with them, but they didn't have to spend evenings and nights on their own, when I had no one to turn to for help.

When on an evening or night shift, I would take the routine readings, and then put the alarm system through to the OCA. I spent most of my time there with the other shift people. If my alarm went off, I would walk down the corridor and hope the problem wasn't too serious.

There was one night when we were expecting a TV crew to arrive early in the morning. The plan was to film the action as we received a regular TV news update from America that was to be shown on the BBC Breakfast Show. The intention was to show what was involved in receiving the daily news from America, and I think the scheduled satellite broadcast was to be at 5:00.

Well, no-one turned up, and we simply received the programme from America and sent to London as normal. We were slightly miffed to not hear anything, but accepted that was the way of television.

Then about an hour later than expected, the door alarm rang, and it was the TV crew. They had got mixed up between GMT and British time.

Their visit was not wasted, and they simply filmed us pretending to receive the broadcast. It involved a lovely moment for me. We made the satellite phone ring, and I answered it and supposedly greeted the Andover Earth Station. The rest was just shots of the TV man and the test equipment showing bogus signals.

With all the charade over, the TV crew left before the actual programme went out on the television. We watched to see how it went, and I was over the moon to see my fingers pushing the button on the satellite switchboard, and my words to Andover.

In the OCA I was with a new group of men now, and would soon gel with them. The television duties were looked after by

Alastair, and the West Wing was the responsibility of Pip. They were the people I was closest to, and as Pip lived on the same estate as us, we quickly began to share transport to and from work.

After another Christmas where I spent much of the time away from Deb and the children, I settled down to a new year with many new things happening in my life.

First Aid Instructor Refresher

I continued to go on various training courses, to get me to an acceptable level of skill to work in the East Wing, but there was another important course to attend.

It had been three years since I became a First Aid Instructor, and I had to refresh my instructor skills, and be re-examined. During those three years I had presented two or three courses a year to train new first aiders at Goonhilly, and I was much more confident standing in front of my audiences.

This greatly helped me when I returned to Manor Gardens in London for the instructor course, and I came away after a successful week with even more skills, and was praised by the instructing team.

Our family was growing up

Andrew would soon be six years old, and had graduated from Playgroup, to proper school. This was just at the top of our estate and less than a ten-minute stroll. Lynsey would accompany Deb or me as we took Andrew to the school gate to get her used to the idea of school as well.

Lynsey was now a part of that same Playgroup where Deb was one of the helpers. When my shifts allowed, I took my turn to take and collect Lynsey, and was well known by the Playgroup mums.

It was a bit of a social thing as well with tea and cakes in the different parent houses, or visits to the pub occasionally. One of the best bits of Playgroup was an informal baby-sitting service that worked on a credit basis. If you performed an evening babysitting, you gained a credit to pay one of the other parents to return the service.

Deb Changes Job

Deb was thoroughly enjoying her job at the swimming pool. It was just a few hours a week, and an informal child-minding arrangement with a Playgroup mum meant that Lynsey was looked after by someone she knew, when I was not around.

The job wasn't hard work, and after a little while she expanded her role to look after some of the administration duties as well. Being able to have a regular free swim was also a bonus.

She was enjoying things so much, that when a slightly different role was advertised at the nearby Carn Brea Leisure Centre, Deb went for the challenge. This time it was far more administration than just being a receptionist, and also more hours.

Brand New Car

Things were becoming more comfortable on the money front.

We decided that it was time to have a new car. Actually, it was **ME** who decided **WE** needed a new car. I was fed up with dodgy rust buckets, so I visited a dealer where the salesman was the son of someone I worked with. Initially I was looking at nearly new cars, but when he sat me in a shiny new Ford Fiesta, and tempted me with a good trade in deal, I was hooked.

So late in 1986 we finally beat the sickness of second-hand cars, and I drove away with a delightful blue/grey Ford Fiesta. It smelt so wonderful with pristine paintwork, comfortable interior, and trustworthy reliability. This was a feeling I remembered from 1972 when I bought my new mini. There was a smile on my face instead of a concern as I leapt into our car.

Life was changing however, as we'd had a second car for some time. Deb was now driving, back and forth to her new job, and with my regular trips to training courses, she needed transport.

That second car was not so new and reliable, so I often drove that one, and left Deb to enjoy our new car.

1987 - What a very full year

Snowed in at Goonhilly

Cornwall doesn't normally have serious snow fall, and it rarely stays around for long, but on the morning of 12th January 1987, I woke up to some serious white stuff.

It was a day when I was about to begin running a First Aid course at Goonhilly, and I knew I had to get to work. The normally 20-minute drive was difficult as I drove slowly along snow covered roads, and kept my distance from the cars in front. I was frightened on the bendy down-hill sections, knowing I had to keep some speed for the up-hill sections to follow.

I eventually crunched and slid my way into the car park, and trudged through several centimetres of snow into the building, long before I was needed to be there.

It was still snowing, and the freezing easterly wind was whipping up the snow and it stung my eyes, and quickly chilled my fingers.

I was very early, and my first priority was a hot drink in the OCA. The night shift crew were still working, and a small number of the day shift who had managed to get in, were chatting to them. There were a number of phone calls from other members of the expected day shift to say they couldn't get in, and from day people who were also struggling. The message from the managers was to not attempt to get in until the roads had been cleared. One or two of the night shift who had been relieved, were going to go home, but others decided to stay at Goonhilly, in the hopes that the weather would improve, before attempting any journey.

My first aid course was cancelled, but there was no way I was attempting to go home, and the snow was continuing to fall, and in fact it was getting worse.

The decision was soon made to shut the gates to the station, and we were officially snowed in. We were given access to the station kitchen, allowing us to raid the fridge and freezers to feed ourselves. We had no idea of how long the situation would continue, but hot food was imperative, as it really was very cold.

At one point during the day, there were discussions about organising a rescue mission from nearby Culdrose, to use a helicopter to get the previous shift people home. I think the idea sounded good, but no one seemed interested. To be honest I was dreading the possibility of a helicopter rescue, so very happy with the idea being ignored.

Most of us assumed the roads would soon be clear, as snow never lasts long in Cornwall.

Well, how wrong we were. The snow continued to fall, and the temperature never got above freezing all day.

There was one rather weird moment, when there was a telephone call from the local BBC news who had driven in a 4 x 4 Jeep to Goonhilly, and were asking if they could come in to film the scene. It seemed so strange that we had been officially classed as snowed in, but a TV crew had managed to get through to us.

Anyway, it was quite special, and Deb always said she knew where I was, as I turned up on the 6:30 Spotlight TV news.

During the afternoon there were new thoughts about getting people home, and one of the drivers (I think it was Les) volunteered to have a go at getting a couple of people back to Helston. The idea was not seen as being very sensible, but off he went. As well as the two men from Helston, my shift buddy Pip went along as well rather than leaving the driver on his own for the return journey.

Well, they did get to Helston, and the two guys were dropped off close enough to walk home.

The return journey to Goonhilly was not so successful. The snow was still falling, and the wind was creating drifts on the exposed road running past Culdrose. Eventually Les got completely stuck, and along with Pip they began to walk.

I spoke to Les on many occasions since then, and he always said that Pip saved his life that day. Les was getting colder and colder, and reached a point where he just wanted to lie down and go to sleep. Pip shouted at him to carry on, and after much swearing and encouragement, they reached the main gate at Culdrose and were brought inside to warm up.

They were safely returned to us at Goonhilly in a Navy 4 x 4 Jeep.

The evening finally saw the end of the falling snow, but it was perishingly cold. It was so bad that the heating failed in some parts of the station. I remember going outside sometime after midnight and was amazed by the beauty of the smooth clean snow, and drifts hiding the familiar features of Goonhilly. I didn't stay out there too long, and the cold was just incredible.

We were all there for another day and night, before the temperature began to rise and thaw the white world around us. The roads were cleared, and the management agreed to get us all home and begin a normal shift rota once more.

It had been another example of the amazing experiences I had while working at Goonhilly. Without the camaraderie of the guys, it would have been a nightmare, but we all shared the work that was necessary, and would look back and laugh at the situation as the years went by.

Watching Live Television

One of the thrills that I enjoyed during my time at Goonhilly, was the chance to see news broadcasts from all over the world being received, before anyone else in the country had seen them.

At the end of January 1987, one of those news items should have just been a routine few minutes of video, but it turned out to be a horrendous story.

NASA had spent quite a while launching their Space Shuttles, and while still an amazing feat of engineering, it was becoming routine *'same old, same old'* news. Early afternoon on the 28th January, I was hiding away in the OCA, and a television news item was being received showing the launch of the Challenger Shuttle.

The initial launch was just as it should have been, and the cameras were following the rocket and vapour trail as it blasted up into the sky.

Then without warning, the rocket and shuttle exploded.

We had been chatting noisily amongst ourselves without paying much attention to the television pictures, but now it went silent. We heard the voice of the American reporter trying to describe the scene, and the NASA commentary attempting to make contact with the Shuttle crew. It was all in vain. They had been vapourised as the bomb they were riding on exploded into a million pieces.

For a few moments, our little gang at Goonhilly, the engineers in the BT Tower, and the television company, were the only ones in Britain to know what had happened.

We regularly saw quite dramatic video pictures of wars, earthquakes, floods, and famine from all over the world, and quite often the footage that eventually shown on the domestic television news had been sanitised. We were desensitised to much of the horrors we witnessed, but the Challenger disaster was watched live, and has stayed in my mind.

A regular experience of receiving International TV News was getting to recognise the reporters. One of the regular reporters (who I will not name) was a lady that I think worked for the BBC. If there was an earth quake, or a terrorist bomb somewhere in the world, she would often appear within hours of the incident. We often joked when we saw her in front of the camera, that the situation must be serious for her to turn up.

Just before one broadcast began, we saw the reporter preparing herself. It might have been simply playing to the camera, but she was sitting watching a monitor as she stared into the camera. This straight-faced professional BBC reporter appeared to be using the camera and monitor to squeeze spots on her face. I really don't know if she knew this was being shown live on the satellite.

Going on Strike

I don't suppose anyone begins a job expecting to be asked to go on strike. I certainly didn't, and although a member of the union that supported us, it was a shock when it became apparent that we might be called upon to go on strike.

It was nearing the end of February, and rumours suggested that BT were trying to impose some changes to working practices following a pay rise agreement. The union (as they do) rebelled against the changes, and long drawn-out discussions between the union and the management began.

Eventually BT suspended some workers at the BT Tower in London for refusing to abide by the new practices. That was the catalyst the union were waiting for, and within a couple of days, all of the engineers in BT were told to down tools and go on strike.

My personal view was that the strike was justified, but along with many other less militant engineers, we believed the union were spoiling for a fight, and the guys in London simply took the bait.

The problem with striking is that you have no idea of the eventual outcome. It might only last a couple of days, or it might go on for weeks or months. Well, our strike was one that didn't have an obvious solution, so we had regular meetings, and most of us spent time standing outside of the gates at Goonhilly to attempt to change the mind of the union members that refused to strike. The management of BT continued to work as normal, and also used their skills to maintain as good a standard of service as they could. So we spoke to our management colleagues, who were also our friends, but they were not a part of the strike, and continued to cover our roles.

After four long weeks away from work, I was struggling with the concept of striking that was against all the things I had been brought up with. I had always been told that *'an honest day's work for an honest day's pay', was* what I should do, and striking made me feel so uncomfortable.

There was also a serious dent made to our savings.

At the end of those four weeks, I decided it was time to go back, and defy the union's orders. I spoke to my union secretary to say what I was about to do, and although he was unhappy with my decision, he understood and accepted it.

When I returned on the Monday morning, I had to sign a form saying I would perform my duties as normal, and with a heavy heart I scribbled my signature on the paper.

As it happened, the strike ended almost immediately, and life returned to near normal. There was a bit of an atmosphere between the strikers, and those non-union guys who had continued to work normally throughout the strike. Some of them openly laughed at us for losing our pay, while achieving nothing, and it was many months before the air cleared.

The strike left a very sour taste in my mouth, and I am quite sure I inwardly decided never to go on strike again.

A Better Moment
Deb was so involved with the social side of my work, and had almost become an unofficial member of Goonhilly. This led to a very special bit of fun during the summer. Someone had seen an advert for a quiz league, and we decided that it would be a

good laugh to enter a team. As usual, it was easy to find a few people to take part occasionally, but committing to turning out once a week was not so simple. Hence Deb volunteered to be a part of our team of four, and we turned up each week at a popular pub in Mullion called the Mount's Bay Hotel.

There were perhaps eight teams in total with fishermen, football teams, various pub teams and ourselves.

As well as Deb and myself, there was Dave Goss (controller at Goonhilly) and Roy Richards who worked in the West Wing. It quickly became apparent that we were rather good, although I was probably the weak link. For the first time I was realising that Deb was someone who could amass and recall facts and trivia at ease.

It was becoming quite serious, and we even had sweatshirts with a picture of Goonhilly 1 on them as we competed each week. Then on the last week of the summer competition, we were crowned champions and awarded little plaques plus a trophy.

On that final evening a photographer from the Helston Packet Newspaper took our pictures, and we had a lovely write up in the paper plus a picture of the team in our sweatshirts.

As a little post-script, the next year we entered a team again, and were once again very successful, but eventually were runners up in the final to a team from the Porthleven Cricket Club. We weren't upset, as the mind challenging evenings were always a very good excuse for alcohol, with plenty of laughs.

Holidays in 1987

We had several holidays away this year. Once again they were with Pontins, and as well as a week in Devon, we travelled a little further to a camp called South Downs on the south coast. Andrew and Lynsey were old enough to make the most of the clubs by now, and this left Deb and I more time to relax.

As a family we explored the local area around the Holiday Camps, and on one day we had a morning in Portsmouth that included a visit to the Mary Rose museum. The flagship of Henry VIII had only recently been recovered from the bottom of the sea, and was on display in this purpose-built museum. It was fascinating to see the constant spray of water over the timbers to preserve them. Deb and I could understand the magnitude of what we were seeing, but I am not so sure it meant too much to our children.

Fortunately, there were always wildlife parks and animals to touch, and playgrounds to exhaust them.

We also enjoyed the various competitions at the holiday camp, and having given up on the knobbly knees challenge, I leapt at the chance to play table tennis. This was even better when I had a game with Chester Barnes (ex English Champion). When I say 'game', I actually mean humiliation, but I enjoyed the experience. If I remember correctly, I believe Andrew scored more points when he played Chester than I did.

Although not a holiday, we also travelled to Romford for the wedding of one of Deb's cousins. Our adventures with the children were getting further away from home, and proving that we could spread our wings a little further.

There was also one weekend when Deb and I had a trip away without the children. This was linked to my First Aid duties at Goonhilly. I enjoyed having practical training exercises with people, and had managed to put together a group of young lads willing to make up a competitive team for a First Aid competition.

It was held at Brean Sands (Pontins) in Somerset and involved in each member of the team having an individual incident to show off their skills, and then a final team exercise. We had no idea of what the incidents would be, and it was very professional with members of the Casualty Union made up amazingly to appear injured.

Anyway, we were approaching this as a bit of a laugh. Most of the teams had been doing this for several years, and were far more experienced in First Aid, and these competitive events. On the Friday evening we had our meal together with a social event to follow. Yes, there was a lot of alcohol consumed, and I remember one stupid moment, when one of the lads bought a small sponge toy representing a crocodile.

Pontins had a crocodile club for the children, and my *not so young* Goonhilly children, thought it would be fun to buy one.

Well, with the appearance of this bendy sponge crocodile, it wasn't long before three of them were kneeling on the floor around the 30cm long crocodile, giving it CPR. The spectacle was being watched by many of the surrounding tables, and that was when the Goonhilly First Aid Team became known as being totally mad, but a really good laugh.

The next day in the competition, we also became known as not very good at First Aid in these situations. We came last, but we were still known as being a really good laugh.

Helston St John Ambulance
Continuing with the First Aid theme, I finally became a member of the Helston St John Brigade. I now had a chance to use my Instructor skills to give training to the men and women volunteers, and I eventually began to run public First Aid courses.

At the same time my own First Aid skills were improving, and I added the ability to drive the ambulance, and attend local events in case of accidents.

The Helston division had a good membership of men and women, plus a large number of children who were our cadets. Our headquarters was in Wendron Street and still exists, but now as a private residential dwelling. At least the St John's Cross remains on the frontage as a reminder of its past.

Behind the garage area, our ambulance station had a large room, where we met, and where training sessions, and courses were run. There was a kitchen behind it for the obligatory cups of tea while we chatted at the end of our weekly meetings. Above the garage section there was another room that once had a snooker table for those who were interested, but the underused table was eventually sold off, and the room became an overflow training room.

Although there had been two ambulances in the past, during my time there, we just had one rather aging vehicle. It was difficult to consider changing the ambulance because the garage had a low ceiling, and it wouldn't allow a full-size vehicle. It was quite a challenge for me to drive the ambulance, but only because of getting it back into the garage. It had to be reversed in, and the street is not very wide. Over the months I think I became more proficient, but I have to admit, reversing any vehicle is not my favourite part of driving.

Over the summer I spent several weekends, when I wasn't working, watching motor sports, or horse shows, and attending fetes to offer assistance for minor cuts, bruises, and wasp stings. I seemed to be a lucky talisman, as throughout my time with the brigade, there was only one single event where we had to get a patient to hospital.

This was when we were covering some sort of event at Mullion Cove. We were asked to look after a lady who had been bitten by an adder, and we instantly decided we had to get her to hospital. She was brought to the ambulance, and her wound was washed and dressed, but then when the time came to set off for Truro, we discovered we had a flat battery.

Total humiliation!

We had to ring for an ambulance from the County, while we awaited the arrival of the RAC to get us out of trouble.

The flat battery was just another of the faults and niggles that we were experiencing with the ambulance. It was the moment when I began to think we should be looking for a new vehicle, if we were going to be able to look after the safety of the people who donated the money for us to exist.

Moving House Again

I thoroughly loved our little semi-detached house in West View. We had converted a rocky hillside into a terraced garden, with lawns, and areas for fruit and vegetables. Inside we replaced the open fire with a far easier and cleaner gas fire, to back up the electric night storage radiators. This meant using a local man (Gary the Gas Man) to run pipework to gas cylinders outside. There was no mains gas available at that time.

The house had been totally decorated, and was comfortable, but with Lynsey growing fast, the third bedroom was not big enough for her.

Deb and I began to search estate agent adverts, and drove around looking at the outsides of houses for sale. We'd checked with our building society about the level of mortgage we could afford, and the time came to put our house up for sale.

Our search for a new home centred on Helston and Porthleven, and after several frustrating weeks, we found one that looked perfect, less than 100metres away at the top of the estate we were already living in. Things came together, as we also had an offer made on our old house, and the move was organised.

The new house was a chalet bungalow with two main bedrooms and a smaller third one in an extension. More importantly, there was a huge lounge, and an equally large kitchen dining room. Our plan was to divide the kitchen diner into two, and make one side a bedroom for Lynsey. This would be perfect for us.

That house in Tregunna Close, had been owned by a coalman, and they used an AGA stove for heating and hot water, as well as for cooking. The coalman obviously made the most of his product, and the house stank of sooty smoke, because the stove was not totally sealed.

So, almost as soon as we moved in, we organised Gary the Gas to instal gas from cylinders outside, with a gas stove with a back boiler to replace the AGA. It allowed us a few weeks to use the AGA and it was an amazing stove, but it was really not in a good condition, and eventually it was stripped down and given away to someone for free.

Having decided to use one end of the lounge as a dining room, I built a stud wall across the kitchen. This created a third bedroom from what was the original dining area. It wasn't a major task, and made easier by asking Chris Warner (still a good mate at that time) to plaster the new wall.

The kitchen became my first plumbing project, as it needed new units. I discovered I rather enjoyed plumbing, although I perhaps was a little over cautious with my handiwork, that probably meant I spent too much on expensive things a proper plumber would have done quicker and cheaper.

The alterations didn't take too long, and then I began the biggest challenge of putting in central heating. This was something that tested my new plumbing skills, and there were a few issues due to my naivety about pumps, header tanks, expansion tanks and soldering in tricky places. After several weeks of minor leaks, major leaks, charred wooden beams, clunking pipework, and much swearing, the heating system was working.

Now we could turn our attention to the garden.

Porthleven Town Council
Sandwiched between a new job, new car, and a new home, I was also about to take on a new role.

At Goonhilly I was regularly getting into discussions with Renfrew Bray. Many of these chats were about gossip, but he was also making me think about local politics. Renfrew had been on the Porthleven Town Council for many years, but was now stepping down, and he was attempting to get me interested in standing for the council.

After many discussions with him, and with Deb, I agreed to give it a go, but wasn't confident of getting through the election. I have a suspicion that Renfrew had probably been involved in some quiet canvassing for me, but I wasn't really very well known around Porthleven.

Anyway, the election day was in May and I dressed tidily, and spent several hours during the day standing outside of the election polling station. It was a very alien situation for me as I smiled and welcomed total strangers before they went inside to cast their votes. I was obviously turning some heads, and there was quite an amusing moment that cheered me up. As I said, I dressed tidily, and wore a jacket and tie. My wardrobe didn't have many ties, and I selected a blue one.

I was standing in the elections as an independent person, but one woman came out and quietly whispered in my ear.

Pointing to my tie, she said:

"I know you say you are an independent candidate, but I can see who you are really representing, and that's why I voted for you".

Once out of sight, I quietly had a giggle to myself. She really had no idea of my true politics, and I really was intending to be independent, but my personal views were actually a long way to the left of the Tory party.

Late in the evening, the polling station closed, and there were just the officials, counters, and candidates locked inside. Two of the candidates would fail to get enough votes, and I was far from confident of being successful.

The little piles of ballot slips were quite similar for each candidate, and when the announcement was made, I was over the moon to discover I had been elected to the Porthleven Town Council.

It wasn't a very taxing role, but I was expected to attend council meetings once a month, as well as ad-hoc meetings when there was something urgent to discuss. Initially as a new member, I kept reasonably quiet at the meetings, and although getting involved by voicing my opinions, much of the serious activity was between the more established councillors.

That would change as the months progressed.

One Last 1987 Moment
There was one other major moment in 1987.

It was 25 years since that very first satellite broadcast in 1962.

... and of course, there was a special celebration.

The main event was a gathering with VIPs from BT, television companies, and newspaper journalists. Goonhilly had been spruced up, and freshly painted walls, polished woodwork, and spotless carpets welcomed our guests.

Although I was supposed to be on duty in the East Wing, I spent a lot of the day watching the activity that was predominantly going on in the OCA.

Goonhilly had been allowing visitors to look around the site for some time, but they were never allowed to physically walk around the OCA. To give them a peek at what happened in the nerve centre, there was a gallery accessible from the main foyer, with windows that allowed visitors to watch the goings on in the OCA.

To be honest, the rota staff were never overly keen on the visitors, as we never knew when the next bus load of tourists would quietly enter the gallery to watch us. So, a pressure switch had been installed under the gallery carpet to ring a buzzer when anyone entered. As the months went by, we learnt to ignore the visitors, but that buzzer was very valuable to alert us when we were up to mischief.

One of the biggest mischief makers was Pip Greenaway. One Sunday morning, he brought in a huge teddy bear, and before the visitors began to arrive, he set up his prank for the day. The teddy bear was sat in the controller's chair and turned away from the gallery. Then strings were attached to the swivel chair and taken to another part of the room that could not be seen by any visitors.

With his equipment ready, and the first visitors expected, we all hid away and waited for the gallery to fill. Then Pip carefully pulled his strings to turn the controller's chair around to expose the teddy bear.

I'm quite sure some of the adults were amused by the scene, but certainly the children thought it was hilarious.

Anyway, back to the anniversary celebrations. I was not allowed in the OCA which had been restricted to operational people (plus VIPs) to stop it getting overcrowded. So, I was standing in the gallery watching, and my shift buddy Pip was standing with me. Someone else entered the gallery, and we turned to see Raymond Baxter coming in to see what was going on as well.

This was a moment I have treasured. This giant of a man stood and chatted to us. He talked about that first night in 1962, and marvelled at how much had changed. He was so down to earth and approachable, and believe me, some of the journalists we had witnessed over the years were far from approachable. The three of us talked for perhaps five minutes before he excused himself to go back to the cameras, and Pip and I were left smiling at that magical moment.

The identical thought occurred to both of us. How on earth did this towering man ever squeeze himself into the cockpit of a Spitfire during the Battle of Britain?

The day passed smoothly, and by the evening most of the visiting dignitaries had left, and it was time for a social event for the staff and wives. It was a very special moment with buses to allow us to enjoy ourselves, and lots of free alcohol, food, and music. There was even a firework display to round off the evening.

It was a wonderful day, and I was so proud of being one small part of the story.

A Bit More History

As a way of finishing my round up of 1987, perhaps this is a perfect moment to bring you up to date on Goonhilly, and satellite communications after its first 25 years.

Satellite Communications was probably approaching its greatest period. There were satellite stations all over the world in a network that was operating with multiple satellites over the three major oceans. It was no longer possible to service the demands with a single satellite per ocean, and of course that meant the need for multiple antennas to be able to operate with them.

Goonhilly now had four 30 metre diameter dishes, numbers 1,2,3 and 6. Alongside these giants there were numerous smaller dishes, with antenna number 4 and 5 plus others with specific services, and for experimental use.

At Goonhilly, the majority of the traffic carried was for the Atlantic region, the Indian Ocean services were predominantly being operated via the new station in Herefordshire called Madley.

Even these two sites were not enough. In the Docklands area of London, a much smaller site was constructed which only had small dishes. It was known as London Teleport at the time, and really concentrated on digital services, plus television. It would eventually become one of the sites used by Sky Television for domestic viewers.

The use of smaller dishes was becoming the way forward. Satellites became bigger with greater traffic capacity, made possible with increased power from more efficient solar cell technology. But more importantly the equipment in space and on the ground, was also improving by mind boggling leaps forward.

Of course, one of the other major drivers for satellite communications, was the use of digital services which could operate with much lower transmission powers from the satellite, and hence requiring smaller dishes on earth.

Sadly, there were already rumours and whispers that Britain perhaps had too much satellite capacity with the two large stations and the smaller London Teleport. Although there seemed to be no immediate threat of change, the longer term plan was already looking at the possibility of closing either Goonhilly or Madley.

Our life at Goonhilly was as good as it had ever been. As well as a friendly atmosphere at work, we also had an amazing range of social opportunities. There was the bar with its darts board and pool table that was used regularly with social functions and evening opening times. Elsewhere we had snooker and table tennis in a wooden cabin and the station had teams for both in the local leagues.

As a more active alternative there was a sport's field that had a good-sized football pitch, plus room for a cricket pitch where the actual wicket area was separate from the football pitch. There was a large pavilion for getting changed and to house the cricket equipment. We had a practice net which was used throughout the summer at lunchtimes to build up batting and bowling skills.

The football team was also in a league and was of a good standard. I had tried to carry on playing football, but I was too slow to avoid getting hurt in tackles, so I turned my attention to cricket. We had matches most summer weeks on a Thursday evening, and we were rather good, and rarely beaten. As with football, I was not the best of players, but I could be relied upon to make a few runs as one of the last batsmen, and I somehow managed to confuse many of the opposing batsmen with slow but effective bowling. Deb would regularly come along to home matches to watch, and to enjoy a drink in the bar afterwards.

Not far away from Goonhilly at Porthcurno, there was a training centre for Cable and Wireless engineers from all over the world. They would come to Goonhilly for a day as a part of their training to see our busy earth station, and one day there was a group of West Indian engineers who took an interest in our lunchtime practice session.

They were invited to join us, and eventually one was asked if he fancied a game that evening.

He returned and was thrilled to have a game. Unfortunately, we had to tell him to calm down his bowling, as he turned out to be just a little too fast for our less than smooth wicket. We had a few complaints from the opposition that night about having a guest player.

We won again of course.

Goonhilly had managed to continue to operate in a rapidly growing business environment as if we were a family. There was the obvious management and engineer divide, but it didn't stop us chatting together, laughing with each other, and socialising at the bar.

I still believed I had found the most amazing job, and was enjoying it. I just wished I could have a role away from the East Wing where I was struggling with the technology.

Life Goes on in 1988

This was a year that I have very few memories of what I was doing at work. I know I spent a lot of time on training courses that were attempting to make me competent for the equipment I was responsible for, but I was not feeling any more confident.

For the first time, since those early days of being shown around Goonhilly, I felt out of my depth, and was almost frightened by the job I was doing. I couldn't do my duty to the standards I set myself, and life at work was not quite so enjoyable.

My only relief was that once the day people had gone home, I could join my buddies in the OCA, and between the occasional alarms that took me back to the East Wing, I was happy.

... and of course, there were my First Aid commitments.

First Aid

Because I was in charge of first aid at Goonhilly, I was given a small amount of official time to look after the emergency boxes, and stocking supplies of plasters. We were very fortunate to have quite safety conscious people, and we rarely used anything other than plasters when there had been a minor accident.

I also ensured the site first aiders were up to date with their qualifications, and then scheduled courses when they were due. Sometimes we offered places on courses to other BT people to fill the course numbers, and I was also occasionally asked to run courses elsewhere in the Country.

Away from Goonhilly I became more and more involved with the Helston St John. I kept everyone as well trained as I could, and delivered courses to the public. This was very rewarding to know that perhaps one day, one of these people might save a life.

But there was also a moment on one of these events where I really doubted if I was doing the right thing.

It was a typical course with a mix of men and women of various ages. As usual some struggled with the practical elements but soon they grasped the principles of CPR, and immobilising arms and legs with triangular bandages.

One evening, as I neared the end of the course, it was time to discuss Carbon Monoxide poisoning. The subject also raised the topic of people taking their own lives using a car's exhaust, but these discussions were quite normal, and I thought no more about it as I said goodnight to the class.

The next week, one man was missing. I had no idea of why he wasn't there, but didn't panic as people often missed the odd lesson. It was only a few days later that I saw a local newspaper story of a man committing suicide. It was my missing person, and he had taken his own life by Carbon Monoxide poisoning.

I felt absolutely awful, and responsible. I spent a long time questioning if I was doing the correct thing. After talking to a lot of people, I eventually realised that I could never have foreseen what was on his mind. I did continue to present First Aid courses, but took the greatest of care when dealing with that subject from then on.

The Helston St John was quite a large Brigade, with men, women and cadets. We attended a lot of public events to provide First Aid cover, but the biggest annual event was Flora Day. St John ambulances and their crews came from several towns for the day, and it was very special to host so many volunteers.

A control centre was set up at our ambulance hall to coordinate activities, as well as being a place for a rest period for the crews.

There were always trips and slips to deal with, and occasional serious accidents that needed to go to hospital. The roads were always packed with thousands of people, and squeezing an ambulance through the crowds was often a nightmare. The County ambulance teams could not be tied up in Helston because of the thousands of visitors, so the St John ambulances were used to transport a patient to a point near the edge of the town where the county ambulance service could take over.

Anyway, when I was on duty, I kept up my record of never being required to treat a serious incident. I was certainly a bit of a lucky charm to the public near to me, but other crews were rarely as quiet.

At the end of the year, I also had a week in London for the re-exam of my Instructor's qualification. I was becoming an old hand at this by now, and I was no longer frightened of being a presenter. I continued to show an eagerness to succeed, and was becoming quite respected by the team responsible for these courses. I believe the lady who led the training was called Jackie Burrows, and her assistant was Bill Harrup. I had great respect for Jackie, but I could still be a bit of a joker.

One of Jackie's pet topics was the use of overhead projection slides. They made up a high percentage of the training material, and so we had to be seen to follow the guidelines of using them. One thing she insisted on was to set up and check the projector before we began each training session. Its size on the screen, and focussing had to be perfect, but once we had completed setting it up, we were not supposed to ever look at the screen which was behind us. Our attention had to always be to the delegates in front of us.

She was a stickler for this, and always *'tutted'* at us if we looked around at the screen during a presentation. One day during one of her own presentations, she had to leave the room to take a phone call. My mischievous mind couldn't resist the temptation, and I slightly moved the overhead projector, so ensuring the display would be out of focus. On her return, Jackie immediately switched on the projector and continued from where she had left off.

The display was out of focus, and none of us could see what she was trying to show us. The class remained amazingly quiet, although obvious grins were appearing. After perhaps five minutes, I couldn't stand it any longer. I stopped her politely, and apologised that I had de-focussed her display. The class then erupted in laughter. I was publicly told off, but a twinkle in her eye suggested she had also seen the funny side ... well just about.

I passed my assessment, and Jackie suggested that I might soon be ready to move to the next level, of training and assessing new trainers. I was also on first name terms with the company doctor (Dr Patterson), who often examined my courses.

First Aid was becoming quite a serious part of my life.

Swimming
Meanwhile, Deb was working hard at Carn Brea, and we were all getting involved with swimming at the Helston Pool. There was no competitive swimming, but there were lessons for Andrew and Lynsey to learn the basics of swimming, and also the more fun side of survival techniques and lifesaving.

I also took on the challenge and learnt to swim. Until that moment, my time in the water was more about floundering to the poolside, rather than showing any finesse of front crawl or breast-stroke. Like many Cornish people, I was brought up to have fun in the sea, and avoid drowning. There was rarely any need to swim fast for more than a few seconds between waves, and that avoided the need to do more than hold your breath.

Now I was slowly building up stamina, and moving reasonably smoothly from end to end of the pool. I was never going to be any good at lifesaving, although I did reach a standard where I received a bronze medal, and took the odd spell in the life guard chair watching the lessons. To be honest, I was never happy in the chair, as even at just over a metre above the ground, my fear of heights was kicking in.

Deb and the children were meanwhile becoming very proficient, and Deb even took the challenge to become open water trained. She put the training into practice during the summer months, and lifeguarded on the beach at Porthleven.

Holidays
As well as the usual trip to Oxfordshire to see Jim and Jean, 1988 saw us going on a holiday to the Isle of Wight, and the 'Little Canada' holiday camp. Andrew and Lynsey were at a more than usual level of excitement. They knew we would be going on a ferry as a part of getting to the holiday destination, and they saw it as going abroad. The ferry lived up to expectations, and the children smiled and laughed as we set off across the short stretch of water to the island.

It wasn't long before we were entering the holiday camp, and being shown to our delightful log cabin.

The holiday was tremendous. The weather was good, the campsite perfect, and we all enjoyed our time on the Isle of Wight. There were loads of places to visit and keep children amused, and the island also had more grown-up places for the adults.

We went back to the island several times over the next few years, and I don't remember a bad experience.

Deb took Andrew on a special trip for his birthday. She took him to Legoland in Denmark. Their journey began with a night sleeper from Penzance, and then a plane to Denmark. I stayed at home and looked after Lynsey. Deb and Andrew had a wonderful few days, while I was more than happy to stay at home and look after Lynsey to avoid going on a plane.

Life in Tregunna Close
Our house in Tregunna Close quickly became a lovely home, and the larger, and flat, back garden allowed far more space for the children to play in. Deb and I did what we could to put our stamp on the garden with flowers and bushes. There was a

swing for the children (and their friends) to play on, and soon a large Wendy House was bought as well. This brought a bit of unexpected amusement one day.

We tended to leave the Wendy House overnight in the garden, but one night we missed the weather forecast that warned of another storm. We were quite used to the wind and rain lashing on our bedroom window, and didn't consider what might have been going on in the garden.

Half way through the following morning, there was a knock on the front door. A neighbour from several houses away asked if we had lost a large Wendy House. They found one in their garden and thought it might have come from our direction. After much hilarity I went around to the neighbour's house and retrieved our brightly coloured plastic house, and thanked the strangers for being so thoughtful.

Amazingly, the Wendy House was undamaged after its adventure, but was destined to be brought indoors at night from then on.

It wasn't long before our cat Sandy was joined by a pair of rabbits to share our lives. This proved disappointing, as they didn't seem to enjoy my company. Their overnight accommodation was in a hutch that stood in a covered area outside of the back door, and I constructed a portable wood and wire pen for them to run around in the garden. The children enjoyed their new furry friends, but they were proving to be rebels, and insisted on trying to dig their way out of their pen as soon as our backs were turned. When brought in (each night) I was responsible for feeding them, but whenever I put my hands inside their hutch, they would attack me by kicking and biting.

After rounding the pair up after numerous escapes from their garden cage, and their less than friendly attitude towards me, the pair of rabbits were given their marching orders. They were given to a nearby workmate called Shaun Bew who had children of a similar age to us, and the rabbits continued their pampered life. Their rebellious streak also stopped, so it really must have been all my fault.

I also set about fulfilling one of my ambitions, and dug a big hole in the front garden to create a small fish pond. We had a little tank indoors with a few goldfish, but it was time for a bigger home. The pond at least solved a problem we had with one of the fish. He (or she) was a white fish, and seemed to adore attempting to eat the small pebbles in the tank. The pebbles were always too big to be swallowed, and also too big to be spat out again. I had to perform a number of first aid rescues by gently capturing the stupid fish, and prizing the pebbles out of its mouth.

Whatever he (or she) did in the pond was out of sight, but I never noticed any similar emergencies.

Both of the children were going to the proper school in this year. The walk to and from the school was less than five minutes from our new home, and many of their friends lived on the estate, or nearby as well. We regularly had friends coming to play in the garden, or in the children's bedrooms. Many had moved with Andrew and Lynsey from playgroup, so we maintained a friendship with parents as well. Our children were happy in school, and while Lynsey was establishing herself with her peers, Andrew was showing himself to be a bit special with his knowledge and ability in mathematics. The headmaster expressed his excitement about Andrew, and the term '*Gifted Child*' was being used, but he was also down to earth, and enjoyed playing with his friends.

New Car Time Again

Later in the year, I decided to change the car again. I was making the most of having spare money, and set off to the garages. I continued with looking at a Ford, but this time it was at Flora Motors near the Park in Helston. The owner of the garage was one of the gang that I spent time with during my teenage years, so once again I hoped for a good deal.

I went up in size this time, and bought a shiny new Ford Escort. It had that brand new smell again, and the extra size gave us all a bit more space.

Less than a fortnight later, Deb set off for work while I was looking after the children. This was quite a normal situation, but about 45 minutes later, Deb rushed in through the front door in tears.

She had been in an accident, and all she could say between the tears was, "**I've written off the car**". Luckily, everyone involved in the accident were unharmed, but our brand-new car was no more.

It took several days for Deb to relax.

I went to the garage where we had bought the car, and where the sad wreck was now being stored. It was confirmed as a *'write off'*, and I began the arduous task of replacing it. This wasn't straight forward, as although it was insured, we didn't have the special cover to protect a brand-new car against major accidents in the first few days. The insurance company would only give the current value of the car back, rather than replacing it with another new vehicle. Even after just a few days, it had already devalued considerably.

I ended up having to choose a slightly lower specification of car, and pay more.

OK, it was an annoying moment, but we eventually had a new car again, and Deb survived quite a serious accident without being injured.

1989 - Community Activities

Town Council

During my monthly Porthleven Council meetings in the Old Institute building, I was becoming more vocal as I understood the way things worked. In 1989 I no longer sat back and listened, I was chipping in with comments and questioning other peoples' views.

To be honest it was hardly very complicated, as our roles as Parish councillors didn't have a lot of responsibility. We had a duty to respond to Street Lighting issues, ensure the graveyard was kept tidy, and make initial responses to complaints from the residents. But the main function that took up most of our meetings, was to receive planning permission requests, and offer first comments to the main council planning group.

We couldn't actually pass or reject a planning request, but we could offer reasons to recommend one, or more commonly, to reject them. Most planning requests were rejected because the village sewerage system was overloaded, and we were trying to pressurise South West Water to implement a new system.

So, if a request involved any possible sewage or waste water increase, we would object seriously, giving the reason as being the impact on the current sewerage system. For most planning requests, we only had to discuss them briefly before politely passing on our objections. However, as time went by, there were more and more objections, and resubmissions of planning requests, to which we repeatedly said *"No Thank-you"*.

It was sometimes embarrassing, and our very firm stance even became farcical at times. I remember one application for a small extension to allow a second bathroom. There was no increase in living space or number of bedrooms, it was just to make life a little easier.

The plan was instantly rejected.

I felt uncomfortable and asked how this could put any extra load on the sewage system? There was no increase in resident numbers, so no increase in waste produced. This brought a flurry of views for and against the proposal, but to no avail.

The plan remained rejected.

I think this might have been one of the first times the reporter from the local newspaper actually mentioned my name, but soon I became the subject of a headline.

At that time, the village had a problem with stray dogs wandering everywhere, and regularly *'depositing what they deposit best'*. There was a serious dog waste issue, and some of the worst examples were on the unlit footpaths where their *'offerings'* couldn't be seen at night. Sadly, the reason for many of these stray dogs, was that working people would often simply turn their dogs out when they went to work, and left them to wander at will.

The discussions turned to the added problem that our wandering dogs also spent time on the beach. Some of the more bad-tempered animals upset walkers, and many dogs did their business in the sand, leaving hidden treasures for people to stand on.

I expressed my views that there should perhaps be dog wardens to capture stray dogs. The response was to question what could be done with these captured dogs. After several minutes of back-and-forth comments, I suggested that perhaps in the end, if no other solution was available to deal with the dogs, they might have to be put down. Somewhere in the words that I used, there must have been a mention of **'*being shot*'**, and the reporter was going mad with his shorthand scribbles.

A few days later I was awarded the honour of a headline:

"Councillor Williams suggests shooting stray dogs".

I learnt a lesson from that incident. Never get too carried away with an argument when a reporter is present. The incident also came in useful in another way. I realised that if I was aware of a topic was to be raised that I had an interest in, I should have a quick word with the reporter before the meeting. This ensured I would get star billing in any report.

I also had his name and number, and would give him a call if I wanted to get an article in the paper. This was very useful for advertising my public First Aid courses, and soon I would be regularly calling on that reporter to raise the profile of the St John Ambulance Brigade.

St John Ambulance
My First Aid activities continued at Goonhilly, but things were getting serious with the St John in Helston.

I was becoming far more involved with training, and when my job allowed, I would go out on the majority of public duties. I enjoyed being dressed in my uniform and attending the fetes, gymkhanas, and motor sports events. I had passed my ambulance driving test, and this included a very special moment when I was told to use the blue lights and horns as I was driving around Truro.

At that time the Superintendent of the Helston Division was Billy Kendal, who was a friend of our family, and I had known him for many years. He was looking towards retirement from his role, and this would be quite a serious moment as he had been running the division for many years. Before Mr Kendal, I only knew of one other Superintendent, and he was called Mr Rodda. In my limited time of seeing him, I had the feeling he was a very strict man, but perhaps that was because I was a child at that time, and children were treated differently from the men that he worked alongside.

One weekend I was sent to a training course in Newquay, where men and women earmarked for possible officer roles were taught all about their responsibilities. We were also shown how to drill a group of people as if on a parade. Putting this into practice was quite a challenge, as there was no way of hiding while giving orders. Shouting out commands to come to attention, or *"By the Left, quick march"* or *"Left Turn"* and *"Halt"* was quite alien to me, especially when I have never had a loud voice.

Anyway, while I was at the event, I had a chat with one of the senior officers for the County, and was asked if I had considered taking on the role of Superintendent. The idea thrilled me, and while it was most certainly something I wanted to do, I also knew it would delight my mum.

So, a few weeks later I was officially announced as the new Superintendent looking after one of the major St John Brigade Divisions in the County. I had a new hat, and pips to put on my shoulder.

… and yes, my mum really was over the moon.

During the summer I began my campaign to get a new ambulance. This was not an easy task, as there were some people who thought it was a waste of money, but many other people supported me, so I looked around at the possible vehicles.

Sadly, the very low ceiling of our garage meant we couldn't consider the normal option of purchasing a second-hand ambulance from the County. I had to contact garages to ask if they could source a suitable vehicle, and after several attempts, I found a Mercedes garage in Truro who could get a factory converted vehicle to suit our needs.

It was very expensive, and I truly wonder in hindsight, if I did the right thing.

Around the same time, one of the men managed to get hold of a Ford Escort estate car, that was converted to an official Staff Car, with plenty of room as a rapid response first aid vehicle. So, during the summer our division had the older ambulance plus this new staff car, and a new Superintendent.

Was it Time to Consider the Future?

I had been working at Goonhilly for over 20 years. During those two decades I had changed from someone who had very few aims in life, other than a serious interest in consuming alcohol, into a quite steady family man who was involved with community-based hobbies.

I was content with my life, but no longer quite as thrilled with my job.

Goonhilly was still an amazing place to work, and I was proud to be a part of the history of Satellite Communications. I began working there when it was just changing from experimental to mainstream use of satellites, and it felt as if I had been involved with science fiction, that had evolved into science fact.

I adored the atmosphere in the OCA with the television screens, twinkling alarm lights, people standing at the console talking on the telephone with colleagues around the station, and the general hub bub and energy as Goonhilly took its place in a busy worldwide communications system.

When I first saw the OCA, it had a single board on an easel showing a list of carriers and earth stations it worked with. Now there was a row of boards several metres long on the wall above the viewing gallery, where hundreds of visitors witnessed the scene every week.

… and hopefully looked at me and wondered what magic I might be getting up to.

The problem with this idyllic job, was that I didn't work in the OCA anymore. In fact, my job didn't even involve satellite equipment, I just looked after the telephone calls, data services, and television channels going to and from London.

Worse still, there were many occasions when I really didn't understand what I was doing.

My children were at an age when I wanted to see more of them as they grew, and my shift work meant I couldn't see them every evening, read them a bedtime story, and I regularly missed them completely over a weekend.

I could have asked to come off shift and have a normal 8:00 to 4:30 job, but that would mean far less income for a lifestyle we were getting accustomed to.

I didn't discuss this with Deb at the beginning of 1989, but my head was pondering over possible ways to change my life.

Training Courses

I had always hoped that one day I could get promotion and become a manager, but Goonhilly ran along the usual Civil Service traditions of promoting people based on length of service, rather than ability.

My intention was to be ready if the opportunity ever came about, so I was always enthusiastic to go on training courses. A good number of these courses were to enhance my knowledge of the equipment I was working with in the East wing, but I always put my hand up if something else appealed.

On site at Goonhilly I volunteered to be trained on the Standby Diesel Generators. This was a requirement of anyone performing temporary cover of the Controller's post in the OCA. These opportunities came up quite regularly as Controllers took annual leave, or were sick, and I wanted to be on the list of people available.

During 1989 I did have a couple of periods of covering the post. It meant I could get away from the East Wing for a few shifts, but more importantly it gave me a wonderful feeling of having made it. This was a role I had always seen as special, and now I was sitting in the best chair in the OCA.

One of the courses I had in the summer of 1989 was my first experience of Computer Based Training or CBT. It was held in a specially created room in Truro where there were several rows of computers in booths. Multiple courses could be run at the same time, but they could be on different subjects, and start or finish at different times.

My course was designed to train people on a rack of transmission equipment that we were using at Goonhilly, but the training was purely working through a series of computer screen slides with photographs and words. At the end there was a test to supposedly check if we had absorbed the necessary information.

Sadly, the training package was one of the very early examples of CBT, and less than interesting or sufficiently dynamic to be effective. The test was simply choosing the correct answer from a list, and if you got too many questions wrong, you could repeat the test and try a different answer.

That first experience of CBT was not very positive, and I felt that the material had been created by someone who understood the equipment, and who had not considered how to describe it to people who were **not** familiar with it. This was how I found many training courses at that time, and something I continually found frustrating.

I also had to go to Leafield for another course, and this time it was my refresher training to keep my certification to work on Submarine Cables. It was a full week of tutor led instruction, and practical work with equipment. A lot of the course theory was very dry, as we had to be taken through all the safety and procedural information. The presenter also had to go through the training course to be licensed to deliver it, so he understood how boring the documentation sessions could be. Hence there was a lot of red herring breaks to keep our minds active, and questions to check we were understanding the hundreds of instructions of pages of procedures.

This event was not long after the CBT event in Truro, and I really appreciated how much better a trainer led event could be.

The week in Leafield also gave me a chance to chat with people I had worked with in the 1970s, and I spent a long time talking with Barry Strange who had been a trainer, but was now the manager of the radio courses. Those few days brought back a lot of happy memories, and the feeling of teamwork was still very evident.

I also had a course in a completely different environment, and that was at a BT Training School in Staffordshire called Stone. The course involved a lot of theory, but there was a chance to work on the equipment as well. It felt different to my experiences of Leafield. Unlike Leafield where we had coffee with the instructors, the training staff at Stone didn't mix with the students outside of the training rooms, and it almost felt like an *'us and them'* situation. I enjoyed the course because it was well designed, with a lot of practical work, but I wasn't overly impressed by Stone itself.

It was a busy summer of training, and I was soon back at Leafield to try and learn how to use a piece of test equipment. I didn't really enjoy this event as it was equipment that I had rarely used, but at least it was another opportunity to catch up with the training team that I had worked with many years before. This time my discussions with Barry Strange were more about the work his team were doing now, and he talked a lot about his plans for expansion in the near future.

Somehow, a question was raised as to if I ever felt like coming back into training.

Family Life
Deb was really enjoying her job. It allowed her to have time away from the house, and something to make her feel useful.

... and of course, there was some pocket money as well.

One of the perks of being involved with the running of a leisure centre, is that she could book activity sessions for birthday parties. Andrew and Lynsey both had a party with time in the main hall for various sports, plus a swimming session, and a tea with jelly and ice-cream. Their friends enjoyed these parties, and many of the parents would get together at the bar for a drink while the children shouted and screamed in their own little world.

Meanwhile, Lynsey had a few weeks learning ballet, and had a pretty pink outfit. It was all at a very basic level, but it entertained the children on a Saturday morning. Both children had school concerts, and dressed up to entertain the parents. I am sure there was singing and dancing involved. Lynsey also took part in races at the School Sports Day, but these events were a long time ago, and it is only the photographs that remind us.

We went on holidays of course, and I am sure we would have spent time at a Pontins somewhere in South Devon. The photograph album has no record of where we went, except for some pictures of Blenheim Palace on the annual visit to see Jim and Jean in Oxfordshire.

My mum occasionally babysat for us to go out in the evening, allowing Deb and I to go to numerous social events at Goonhilly. We worked behind the bar sometimes, and the entertainment was supplied by Goonhilly's own musical group. Called 'SFA' the group consisted of Des Prouse (guitar), Mike Young (keyboard), Graham Rogers (guitar), Anthony Sutton (bass guitar), and Martin Webster who started on the drums and also sang. They played a mixture of rock and pop and were very good ... to my ears anyway.

I had a role as well. I would use the record decks and pretend to be a disk jockey while the group had their break. I was not very good, but it amused me, and a few people would get up and dance along. The group also had a few gigs away from Goonhilly, and I would often tag along to help with the lifting and carrying, plus the disco session in the break.

Everything was going very well in our lives, but as summer faded, things were about to change dramatically.

The Final Straw

I had been working in the East Wing for three years, but I still felt out of my depth. It was going to get worse, with many of the traditional analogue services becoming digital, and although I could quite happily learn about the new technology, it was yet another load of new things to get to terms with. Then came the news that we were about to get a very large submarine cable, which would be using fibre optic technology, and have completely new ways of working.

During almost every day I would watch the shift TO responsible for television broadcasts, and think to myself that I could do that.

... and then came the final straw.

I was scheduled to cover the controller, and looking forward to a week's break from the East Wing, but one Monday morning at the end of a night shift, a TO from another section came to give me some news.

He was senior to me in years of service, and had been talking to the manager, and demanded that he should be covering the controller shifts rather than me. The section he worked for was not one that mixed with the OCA, and I believed I was better qualified for the job.

We argued.

Yes, we **really** argued, and I admit to being very angry. This was the first of just two occasions in my life when I have truly lost my temper with someone.

I eventually accepted the situation and went home, but my head was in a very bad place.

I was not due back into work until the Thursday, and I shared my anger and frustration with Deb. We talked through some options, and Deb assured me she would support whatever I decided to do.

When I arrived at work on the Thursday, I rang Barry Strange at Leafield, and asked if there was any chance of a job.

Barry told me that an advert was about to be published for new people, who would be primarily expected to design and then deliver training for new digital services. The roles would also involve training for Satellite Communications, and possibly television. The jobs would mean promotion, and include assisted transfer terms to move house from Cornwall to Oxfordshire.

Although I would have to apply and be interviewed if I wanted the post, I was in a very good position in terms of experience.

It was nearing the Autumn of 1989, and that evening it was time to have a deep discussion with Deb about our futures.

By the time I went back to work on Friday, the decision was made. When the job advert appeared, I would apply for a job at Leafield, and this time it would be a permanent move away from Goonhilly, and Cornwall.

A Frantic End to 1989

It was the end of the Summer, and the next month was a roller coaster of emotions and excitement. The job advert appeared, I made my application and sat back for the outcome. I had told everyone in my work circle of what I was doing, and I received a lot of advice suggesting I was doing the wrong thing, but my mind was made up.

Barry Strange eventually rang me to say I had got through the paper sift, and a date was set for a trip to Leafield for an interview.

In 1989, the interview process was very informal, and I believe the questions I was asked were very much targeted at my strengths.

By the time I was back in work, I had already received a phone call to say I had been successful, and subject to the usual trial period, the job was mine.

My head was spinning.

In less than a month, I had told family and friends of what I was doing, and resigned from the Town Council, and also from the Helston St John Ambulance. There was hardly time to draw breath before I was about to say goodbye to Goonhilly.

Sadly, my last day was a very disappointing occasion.

There was no send off, and after signing a few forms, I emptied my locker, and sat in the bar area to have a drink to say goodbye. Only a couple of people turned up, and they were from the East Wing. One of them was about to get my shift job, and I knew he should have had it instead of me, so justice was done.

Angry at the lack of the usual farewell from the management, I went to my car, drove to the gatehouse, and threw my security pass into the temporary pass bin, before driving away from Goonhilly after 21 years.

It was the end of a major period in my life where I had been so happy, but it was time to move on.

I would no longer be on shift duties, so there would be more time spent with my family, and with promotion to make us financially secure, a new life beckoned.

Goodbye Cornwall

For several weeks, I travelled back and forth between Porthleven and Leafield. Deb and the children remained at our house in Tregunna Close, but came to Oxfordshire on a couple of weekends while we went searching for a new home.

Eventually we had an offer accepted on a brand-new house in Witney, but it involved a very quick move. We had to complete the purchase on Boxing Day of 1989, and we had little more than a couple of weeks to organise the move.

Just before Christmas, Deb and the children made their final move to Oxfordshire. I stayed for another day in an eerily empty house with Sandy our cat. There was a truly severe gale blowing that night, and I listened to the roof tiles rattling for the final time.

In the morning I went for a walk down to the harbour for a last look, and realised just how bad the night's storm had been. A section of the harbour wall and road had been washed away. Buildings had been smashed to pieces and lay all over the harbour area. I had never seen destruction like that before, and pitied my council colleagues who would be spending many months overseeing a major rebuilding project.

I packed the car with my final suitcases, plus the cat and her box, then drove into Helston to hand over the keys. Then it was a six-hour drive to Leafield to spend Christmas with Jim and Jean.

I was sure working at Leafield would be a wonderful career move, and living in Witney would open up so many new possibilities for Deb and the children.

Driving down the hill out of Launceston, I crossed the bridge where the county sign told me I was entering Devon. I was looking forward to a new life, but I shed a little tear and said:

"**Goodbye Cornwall**".

Goonhilly through the years

After I left Goonhilly, the station continued as the biggest earth station in the world. There was one further major aerial constructed, but Aerial 7 was just 19metres in diameter, and used for the Maritime system.

Meanwhile the Madley Earth Station was expanding, and became very busy. There was an International Switching System added to the site meaning it became the equivalent of a London Exchange Centre.

Rumours had been doing the rounds even before I left Cornwall, that either Madley or Goonhilly would eventually be closed. We always considered the additional responsibility of having Submarine Cables would protect Goonhilly, but Madley had advantages as well.

My years in training meant often staying in hotels, and on one trip the hotel I was using, also had a number of managers from the Satellite Group Headquarters' team. I was well known by them, and spent an evening chatting over a few beers. One of the topics discussed was that Goonhilly was almost certain to close in the near future because of the high cost of getting the services to and from London Exchanges.

Perhaps I should never have been told this, and I realised I had to keep quiet about it.

Eventually the decision was confirmed, and in 2008 Goonhilly ceased its operational role.

It was a sad moment, with most of the people I worked with being made redundant, or forced to move to jobs elsewhere within BT. Fortunately the redundancy terms were generous, and few people I have met complained about the deal they received.

As I have already mentioned, Aerial 2 was demolished, and so was Aerial 5 that I had been involved with. Several engineers remained on site to maintain the equipment, but I couldn't see any real future for this amazing place.

What I didn't know, was that plans and discussions were ongoing about a future for Goonhilly.

Over the years several groups of people had taken an interest in various Space style projects, and the site began to thrive again. Then in the quite recent few years, there were rumours about Cornwall being the location for Space Travel, and the possibility of Goonhilly becoming involved for control and monitoring.

As of now (2021) these plans are becoming reality, and the three remaining large diameter dishes are preparing to be used again for Deep Space technology. The three remaining large dishes may not be tracking satellites anymore, but they will remain looking into space as radio telescopes.

While I was working there, the dishes were looking at a satellite about 36,000km away from earth. Those dishes are now looking deeper into space, and even tracking NASA exploration probes. Currently, Aerial 6 is focussed on activities on Mars, which is over 200,000,000km from earth.

Goonhilly will almost certainly be keeping its giant ears on space for a while longer yet.

So, What Happened to me?

After two decades at Goonhilly, I had decided to move on to another phase of my career. I was going to be in a full-time training role, and this time there was no way back.

My head was spinning with questions:

- Was this the right decision?
- Should I have waited a while, and thought through the idea?
- Would I enjoy being in training?
- Would the children accept a new way of life?
- Would Deb accept the change?
- Would I miss Cornwall?

There was only one question I could answer. Yes, I would miss Cornwall.

How on earth could I be deciding to go into training. In school my stubborn brain and rebellious attitude had convinced me that education, and learning new things was a waste of time. Although deep down I knew my persona was hindering any chance of making a success of life, teenage hormones are more powerful than sense.

After more than 50 years, I believe the catalyst that changed my mindset was the determination of my English teacher to not give up on me. Miss Lomas rarely showed anger, but her frustration with my attitude was always very apparent. But strangely I really enjoyed her lessons. I struggled with adverbs verses adjectives, and never knew if I was using a pronoun, and was it time to insert a comma yet?

The positive side of her lessons were when she read a book to us. Miss Lomas was a lover of books; she even had a book shop in Mullion when she retired. It wasn't every lesson, but there were regular moments when she sat on the edge of her desk and read a passage. Her ability to bring the words to life were amazing, and I often felt as if I could see, or even feel the descriptions.

My problem was that I just couldn't produce anything similar to these words.

Then Miss Lomas found the ultimate *'kick in the backside'* moment. It was time for the annual school show, and most lunchtimes I was rehearsing a part in the chorus of a Gilbert and Sullivan Opera. I adored this experience, and was putting a lot of effort into it. She obviously saw and understood my enjoyment.

I was called to see her, and she announced that as I was unwilling to demonstrate the same enthusiasm for the academic side of school, I could no longer be involved in the show. It was a cruel punishment, but somewhere deep inside my head I realised what she was telling me.

That moment was a little before my 'O' Level exams. It was too late to improve my performance, but it did gently nudge me to turn a corner.

Now, a little over 20 years later, I was leaving Goonhilly, and about to commit myself to full time training.

… yes education.

Was it a *'Poacher turned Gamekeeper'* moment, or had several years of unsuitable training, given me something to address. Whatever the reason, I think I made quite a success of training design and delivery over the next 20 years.

Regrets
There were regrets about moving away from Cornwall of course.

My most personal regret was losing contact with my family and friends.

I know my fleeting visits to Cornwall were welcomed by my mother, but when we returned home, I knew my mother would be crying before we had got to the end of her road. Fortunately, as well as holidays, I had numerous visits to deliver training locally, so I could spend time with mum, and catch up with my brothers.

My job kept me busy, and visits to Cornwall were short, and a long way apart. On one trip I was away in Yorkshire for a week, followed by a few days in London. As I was in a meeting with my training sponsor at the BT Tower, I had a phone call from my brother Ronald. It was the news that was always going to happen one day. My mother was very ill, and would not be getting any better.

Sadly, after the funeral a couple of weeks later, visits to Cornwall became even rarer. We managed little more than short breaks in the Spring and Autumn to have a meal and chat with my brothers.

When it comes to friends, it was even worse. After I left Cornwall in 1989, I never saw my closest mate Chris Warner again. He broke up with his wife, and disappeared off the face of the earth. We rarely saw any of the other gang members, except a fleeting *"Hello"* on Flora Day with some. Perry and wife Linda came to visit us once, and we said we would do our best to meet up in Cornwall soon. Well, that was in 2019 and over a meal seven of us chatted and drank the evening away. When Keith Pankhurst and his wife (Heather) came into the restaurant, he greeted me with a painfully telling question:

"Hello George, where have you been for the last 30 years?"

We all made promises to meet up again soon, but Covid stepped in to put those plans on hold for a little longer.

As far as my working colleagues are concerned, it was restricted yet again to a Flora Day moment when we spotted each other in the crowd. Many of the smiling faces I remember have sadly left the rest of us behind, and the remaining few are all getting older. Deb and I have been to a couple of reunions, and for a few hours it was as if nothing had changed, except for the numbers getting less.

As far as regrets about our lives away from Cornwall, the first three years of my new job in Leafield were wonderful. Our home in Witney gave the family so many new options, and there were good schools for the children. Deb found another job in the Leisure Centre, and that allowed all four of us to become involved in competitive swimming. We made a host of new friends through the swimming club, and it provided Deb and I with a hobby for almost 15 years.

But sadly, it all went wrong.

The training school was closed in 1993, and we were forced to move to Staffordshire where I continued the job at BT's Central Training School. This was a different working environment with out-of-date Civil Service attitudes. The work was initially exciting, but as the years rolled by, my enthusiasm was drained, and for several years I longed for retirement.

Staffordshire is a lovely area of the country, but it didn't feel right for me. So, when we retired at the end of 2011, we soon made plans to move away. By 2014 we were living in the Herefordshire countryside, just three miles from the Madley Earth Station. Life was good again, and I finally began to write books in an attempt to recreate the style which Miss Lomas had fascinated me with. I will never reach that level of writing, but at least I have left something of my life for others to read, and compare to their own lives.

In 2019 Deb and I moved back to Cornwall. Our son lives in Cannock, and our daughter is in Bridgewater with her husband and our grandson. Our home is 20 miles from Goonhilly. The dishes no longer chase satellites across the sky, but Goonhilly is still actively involved in space.

In February 2021, Aerial 6 focussed its huge reflector on NASA's Perseverance probe as it landed on the planet of Mars.

I am still so proud of being a part of Goonhilly.

p.s. *If I maintain my enthusiasm for writing, there should one day be another book to bring the life of this Cornishman up to date.*

Printed in Great Britain
by Amazon